Dr. Youd Sinh Chao's book c   and easy to read. It seems ve,   and other cultures in South East Asia dealing with the communication within the family structures. Even though I have worked with Mien and Lao people, this paper gave me new information which will be very helpful as I continue ministry in South East Asia. I would recommend this as a must reading for those working with Mien and Lao people both in the United States and Asia since many of the struggles they experience are not apparent to those from a Western world view. The research is extensive and well communicated in the paper.

Lorna Frickel, MA in Religious Education from Grand Rapids Baptist Seminary and author of research paper entitled *"Learning Styles In South East Asian Cultures"* 1999.

"How fascinating!" I thought as I was reading this book. My dear friend Dr. Youd Sinh Chao has drawn many practical comparisons between his own people group, the Mien, with other ethnic groups and modern American culture. In the process he has drawn very practical applications as to how to have happy family relationships. Thus this book will be a valuable help not only to Mien youth and their elders but to westerners as well trying to live harmoniously in this fast paced and hectic century. Born in Laos, fleeing to Thailand, coming to America as a refugee, progressing here educationally, and now holding responsible positions both in Mien and American society he has seen many dysfunctional as well as well-adjusted families in many cultures. He is thus in a unique position to present this study. I highly recommend it to you.

C. W. Callaway, retired missionary to Mien people for over 60 years both overseas and in the U.S.

P. O. Box 5027, Vallejo, CA 94591
Tel. (707) 554-4184 e-mail: cwcall@att.net
www.mcya.net www.yidg.org www.motherteacher.org/mien

This is the first book about the Mien people with a focus on marriages and family relationships. Written from an emic view, the book clearly portrays Mien cultural practices, family relationships, gender roles, and communication styles. The book provides many insights about the ever-changing Mien family dynamics especially helpful to social service workers and therapists/counselors working with Mien families. It is also a resource for the second generation Mien to understand their cultural heritage and family matters. I highly recommend it.

Chiem-Seng Yaangh, PhD/MSW
Educator, Researcher, Community Leader
Board President of United Iu-Mien Community, Inc.
Sacramento, California

Intercultural Communication: Impacts on Marriage and Family Relationships

Youd Sinh Chao

WestBow Press

Copyright © 2012 by Youd Sinh Chao.

All rights reserved. No part of this book may be used or reproduced by any means, graphic, electronic, or mechanical, including photocopying, recording, taping or by any information storage retrieval system without the written permission of the publisher except in the case of brief quotations embodied in critical articles and reviews.

WestBow Press books may be ordered through booksellers or by contacting:

WestBow Press
A Division of Thomas Nelson
1663 Liberty Drive
Bloomington, IN 47403
www.westbowpress.com
1-(866) 928-1240

Because of the dynamic nature of the Internet, any web addresses or links contained in this book may have changed since publication and may no longer be valid. The views expressed in this work are solely those of the author and do not necessarily reflect the views of the publisher, and the publisher hereby disclaims any responsibility for them.

Any people depicted in stock imagery provided by Thinkstock are models, and such images are being used for illustrative purposes only.

Certain stock imagery © Thinkstock.

ISBN: 978-1-4497-6451-7 (hc)
ISBN: 978-1-4497-6452-4 (sc)
ISBN: 978-1-4497-6453-1 (e)

Library of Congress Control Number: 2012915172

Printed in the United States of America

WestBow Press rev. date: 10/01/2012

TABLE OF CONTENTS

List of Tables i

List of Figures ii

Introduction: Intercultural Communication: Impacts on Marriage and Family Relationships ix

Chapter 1: Changing Land, Changing People 1

Chapter 2: Mien Cultural Traits 8
- Who are the Mien? 8
- Children in Refugee Camps 13
- Psychological Impact of Life in Camps on Mental Health and Personalities of Mien and other Southeast Asian Children 15
- War/Trauma Experience 16
- Displacement 17
- What does it mean to be Mien? 22
- What is Family? 23
- Family Relationships 25
- Family Life and the Status of Women 26
- The Role of Mien Women 27
- Love and Sex 30
- Marriage and Divorce 32
- Parents and Children 34
- Marital Issues 36
- Types of Family Structure 40

Chapter 3: Mien Families in America 46
- Religious Points of View on Marriage 52
- Changes in Mien Marriages and Families in the U.S. 58
- Family Matters 62
- The Results of Unhealthy Communication 64

                How Achieving the "American Dream" can
                    Help or Hurt Mien Marriages and Families? 68

Chapter 4: Different Mien Groups in the United States............73
               The Non-Christian Mien..................................74
                  The Traditional Group..............................74
                  The Integrator Group 77
                  The contemporary group 80
               The Christian Mien 82
                  The Nominal Group..................................82
                  The marginal group 88
                  The Conservative Group...........................89

Chapter 5: Survey Construction 93
               Survey Construction 93
               Distribution of the Survey................................93
               Content of the Survey......................................94

Chapter 6: Results of Questionnaire Survey..................106
               Questionnaire Survey Results.........................106
                  Educational Achievement.......................107
                  Religious Belief Systems 109
                  Intercultural Communication 116
                  Conflict Management 120
                  Why Conflict Develops 121
                  Love and Respect 132

Chapter 7: Intercultural Communication 144
               Inverse Communication Styles.......................144
               Communication Difficulty 148
               The Role of Culture in the Communication
                  Process 152
               Filial Piety..154
               Direction of Parent-Child Communications 155
               Self-control in Emotional Expression 156
               Well-defined Social Roles and Expectations 156
               Shame as a Behavioral Influence......................158
               Circular Communication Style 160

	Two-Sided Communication 165
	Communication and Gender 167
	Social-Emotional Interactions 169
	Manners and Gestures...170
	Levels of Communication 171
	Negative Interactional Patterns...........................173
Chapter 8:	Mien Cultural and Marital Issues 177
	Changing Roles of Mien American Families...........177
	Parenthood 181
	Marriage 183
	Mien Marriage Problems.....................................186
Chapter 9:	What Marriage is and What Marriage is Not 191
	What "Marriage" is NOT:....................................194
	Marriage is NOT a game. 194
	Marriage is NOT a sport..................................195
	Marriage is NOT a business.............................195
	Marriage is NOT a contract.............................196
	What "Marriage" Is...197
	Marriage IS like a tandem bicycle....................197
	Marriage IS like a pair of scissors.....................198
	Marriage IS like a pair of chopsticks................199
	Marriage IS a covenant...................................199
Chapter 10:	Marriage and Relationships...................................201
	The Two Crucial Dimensional Relationships 202
	Horizontal Relationship..................................202
	Vertical Relationship 205
Chapter 11:	Recommendations and Suggestions........................216
	Recommendations for Couples 217
	Love and Respect 218
	Communication 225
	Conflict Management.....................................228
	Religious Belief System 230
	Recommendations for Counselors and Therapists...231
	Counseling Mien Americans 236

  Recommendations for Researchers 239
  Recommendations for Pastors and Laymen 241
  Recommedations for Community Leaders 242

References 245

LIST OF TABLES

Table 1. Turning Points in Mien Family Life 51

Table 2: Mien Christians and Non-Christians in the U.S. 109

Table 3: Comparison of Mien and American
Communication Styles 176

Table 4: Summary of Horizontal and Vertical Relationships 211

Table 5: Asian American Households and Family
Characteristics 216

LIST OF FIGURES

Figure 1: Mien Christians and non-Christians in
 Washington, Oregon and California states. 110

Figure 3: The Five Factors Impacting Mien Marriages and
 Families.. 143

Figure 4: Communication Pattern 146

Preface

Acculturation is a difficult process for any person or people group. When moving from a county ravaged by war, adjusting to life as a refugee, and then having to adapt to a totally different country, individuals and families are confronted with a plethora of new social structures, mores, and communication styles. Family members are faced with changes that reach deeply into the heart. In addition, succeeding generations progress through acculturation differently and at varying rates. When these types of traumatic changes take place, communication and problem solving within the family become monumental challenges.

In his groundbreaking book, Dr. Youd Sinh addresses the impact of these issues on the multi- generational Mien people and families who have immigrated to the United States. Dr. Youd Sinh does not write merely from an academic or philosophical perspective; he has personally experienced these complexities and challenges, having come to the United States in the mid'80s. His discussion not only addresses issues, but challenges readers to interact with the illustrations and examples and to apply the practical help and advice. Change is an inevitable part of life and must be met proactively.

I am reminded of a conversation with an Asian friend regarding family issues in which he spontaneously interjected, "It's all your fault!" "What's my fault?" I asked. He replied, " In my culture, I follow God, my wife follows me, and the children follow my wife. Now I am in your country and everything is turned upside down." After a few seconds of reflection I said, "I have an answer." "You do?" he questioned hopefully. "Yes," I said. "You can go back!" In that instant we both laughed. We both intuitively knew that going back was not a realistic option, as his children were already too adjusted to American life. The reality is, we must move forward. We must adapt to our new environment and the dynamics it presents.

I am reminded of a scripture. "I can do all things through Christ who strengthens me." (Philippians 4:13).

Vincent L. Inzerillo D. Min
Language Missions Director, Northwest Baptist Convention/SBC, 1996-2008
Senior Pastor of New Harvest Church in Portland, Oregon

Forward

With a deep sense of personal compassion and strong connection to the Mien couples and families whose stories he brings us, Dr. Youd Sinh Chao has generated a true gift to the Mien families and other Asian and non-Asian communities. This book, focusing on "Intercultural Communication: Impact on Marriage and Family Relationship," serves not only as an invaluable record of the intersection of traditional and the acculturated communication styles within Mien society but also a moving and often personal memoir of Chao.

Part memoir, part research, part practice – this book details an ambitious and rich account of an emerging and complex social change that is being developed every day within the Mien families. Chao carefully articulate vivid personal and national history in which he guides us through a range of current critical points that have galvanized the community. He deftly interweaves the remarkable history of his people with his own unique journey as a fellow sojourner. From the journey of escape from Laos, the refugee transit in Thailand, to an examination of intergenerational tension in America, this book captures the words and memories of the Mien Americans in the twenty-first century. Chao has also given us a way to examine the challenging reality of what it takes to strengthen family relationship in corporate America whose values oftentimes clash with classic "Asian values" of respecting authority, being modest, etc.

As a marriage therapist and teacher from Asian descent, I often read with an eye to the exquisite cultural treasures I may be able to bring to the classroom and clinical setting. As a journal reviewer, I read research looking for valuable applications to the contemporary world of couples and families. This book offers insights into the Mien culture and family dynamics based on Chao's research on the Mien's couples and his clinical work with them. Chao has given us a truly practitioner-friendly guide in working with the Mien community.

This inspiring book is an important addition to the growing field of Asian American studies.

Karen Quek
Associate Professor and Licensed Marriage and Family Therapist at Alliant International University

ACKNOWLEDGEMENT

First and foremost, all the glory, honor and gratitude go to the Creator God. I praise and thank God for His amazing love, grace, mercy, and provision in helping me to become who I am today. Without His guiding and protecting hands, I would not be alive nor would I have the opportunity to be living in this great land of opportunities called America. My life would have been easily ended during my journey escaping the communists from Laos to Thailand, or during the years of suffering from hunger, thirst and diseases in Thai refugee camps. I can only pray and entrust this book in God's mighty hands that it would become a meaningful resource to my readers.

Secondly, I would like to dedicate this book to my lovely and faithful wife Koy Fou, and our five blessed children: Dorn Fin, Meuy Finh, Sen Finh, Nai Finh, and Faam Finh. Throughout the many years of schooling, researching, and writing of this book, I was absent from their lives for many hours and days. Yet, I always find them to be understanding, forgiving, loving, supporting and inspiring me in my educational endeavor. They provided me the strength and courage that I needed to complete this book.

I am grateful for Dr. Karen Quek, for setting aside her valuable time to edit this book and provide me with many profound insights and thoughts. Her expertise in marriage and family counseling, along with extensive knowledge of Asian cultures counseling, have added valuable inputs to this study.

Last but not least, I would like to thank some of my spiritual mentors and friends Dr. Vincent Inzerillo, Dr. Chiem-Seng Yaangh, Mr. Callaway, Larry Frickel and Lorna Frickel for their emotional and spiritual support and the endorsement of this book.

INTRODUCTION

Intercultural Communication: Impacts on Marriage and Family Relationships

In a marriage, differences in communication styles can act as a stumbling block to the successful growth of the relationship. People from different countries and cultures have different ways of communicating requests, needs, desires, concerns, feelings, and expectations. Many of the communication styles are hidden within the culture of the individuals who make up the extended family. In order to understand expressive or non-expressive, written or verbal mediums of communication, one must become familiar with one's own communication pattern, as well as that of other individuals, groups and their culture.

Men and women do not speak the same relational language even if they are from the same culture, society or family. In order to gain a deeper understanding on how communication styles and cultural differences can greatly impact marriages and families in the United States, this study focuses on one of the ethnic groups from Southeast Asia, known as the Mien people. The Mien are one of the many ethnic minorities in the U.S. confronted by new communication patterns, societal expectations and pressures to maintain a balanced marriage and family. Society as a whole should put forth a strong effort to investigate, acknowledge and understand the different groups of people represented in our communities and the challenges they face, such that strides may be made in the effort to strengthen the family unit. The strength of a society comes from strong, healthy and balanced families. To have a strong nation is to have strong states; a strong state requires strong cities; a strong city requires strong communities, and a strong community requires balanced, secured families. Individual or family issues in one single household can create a ripple effect onto many other members of the community. Too often society ignores family conflicts that, once inflated, harm and weaken our nation.

The research described herein assesses the communication differences between the traditional Mien non-linear (or circular) communication style and the Western linear (or direct) communication style as laid out on table 3 in chapter seven. Several issues are explored through evaluation of responses to a questionnaire survey developed for this study. The advantages and disadvantages of both traditional and modern marriage and family communication techniques are addressed with a general conclusion in the end.

Finally, recommendations are offered that serve to improve marriage and family relationships, and to assist researchers and service providers in better understanding the Mien people and other Asian minority groups in the U.S. The recommendations are based on the evaluation of information obtained through the research described herein and my own personal life experiences as a Mien educator, researcher and family member.

Youd Sinh Chao

Chapter 1

Changing Land, Changing People

"Changing mountains is easier than changing the human mind", a well-known Mien saying, provides a succinct explanation as to the extent to which cultural and environmental factors greatly impact people's lives, particularly for those resettled or resettling in the United States from vastly different lands as refugees or immigrants. The ways people think and believe guide their behaviors within the family and outside the family. A deeply-developed belief system can serve as a lifetime guiding principle that may be very difficult to change or relinquish. As a formal political refugee from Southeast Asia, I have lived and worked with many individuals, married couples and families in the U.S. since 1985. I have witnessed and shared their grief, joy, peace, challenges, and happiness throughout the years. I share similar challenging life experiences with thousands of refugees from Southeast Asia and around the world, including losing many family members during the war, being forced to uproot from my homeland, facing persecution, suffering in a refugee camp, and navigating the language and cultural barriers in our new home, the U.S.

As a proud citizen of the United States, father, community spokesman, language instructor, language interpreter, marriage and family counselor, and conference speaker, I have been greatly heartbroken to see so many marriages and families impacted by today's social and cultural influences, and causing people to drift from traditional values. With the divorce rate on the rise, family relationships are weakening and too often falling apart. The gaps between parents and children, grandparents and grandchildren are widening, causing great concern and demanding attention from service providers in our communities. As current studies and other information resources regarding marriage and family issues within the Asian community are very limited, especially for the Mien ethnic minority from Laos and Thailand, this study was designed to examine some of the major issues impacting the health and wellness of Mien marriages and families in the U.S. Such a study on the success and failure of Mien marriages and families has not yet been done, and it is my honor and privilege to take on this crucial task.

As we see all around us, many people from around the world have been forced to relocate from one place to another for different reasons. This impacts their marriages and families on many different levels. People migrate from one country to another for a better life, to be united with their families and friends, while others are forced to leave their home countries for political, economic or other forms of persecution. Moving internationally itself is not an easy task for anyone, especially for those who live in remote or underdeveloped places. For anyone leaving his or her own familiar environment and moving to a foreign environment, fears, anxieties, and/or dangers can occur. Changes in a person's life can be positive or negative experiences, and can create hope or bring despair to an individual, a family or a community.

In some unforeseen situations people must go through stages of unexpected change. Some of these changes include the adaptation of new cultural and social dynamics. For instance, marriage to someone outside of the culture which creates another layer of marriage and family challenges, not only for the married couple, but also for their immediate families and their communities as well. These people become parents and create a new or different chapter of life. The couples are given new responsibilities to their families. Their personal life goals and cultural expectations may not match or fit into their traditional norms and cultural expectations. The experience of migration from one's homeland can be as much a challenging and bewildering as it is creative and cultivating. The experiences become permanent scars on the migrants' hearts, minds and souls. Depending primarily on the nature of their migration experiences, some become better and stronger people while others can become bitter and victimized by their negative encounters.

Leaving one's familiar environment, their home, their family, and their culture leads to a period of life that encourages reflection and exploration of one's roots. An appropriate reflection or exploration of one's past is necessary to understand one's present, and how to move forward into the future. Often people integrate present encounters and aspirations with the past by sharing stories, feelings, hopes and future plans. They may engage in personal life testimonies or make comparisons between the two vastly different places which they have now experienced. Through the social and cultural exchange process, they may discover amongst themselves any conflicting values and lifestyles between the new and the old.

As society evolves, family dynamics and communication methods are also reshaped by different cultural and environmental variables. Traditional family systems are shaken by many factors that force families to accept and adopt foreign forms of family structure that can create relationship barriers within the family circle. Immigrant and refugee families are facing the most challenges in marriage and family life. Mien refugees from Southeast Asia are one of the ethnic minorities in the U.S. who face not only a great intergenerational gap (between children and their parents and grandparents), but also a gap between spouses in their communication styles and conflict resolution. There is a general shift or reversal from the traditional family structure where the father is the leader and provider for the family. In many cases, after moving to the U.S., the mother or the children are forced to be the main provider for the family due to the lack of social, language, or job skills applicable in the U.S. of the father.

There are many factors that contribute to the success or failure of marriages in any society. In order to have a strong and healthy society, we need to have well-balanced and healthy families. Family values shape our society in the past, present and in the future. Family issues in non-parallel communication, problem solving, child rearing, and family structure are not to be ignored. These issues need special attention from researchers, educators, policy-makers and community members in examining the causes of conflict and in order to seek appropriate resolutions. Parents are worried about the future marriages of their children and grandchildren because more families are falling apart and longstanding cultural values are disappearing from today's families. Differences in communication styles among immediate and extended family members has become one of the major obstacles to creating a healthy family relationship. Communication within a marriage (and family) is the strongest force that pulls and pushes people together or apart. Many unresolved conflicts within marriages (and families) have resulted in unwanted separations and divorces.

Since the Mien people began settling in the U.S. between 1975 and late 1990, limited literacy and other cultural differences have caused many social and financial problems which lead to even more serious legal issues and other issues within the family. This study provides pertinent cultural and historical background of the Mien family structure and dynamics in Laos and Thailand. It uses both personal experience and research data to show how marriage and family communication enhances or impedes the Mien peoples' relationships in the U.S. (on the West Coast in particular). The study shows how Mien families living in the U.S. are no longer able to preserve their traditional family structure and value systems. As a result, the divorce rate is escalating as people are acculturating and assimilating into modern society in the U.S. and experiencing different levels of communication. While some families are becoming socially, academically and economically more advanced, many families are falling apart and creating a burden on their communities and social services. Thus, as a concerned citizen and educator among the 30,000 Mien people in the U.S., the rising existence of these issues has led me to conduct this study of the leading causes affecting the Mien people in the U.S.

Mien families struggle with typical "American" problems—the widening gap between children and parents, youth gangs, early pregnancy, high school dropouts, alcoholism, tobacco, drug and gambling addiction, and a general increase in family problems and divorce. However, within the Mien community in the U.S., there has not yet been a primary source of data or research conducted on this particular group of people with regard to the issues of marriage and family. Other ethnic groups have been given much attention by researchers and media but the Mien people have been overlooked. Therefore, this primary research study is much needed.

It is believed that some of the main causes of the rising divorce rate in America arise from cultural differences, language barriers, differing communication styles, incongruent parenting styles, conflicting belief systems, and the gap between traditional, non-traditional and modernized married couples. As a native Mien person, I strive to present an in-depth view of Mien cultural tradition and family dynamics of the Mien people in the U.S. The marriage survey was carefully generated to gather a broad range of data to support the following research questions. The construction of the survey is provided in Chapter Five and the results and final discoveries will be discussed in Chapter Six. As such, the following five questions were designed to elicit the information on which this study is based.

1. How have Mien traditional family values, family structure and expectations impacted their marriages in the U.S.?
2. How have Mien traditional communication styles enhanced or hindered their marriages and family relationships?
3. How have the dominant cultural communication patterns affected today's Mien families and marriages?
4. What role does conflict management play in today's marriages and families for the Mien people? (How does conflict management impact marriages and families?)
5. Does religious belief or faith in God help bind married couples in a "foreign" culture?

In reviewing literature on marital conflicts in other cultures, it is obvious that similarly the communication barrier is threatening Mien spouses, parents and children in the U.S. Fong indicated that the lack of success among other racial minorities is directly attributed to the weakness in their family values and cultures. He explained that, "Social scientists interested in Asian-Americans have tended to focus on race relations issues and broader socio-historical experiences, but have given only cursory attention to Asian families. At the same time, social scientists interested in families have failed to conduct much research on Asian Americans."

The Mien, an ethnic minority group from Southeast Asia, have been under-represented in scientific research for the past two decades; specifically in regard to the family and marriage issues that are confronting these families in the U.S. As a political refugee from

Laos, and a former community leader and spokesman in the U.S., I have personally witnessed many different marriage problems within the Mien communities in the states of Washington, Oregon and California, and also in other countries, such as Canada and Thailand. Because of their limited educational and occupational backgrounds, the Mien people have to overcome many obstacles in order to alleviate family problems. As a result, Mien leaders, elders, and pastors alike are becoming increasingly concerned with the stability of Mien marriages and families in future generations. In response, community leaders, pastors and other service providers in different settings are searching for resources to help Mien individuals, couples and families in need.

As an interpreter and community liaison, I have worked with public school teachers, administrators, social service providers, medical professionals, law enforcement officers, probation officers, and lawyers, both in public settings and in people's homes, for over seventeen years in many different states, and I have taken notice of some of the issues and needs of not only the Mien people, but also of other refugee and immigrant families. In order to provide the most appropriate and highest quality services to these people, it is necessary to gain in-depth knowledge of the people and the specific services they need. With this first-hand knowledge of the issues facing the Mien people, I created a "Marriage Communication Survey" and studied one hundred married couples, fifty Christian married couples and fifty non-Christian married couples in the State of Washington.

Since the large majority of first generational couples are not literate either in English or in the Mien language, the study was conducted through one-on-one meetings in the participants' homes, telephone interviews, and surveys collected from monthly couples' gatherings and annual retreats. As a native Mien speaker, and language and cultural consultant, I have had the honor and privilege of completing the primary research using the Mien language with very minimal language or cultural barriers as would typically be the case for a non-native Mien researcher or even a native Mien speaker with a less public role in the community. My contact with all of the participants was always very formal, as expected by the study and the Mien culture. The questions were intriguing to the participants as they had never been challenged to think so deeply about their marriages and family relationships. Many of them had to take extra time to fully process the questions prior to giving their responses. Generally, in the Mien culture, people do not probe into others' personal or family issues unless they are being inquired by their parents, grandparents, community leaders or the authorities and generally not to someone outside of the immediate family.

Chapter 2

Mien Cultural Traits

Communication has become one of the most important factors in determining the success or failure of a marriage and family. It is undoubtedly a crucial and essential medium to strengthen or weaken people's lives as they strive to learn, make adjustments and grow together as couples, families and as a community. For this reason, researchers have given much attention to the role communication plays in couples' and families' lives. Communication bridges understanding between two or more people in their recreation, dissolution, and everyday management of marital and social relationships. Good communication opens peoples' eyes and unlocks their minds for better understanding and building stronger relationships. Healthy and balanced communication builds trust and confidence between people. It breaks down barriers and helps people to see and better understand themselves and others amid confusion and frustration. It creates hope and meaning for a broken relationship to find healing and restoration.

Since understanding culture plays a major role in understanding a couple's marital relationship, it is necessary to provide some background literature for better understanding the Mien historical and traditional marriage and family background.

Who are the Mien?

M.I.E.N stands for **M**ountainous, **I**nterdependent, **E**nthusiastic, and **N**omadic people who are originally from central and southern China. The historical roots of the Mien have been studied and documented by various historians and scholars in China and missionaries from different countries and can be traced back as early as 2500 B.C. The Mien peoples' rich and fragmented history is partially linked with an ancient period of Chinese history. The Mien peoples' history has been filled with great pride, as well as disappointments and uncertainties. Many Mien people and educators consider the literature *Jiex-Sen Borngv*, one of the limited resources available in Chinese characters, provides an in-depth historical background about the Mien people. Since this book has not been translated into English or the Mien language, only few Mien elders who are literate in Chinese can understand the full meaning of the text. Although the text has long been viewed as a sacred and important book by Mien scholars and elders, it has not become familiar or well known to many people in modern times. The text has not gained a great deal of acceptance among the majority of young Mien people and educators who are not literate in Chinese. Furthermore, the text has been put aside as historical evidence by the Mien who have become Christians. For many Christian Mien, the more knowledge they gain from the Bible in regards to history and humanity, the more skeptical they become in accepting historical viewpoints that are not aligned with the Bible's teachings. Regardless of the dichotomized viewpoints, most Mien educators speak highly of the text and strongly suggest that their children and grandchildren at least become familiar with it.

In addition to the Mien's *Jiex-Sen Borngv*, there is other literature written by Chinese scholars, historians, other anthropologists, sociologists, and missionaries about the Mien people, their language, culture and history. Mien leaders and educators in the U.S. have worked closely with many Chinese scholars and historians from Thailand, Laos and Vietnam in tracing, recording and producing some historical studies about the Mien people and their origin. In addition, both short-term and long-term Mien missionaries from the U.S. to Laos, Thailand, Vietnam and China have provided much insight into the Mien people, culture, language and history. I have also personally made several trips overseas to gather culturally relevant information for this book.

As a Mien person myself, born and raised in Laos—which I left for political reasons at age seven—then living in a refugee camp in Thailand for more than six years, and then formally educated in the U.S., I have done many years of research and have the privilege of knowing and understanding the Mien culture as an insider. Sadly, the majority of historical literature on the Mien people is presented from an outsiders view. The Mien people have very rich cultural traditions and a complex history. It requires extra effort from any interested person to explore fully the roots, the stem, the branches and the leaves that form the core values in the shaping and transformation of these people. Although it is not the intention of this book to provide such a detailed historical account of the Mien people, it is highly recommended that anyone interested in learning and understanding the Mien culture refer to the references provided in the bibliography for further study. This book, on the other hand, provides only a brief historical overview of the Mien people aimed at illustrating cultural components and cultural norms.

Historically, the Mien were scattered throughout the central, southern, and southwestern provinces as well as some small areas in eastern China and developed a variety of dialects. They inhabited parts of central China in the provinces of Yunnan, Nanking, Kweichow, Kwangsi, and Kwangtung during the latter period of the Han Dynasty (20-220 A.D.). Due to their communication barriers and disadvantaged economic status, the Mien maintained their own livelihood through more primitive forms of agriculture by grazing livestock on hillsides and in mountainous areas. Their basic economy and primitive lifestyle was shaped by their diligent farming skills and familiarity with nature and forestry. They did not possess any sophisticated or industrialized skills but confounded upon their agricultural skills by cultivating terraced fields in the foothills and narrow valleys in order to produce rice, corn, and vegetables to support their families. By becoming friends with their surroundings, they were able to utilize the God-given natural resources to sustain their families. Men were hunters, women were gatherers, and children were helpers and observers. While men hunted wild animals and fished, the women and children gathered berries, fruits, mushrooms, and edible plants to feed the family and their domestic animals. Their language, economy, and way of life were similar to those of the Han (Chinese). Much of their livelihood came from forestry or dry farming in the mountains and jungles. Prior to their migration and relocation into different parts of the country and into Southeast Asia, they were believed to be one of the largest ethnic minorities in Kwantung province, China.

Having lived for many centuries in rural isolation from urban life, the Mien mainly relied on the grace and provision of heaven to provide them rain for their crops. Once they had lived in one location for several years, the land would lose its original nutrients from the constant slash and burn farming process, forcing migration for them to relocate to other more suitable farming areas. In the latter half of the 14th century A.D., the Mien were driven out of the coastal mountains and sailed on the China Sea in search of better land and opportunity for survival. Arability of land, as well as many other factors, caused the Mien to leave China and disperse themselves amongst many other countries in Southeast Asia. The increasing dominance of Chinese populations, resistance to heavy levies imposed by the Chinese government, the desire to search for freedom, and famine and drought in China were all contributing factors that forced the Mien to leave Shantung and central China and into the mountainous regions of Laos, Vietnam and Thailand. There they hoped to be able to continue their diligent, hard-working agricultural lifestyle in order to survive and support their loved ones.

At the end of the Indochinese or Vietnam War in 1975, with the fall of Laos, Cambodia, and South Vietnam, millions of refugees from these three countries fled their homes in search of freedom and safety in Thailand, France, Canada, Australia and the U.S. The Mien were one group of ethnic minorities in Laos that were forced to escape communist persecution due to their connection and involvement with the U.S. Central Intelligence Agency from the early 1960's to 1975. The Mien people who lived in the mountainous regions of Laos as the Hmong (often known as highlanders, hill tribes or montagnards) were the least educated and most unprepared groups of people relocating to nearby countries for survival. With no support from the Laotian government or from any other country, they found themselves in a helpless situation. Without any form of electronic communication or media outlet, they could not reach out for support. The only news they received (by word-of-mouth) was that the Communists had captured the country and they had to flee for their lives.

When the shocking news spread to the small villages, the people realized that in order to stay alive they had to immediately flee from their homes and travel to Thailand, the closest country with some obscured hope.

As they fled, the primary goal was to avoid capture by the enemy during their dangerous and unpredictable journey. They knew that capture by the Communists would mean very little chance for survival. In most cases, capture meant they would be killed instantly, and in very rare cases, those captured were given the liberty to repatriate back to Laos, ultimately making them slaves to the communists.

Thus, the best hope was to safely reach their destination of Thailand, as they travelled the long journey through the rough and unknown terrain, bare-footed. As it was not safe to walk on the main roads where there were bombs and traps, they had to find shortcuts through the forests and jungles. This made the journey even more treacherous, especially for those families travelling with young children.

Throughout the journey, the Mien held on to the hope that they would not be rejected by the Thai government once they made it safely across the border. In the end, some of the new refugees were fortunate enough to reach Thailand, while many others were not. Tens of thousands of innocent people lost their lives along the way from starvation, disease, and from land mines and other traps set by the communists in the jungle and trials. Others committed suicide when the pressures and pain grew more than they could sustain. As an example of the heartache endured, there were some parents who even had to intentionally overdose their infants or children to stop them from crying or making loud noises in order to keep everyone from being caught when the enemy approached.

When the influx of hundreds and thousands of families arrived in Thailand, more grief often struck the new refugee families. In many horrific cases, people were robbed and women and young girls were raped, tortured and abused by Thai farmers or soldiers near the border before they were able to enter the refugee camps. Many families were completely controlled by corrupt Thai soldiers. Tens of thousands of people from Laos, Vietnam and Cambodia were forced to live together with limited food resources, scarce medical supplies and poor shelters in hastily built refugee camps.

Children in Refugee Camps

Children in the refugee camps were restricted in their freedom of movement. The camps were overcrowded and outbreaks of measles, dysentery, meningitis and cholera were increasingly common health problems affecting people of all ages. The bigger the camp, the more health problems would arise.

One major consequence of life in a refugee camp was the nearly inevitable subjugation to a sub-nutritional diet, with a particularly negative long-term affect on growing children. Epidemics of nutrition-related diseases were also common in the refugee camps, caused by the lack of necessary nutrients in the makeshift diets. Many of the health problems affected children's cognitive ability in learning, which often has a lasting effect.

In addition to the serious health problems, many families were broken as a result of the difficult and often deadly journey—and as a result, children were now being cared for by only one parent, or without either parent. In some cases, one child had to assume the role as head of family and care for their younger siblings. Life in the refugee camps also meant that children lost outside role models to guide their development since everyone was locked inside the camps. Individuals with special gifts, knowledge and skills were not able to develop or apply them in a confined refugee camp environment. Even when both parents were present, these children were forced to grow up under abnormal conditions. Just to feed their children, the parents would try to find whatever available gardening space they could and plant any vegetable could possibly grow. Some individuals would risk their lives by sneaking out of the camps to look for physical laboring work from nearby Thai farmers. These risk-taking individuals would leave the camps at night or early in the morning and returned late in the evening. They would work from early morning until late afternoon digging farm lands with shovels and hoes, cultivating the fields with long knives, planting or harvesting corn and rice, or transporting the crops from field to towns with nothing but their backbone. Strong and fast laborers could earn 10 to 20 Thai Baht per day—with that money they would be able to buy a small portion of meat or vegetables, enough to feed a small family for one or two meals.

Children with parents who were able to successfully risk their lives to labor for the small sums of money were fortunate enough to get some protein in their diet. The risks that the parents took, however, came with many severe consequences. The inhumane punishments included cleaning the filthy restrooms, public shaming by adorning a humiliating tag while walking around the refugee camp, a severe physical beating, or being jailed in pits dug by other refugees in the camp which were filled with a mixture of domestic animal wastes.

For those parents who were not able to find any available land to grow vegetables or were not willing to take the huge risk to earn a little money outside of the camp, they ended up depending on hand-outs from their neighbors, relatives and the Thai government. Thus, parents were deprived of their authority; their role as provider for their family was undermined by their dependence on a system over which they had no control.

Parents suffered lack of self-esteem and hopelessness as they had lost their homeland, property, farms, families, relatives, and friends. Many parents, especially fathers, developed emotional and psychological problems as they failed to fulfill their roles as providers and protectors for their families.

Domestic violence and marital conflict clouded the lives of families in the refugee camps. Both men and women suffered anxiety and depression as a consequence of the hopeless situation in which they were living. Substance abuse was a common problem among men. Some turned to depend on opium as a form of comfort or to create numbness to their emotional, psychological and physical suffering.

Children in refugee camps were growing up in conditions that did not permit their socialization according to the values of their own culture. As had long been the tradition, children had no opportunity to acquire agricultural skills working alongside their parents. Boys were no longer able to learn social, leadership, and economic skills from their fathers as they would have at home in Laos.

Psychological Impact of Life in Camps on Mental Health and Personalities of Mien and other Southeast Asian Children

Cleanliness for children in the refugee camp was almost impossible. Sufficient water supply was a large problem. Deep wells were dug and access to water was a challenge for both adults and children. Most wells did not produce sufficient water for the families that relied on it. Clean water was mainly reserved for drinking and cooking. Families who were lucky enough to live at a camp nearby a river would bathe and wash their clothes in it. For families who lived in the Soptuang Refugee Camp, in the Mae Jarim province of Thailand, access to Namwa River was two to three hours walking distance.

In addition to the limited access to water, adequate and clean clothing created another health issue for refugee children. Most children had only one pair of clothing covering their bodies. Inability to keep one's clothing clean increased the incidence of body lice and scabies which also led to serious skin infections. Since relevant medical supplies were not available, the most effective form of treatment for head lice was to remove all of the hair of the individual affected by shaving his or her head.

Although the United Nations High Commissioner for Refugees (UNHCR) ensured that at least primary schools were available for all children in refugee camps, in a day-to-day struggle for survival and basic necessities, education did not constitute a top priority. Even if access to a school was available, and children had proper clothes or uniforms to wear as required by the Thai schooling system, there were many households in refugee camps where the labor of the children was critical to their survival. Parents, usually where a mother was forced to care for her family on her own, often needed their children to share the burdens of cooking, fetching water and firewood, or watching the younger children while she labored elsewhere.

Overall, many refugees were at high risk for mental health problems as a direct result of the refugee experience. Primary factors leading to this increased risk were war/trauma experience and displacement. Many refugees also experienced psychosocial and environmental problems in the host country that negatively affected their mental health. It should be noted that aside from these factors, refugees from Southeast Asia are also subject to the same mental health problems as any other population. Explanations of some of the mental health issues specific to refugees are provided below.

War/Trauma Experience

The Secret War in Laos was a brutal experience that created deep scars and wounds in the minds and souls of Mien refugees. To individuals who have never had the experience, it is simply unimaginable. Through study, we know that even brief contact with war or war-like circumstances has a lasting effect on many people. Mien and other Southeast Asian refugees often experienced far greater brutality than many of the war combatants. Many developed shattered illusions of safety and awareness of vulnerability prior to resettling in the U.S. Many of the traumatic experiences faced by the Mien and other Southeast Asian refugees included witnessing imprisonment, rape and assault of innocent people, often close relatives and friends. Imprisonment of refugees from Southeast Asia was common. For those held in isolation, the experience tends to be most traumatic. Visitors and news media were rarely allowed in the refugee camps so there were few reports or evidence reported on the circumstances and living conditions inside the camps.

Rape and other assaults were far more common than generally reported, as was torture. Common forms of physical torture were beating, genital trauma and rape. Some children witnessed the murdering of their parents and vice versa. Homes and possessions were destroyed or left behind. Personal belongings, jewelry and other valuable items people brought with them on their long journeys were often stolen by soldiers, bandits, or refugee camp guards. Some people had to trade their only jewelry, such as their silver engagement bracelets or other family heirlooms, for food or medicine. The majority of refugees came to the U.S. with nothing but the plain, faded clothes on their backs and unforgettable memories of their former life. Many individuals and families were separated, wounded, or killed. During the fighting or while fleeing, separation of family often occurred; and for various reasons, some members were left behind. Life in a refugee camp, especially in countries of first asylum, was usually difficult and unsafe. Conditions in most camps were primitive and dangerous, with some camps similar to third-world prisons. These and other factors lead to a high incidence of anxiety disorders, especially posttraumatic stress disorder (PTSD) or combat stress reaction (CSR) and to a lesser extent depressive disorders. Grief is a major factor in the lives of many refugees.

Displacement

Mien refugees came from the war-torn country of Laos, left their homeland and culture with little or no hope of return. "Culture shock" was overwhelming, and for older generations with less ability to adapt, the issues only got worse. They entered the U.S. which has a completely new and often incomprehensible cultural system. A lifetime of memories, familiarity, and accomplishment is abandoned. The language, customs, and values of the new world are not only different from Laos and Thailand, but are also perceived as being superior. Adjustment to the U.S. culture is often more difficult for refugees than for immigrants; and is most difficult for older refugees.

Displacement first took place after the Vietnam War in 1975. Many people in Laos decided to leave early, but some were reluctant to leave their homes, farms, and thus waited until there was no choice. The unsafe conditions forced families to leave with only what they could immediately carry on their backs. Brutality occurred before, during and after the dangerous journey to escape. The brutality they experienced included suicides, roadside bombs and traps, getting shot at by soldiers while crossing the river, or being assaulted and tortured. Displacement often caused physical and/or psychological trauma for the Mien and other refugees. These and other mental health problems are compounded by great difficulty accessing and obtaining, on a consistent basis, any sort of effective basic healthcare and an almost complete inability to access mental health services.

The overwhelming circumstances and other cumulative negative effects have contributed to the development, exacerbation, and difficulty resolving the mental and other health problems of refugees. Through many long and difficult processes, the majority of Mien and other Southeast Asians migrated to the U.S. Many of these people living in the U.S. are suffering from post-traumatic stress that dominates their physical, emotional, and psychological well-being.

The Mien people were also known as "*Yao,*" a term given by the Chinese meaning "barbarians." Mien leaders and elders in the U.S. redefined the term to be called "*Iu-Mien.*" "*Iu*" means "a unique ethnic group" and "*Mien*" means "the people". Today one may see many spelling variations of this name, such as *Mien, Mienh, Iu-Mienh, Iuh Mienh, Iu-Mien, Yiu Mienh, Yiu Mien,* or *Yao-Mien*. An "h" at the end of a word indicates a tone marker in the Mien writing system as Mien is a tonal language like Hmong, Lao and Thai. Regardless of the spelling, the names refer to the same ethnic group. Any other ethnic groups are considered outsiders, or, "*janx,*" the non-Mien.

The original written Mien has been interpreted and modified by different groups and individuals in Laos and Thailand. The government, educators and missionaries made several attempts to create different versions of a writing system for the Mien. However, none of the previous scripts that were written in Chinese, Laotian, Vietnamese, Thai or Roman symbols were widely accepted by the Mien since those scripts were far too complex for ordinary Mien farmers to learn. The richness of the Mien culture and language has been preserved and passed on from generation to generation through oral communication. It was not until 1984 that the Romanized Mien script became globally accepted.

Today the Mien live throughout the U.S. and in other countries. They can be found anywhere from California, Oregon, Washington, Texas, Illinois, Alabama, North Carolina, Georgia, Minnesota, Kansas, Oklahoma, or Utah as well as in other countries such as Canada, France, China, Thailand, Laos, and Vietnam. In the U.S., California, Oregon and Washington states have the largest Mien populations. The Mien came to this country from various areas of Laos and Thailand. They speak their own language and possess their own unique cultural traditions. Due to their small size of population, approximately 28,000 people in the U.S., they are not being identified or recognized as a distinctive ethnic group. They are often identified as Asian, Asian-Indian, Laotian or Indonesian by the community and local government.

The Mien came to the U.S. for several reasons. They are unlike other groups of immigrants who came for socio-economic well-being, education or because of religious dissatisfaction. Immigrants who came to the U.S. out of their own free will can choose to stay or return to their home country without restriction or fear of danger. Most immigrants that chose to enter the U.S. for economic or educational development had goals and expectations before they came over. Some of these people have strong educational and occupational skills from their indigenous countries. Upon their arrival to the U.S., they have an easier transition into the modern industrial and technological society. Knowing the language, being familiar with the culture, and possessing the job skills and necessary, education serves as a strong foundation for these immigrants' success in the U.S. They have less social, economical and psychological challenges than the refugees entering the U.S.

The Mien and many other Southeast Asian refugees came to America not because they had heard or seen that the grass is greener in this country, but because the yellow grass was burning their feet and forcing them to move to whatever country would accept them. They could stay and be burned alive or risk their lives with the hope that somehow their ancestors and/or God in heaven would hear their cries and lead them to safety.

While some of the military leaders had heard of or had some limited information about the closest country, Thailand, the majority of women and children had no knowledge about any other places in the world but their familiar villages. Many of the families did not have much to pack. Most of them did not have more than a pair of extra clothes or a blanket, and the clothes they had on their backs. Packing for most families included pots, pans, utensils and uncooked rice. All of their pets, domestic animals, homes and farms had to be abandoned. As soon as they left their villages, their crops, cattle, and domestic animals were free to whoever found them. The only things they could take with them were the shattered images of what they once had in their minds and hearts. For many people, these shattered images do not become just unforgettable memories, but they become un-healed pains and permanent scars. For many people, the emotional wounds are so severe that they become victims of their own pasts.

Mien refugees came to the U.S. fleeing from communists, political persecution, and in search of freedom and peace. Upon arrival, they searched for educational and economic opportunities. They arrived in their new land without any foreknowledge of it and without intention of pursuing 'the American dream', but instead merely in search of a safe place to live and raise their families. They typically did not have much to offer their new neighbors and friends in the U.S., other than the sharing of their rich cultural traditions, diligent work ethic, and a deep appreciation for the protection and solace America would provide. They were and still are proud to offer their agricultural labor, religion, art, food, culture, and language to this multicultural society.

"Immigrants who come to the U.S. often have to deal with two different distinct and dissonant problems. One of these is how to acculturate and adjust to a foreign culture, which often itself is in a state of flux; the other is how to deal with older relatives who still identify with traditions of the native culture while only paying lip service to the new one" (Watkins-Hoffman).

Immigrating from one's only known home country to another unknown country is a complex psychosocial process with lasting effects on a person's identity and social well-being. "The process of acculturation from one's native culture to a new one, is further complicated by the socio-cultural context of the individual, which includes considering such variables as size of the native language group to which the immigrant belongs in this country and whether that group is seen as subordinate politically, culturally, technically, or economically" (Watkins-Hoffman).

American anthropologist, Clyde Kluckhohn, said "Human life should remain as a house of many rooms." The world no longer operates as if human societies are isolated from one another, without the information-sharing effect of mass media, modern technology or contact with outside cultures. According to Clifford, we can no longer speak about other cultures as "primitive", "pre-literate" or "without history and people in different countries now "influence, dominate, parody, translate, and subvert each other . . . . enmeshed in global movements of difference and power". Cultures never hold still-they are alive, constantly evolving, adapting, sharing, and even being forced upon one another. They are like moving pictures on a screen (Wolf). For the Mien people around the world, new trends constantly emerge, both within their own society and from the outside. Cultural difference or ethnicity "is an important issue in the study of the family" (Arcus). Many studies have shown that there are cultural variations in family development from one's birth into a society until his or her departure from this world (Feagin).

People from varying cultures have established unique cultural norms for dating and marriage, parenting, financial management, education, dealing with death and other important aspects of human life (Arcus). Families act as a bridge for the passing of cultural values and traditions from one generation to another and one society to another (Saracho and Spodek). As people migrate into new cultures, their family values and traditions often conflict with those of the larger, more diverse cultural environment (Jim and Suen). Multiculturalism and multilingualism have important implications on family life and societal well-being.

Cultures are not set entities but change over time as they interact with one another and with the environment (Arcus). Porter and Samovar offer the following characterization of culture: "Culture is the deposit of knowledge, experiences, beliefs, values, attitudes, meanings, hierarchies, religion, timing, roles, spatial relations, concepts of the universe, and material objects and possessions acquired by a large group of people in the course of generations through individual and group striving".

It is clear that the world no longer consists of isolated homogeneous societies. People with varying linguistic heritages may live within the same community or close to each other (Saracho and Spodek). Language is communication and communication is language. A language represents a unique communication pattern that a person acquires from his or her social environment. Fuglesang asserts, "[t]he words we learn have cultural connotations and reflect the prejudices, preferences, sympathies, aversions, superstitions, taboos, or myths of that social environment. Mastering a language also means subjecting oneself to verbal habits and value judgments". People consciously and subconsciously develop their native language from the culture and environment in which they live. People may choose to study new skills or are often forced by cultural and environmental demand to acquire new knowledge or skills.

What does it mean to be Mien?

Mien people can easily be deciphered by their traditional clothing. Author Lewis stated that spotting "groups of black-turbaned, red-ruffed women on low stools bending over their embroidery" is sufficient evidence to identify a Mien village. The Mien women wear multi-colored pants, turbans, and red tunics that distinguish them from other ethnic groups like the Hmong, Lisu, Lahu, or Akha. Young Mien children are recognized by their black and indigo-colored caps, covered in finely detailed, hand-sewn embroidery and pompoms. The Mien men are typically seen in loose-fitting black or dark blue pants and matching jackets, embellished with red, black, and white piping or sometimes edged with silver-wound braids.

The colors and styles of the women's clothes are used to identify tribal affiliations of the Mien such as the round turban (*m'nqorngv-beu-ping*) versus the criss-cross turban (*m'nqorngv-beu-paanx*). Round turbans are worn by women in southern parts of Laos and by the Thai Mien who migrated to Thailand in the early 1900s. Criss-cross turbans, on the other hand, are worn by women in northern Laos. The Mien people place high value on their cultural symbols and revere them as important reflections of their culture. As such, to be Mien is to preserve the cultural traditions and leave behind a rich and long-lasting legacy.

To be Mien means to learn and live a lifestyle characteristic of Mien traditions. This includes the language, history, culture, and mannerisms characteristic of the Mien and keeping up traditional values of respect, obedience, and diligence in the household and in the field. In the

Mien traditional value system, the individual serves as a harmonious contributor to the family. Important to the Mien culture, is the belief that one's role in society is to be a good person (*kuv mienh*) and be hard-working (*jienh*), both in bearing and raising children and tending livestock. *Kuv Mienh* involves soothing over differences, cooperation, mutual acceptance, quietness of the heart, and harmonious existence. The *Kuv Mienh's* behavioral expressions need to be in relation to the supernatural and to superiors in respectful, polite and obedient ways. Likewise, mutual assistance and sharing of household chores farming duties reflect the concept of *jienh* (diligence).

Finally, being Mien also means to understand the implicit family structure, and the roles and responsibilities of each household member. The structure of a Mien family is an important indicator of family wealth and wellness. Traditionally, the most important unit of social organization in the Mien culture is the family, headed by the father. As he ages, the father turns his responsibilities over to his eldest son. In the typical Mien family, multiple generations of parents, children (both married and single), and grandchildren live together under one roof. In some cases, when a son is unable to pay the expected bride price to his in-laws, he gives up his typical rights and goes to live with his wife's family, to offer his labor in lieu of the bride price, a tradition known as "*zoux laangh*".

What is Family? What are Its Functions?

There is no single, widely-accepted definition of family. People from different regions and cultures and even from different backgrounds within a single society, have different ideas as to what constitutes a "family". Researchers Mattessich and Hill state that families are groups of people related by kinship, residence, or close emotional attachments that display four systemic features: intimate interdependence, selective boundary maintenance, ability to adapt, change and maintain their identity over time, and performance of their family tasks. Family cohesion is defined as "the emotional bonding that family members have toward one another (Russell)."

Furthermore, the primary functions of the family include physical maintenance, socialization, education, control of social and sexual behavior, maintenance of family morale, motivation of individuals to perform in their familial and societal roles, the acquisition of mature family members by the formation of sexual partnerships, the acquisition of new family members through procreation or adoption, and the launching of juvenile members from the family when mature (Mattlessic and Hill). A family system can also be defined as any social unit in which an individual is intimately involved, and which is governed by "family rules" (Walker and Crocker).

The Mien define family as *hmuangv-doic* or "household", which includes grandparents, parents, children and grandchildren, whether living under the same roof or not. Why, we may ask, does it matter how "family" is defined? For one, there are significant political, economic, legal, and religious interests bound in the definition. Sociologically, the term 'family member' implies differences in the social rights and obligations toward those who are also identified as "family" versus those identified as a stranger, colleague, neighbor, roommate, or friend. From a biblical standpoint, family consists of a legal marriage between a man and a woman, with or without children.

In a typical Mien family, everyone pools their resources and works together as a family unit. As such, household furniture, equipment, tools, and cooking supplies belong to the entire family. The head of the household (in most cases, the father) makes all of the major decisions, settles disputes, and imposes punishment when necessary. He takes on total responsibility for the well-being of his family. He deals with the outside world and faces any challenges that come to any of his family members. When an issue arises, he is to be notified and his instruction is to be followed. When any of his children face a social, physical, emotional or financial problem, it is his duty to resolve it and lead them through resolution. Likewise, he is held responsible for his children's actions. There is a Mien saying, "*Dorn dorngc sic diex dangh jaa*", which means when a son encounters a problem, the consequences fall on his father's neck. In the Mien culture, being a father means one must be equipped not only with survival skills to thrive in the jungle and mountains, but also the skills to guide and discipline his children and to be a successful problem-solver. He constantly stands in the frontline protecting his family. For any internal or external pressures the family faces, he is the first to face them and also must see their resolution through to the end. As Mien husbands say, "*Nziaaux hlo fai mbiungc hlo yaac zuqc mbuo ndaangc,*" meaning, "we are the first to face any rain or storm."

While the husband does have many of the important responsibilities within the family, in return he receives high respect from his family. It is his responsibility to train his children to be hard, diligent workers. He is also responsible for instilling his children with high moral principles, for their own sake, for the family reputation and so that they may, in turn, serves as role models for their younger counterparts. It is also the father's duty to teach and model proper respect, manners, and discipline based on longstanding traditions passed on through generations.

The Mien father is also responsible for passing on the wisdom, and skills he has gained throughout life to his children, particularly his sons. The more sons a man has, the harder he must work to save money for each of their future wives as there is traditionally a bride price involved in a marriage in the Mien culture. This bride price is determined by several conditions. Some of the major considerations include the bride-to-be's reputation in the family and community, her educational and occupational level, her ability to take care of children, her ability to cook and tend livestock, her sewing and embroidering skills, respect and obedience she demonstrates within her family, her beauty, and her physical, emotional and psychological wellness.

Family Relationships

Where does the word family come from? The word 'family' originally comes from the Latin language. The ancient Romans used the word "*familia*" for household property—the fields, the house, money and slaves. The Latin word "*famulus*" referred to servants. According to historian Collins, in ancient Rome, a marriage consisted of a man buying his wife, who was then recognized by the law as part of his property. Like present day society, people throughout history have married for different reasons. According to Collins, our society demands that every child be linked to a father who is legitimately married to his or her mother. The purpose of marriage then, is to produce legitimate children.

Traditionally, the Mien have regarded the family or the community as the societal nucleus, whereas, there has been a shift in beliefs for 'Americanized' Mien immigrants that have come to value themselves as the center, a traditionally Western way of thinking. How individuals attach priority to those things closest to themselves reflects how they value themselves relative to others (Fuglesang). Individualized Mien immigrants in the U.S. would tend to be self-assertive in their request, statement or communication style. Married Mien men traditionally refer to their wives as "my woman" (*Yie nyei m'sieqv dorn*), as opposed to "my wife." Others would say, "so and so's mother" using the child's name for identification as opposed to the woman's, for example, "*La'Gauv nyei maa*" meaning "Gauv's mother".

Family Life and the Status of Women in Mien Culture

Traditionally, in the Mien culture, young people are never given freedom in mate selection (this is especially true for girls). Marriage has traditionally been arranged by the parents on both sides. Unlike in the U.S., the significance of marriage lay not in bringing happiness to individuals through affection nor equality between husband and wife. Likewise, social life is not the based around the "couple" in the traditional Mien society. The Mien society rather is centered around the father-son relationship, whilst the American society, on the other hand, is centered around the husband-wife relationship. In the father-son-centered society, human relationships are based on subordination, obedience and respect. In the husband-wife centered-society, by contrast, human relationships have a foundation of equality.

In the traditional Mien family system, the continuity of the family through patrilineal succession from father to son was of the outmost importance and to which the husband-wife relationship was secondary. At the same time, the women's status within the family is traditionally subordinate to that of the men. Since the Mien people began migrating to the U.S. in the mid-1970s, there has been a great deal of change in the status and role of women in the family unit, in society and in the workforce. The major factors affecting this change include: first, the equal opportunity for education in the U.S.; second, employment opportunities for women outside of the family circle due to industrialization; and third, as a result of family planning efforts, Mien women in the U.S. on average marry at an older age and have fewer children. On average, the size of a Mien family in the U.S. has become smaller, exemplified by the general desire for fewer children. At the same time, traditional thinking has evolved to where parents place equal value on both sons and daughters. The result of these changes is that women are generally happier in their marriages as they are under the same equal protections and provisions in the U.S. family laws as human rights and family court offer the same protection to people of all ages and gender.

The Role of Mien Women

When taking a closer look at the societal role of Mien women over the past several decades, one of the key differences from men is that women traditionally did not have the opportunity for formal education or for pursuing a career.

As is also true of many other cultures, the Mien culture traditionally has considered women to be of inferior status to men. Men were viewed as superior in the home, in the community and in society as a whole. As such, from the beginning, women were treated different from and considered lesser than men. To some extent, this is still evident today.

The Mien community is evolving, however, and increasing number of women are pursuing higher education and finding success in the workforce. According to Chao, there were a total of thirteen Mien college graduates in 1994 in the U.S., ten of whom were women. This reversal represents an important turning point in the educational history of Mien women. Since then, community organizations have begun celebrating educational accomplishments of high school and college graduates and encouraging the pursuit of higher education. Today, there continue to be many more Mien women completing higher education degrees than men.

At the same time, however, Mien women continue to marry young, as expected and encouraged by their tradition-minded parents and grandparents. Some of the underlying reasons for this, as well as the transitional elements essential to change for Mien women are discussed herein below.

To better understand a Mien woman's role in the family, one must first understand how family is valued by the people. The Mien people value the family as the most important unit in society, and this belief has been deeply embedded into the minds of Mien women. They have traditionally accepted that their duty as women is to be good mothers and to impart moral virtue to their children. By contrast, men, on the other hand, pursue a variety of activities, for example, decision-making among clan members, going to school, or building a career. The women did not actively participate in decision-making or go to school and thus did not achieve social or mental maturity. Likewise, they were not allowed individual personal choices. In other words, they typically did not act independently without the presence of their husbands or in-laws and their responsibilities were primarily menial household chores. Inevitably, this limited place in society not only dulled the Mien women's minds, but also limited their potential to thrive in life.

The second reason Mien women marry young is that in this culture they are constantly encouraged by those they respect and look up to marry while still youthful and attractive. Many Mien parents and grandparents use the flower analogy stating that "the beauty of a flower only lasts a limited time; and when flowers are blooming, they are of the best shape and attract the most bees." That being said, the average age of marriage for traditional Mien girls ranges from 14 to 18 years of age. Generally, in any society, it can be said that women mature faster than men and thus men traditionally marry someone younger than them. One of the significant beliefs resulting in the desire for a younger wife is that women become "aged" after several pregnancies or the more children the woman bares, the less physically attractive she becomes. It is this type of belief instilled in girls' minds from a young age that urge them to marry as soon as they can. In other words, girls are often afraid that the longer they wait, the less their chance of finding a suitable partner. Of course, that mindset is changing, especially among the new educated class of Mien women.

Marrying young, the Mien women move directly from childhood into the responsibilities of adulthood and married life. Parental responsibilities then also begin at a young age when as she starts to raise her own family.

A third reason for early marriage is the tradition of arranged marriages. Although arranged marriages are not as common among the Mien in the U.S. as it is in Laos and Thailand, belief in the tradition is still present in some people's minds. In Laos and Thailand, couples do not usually date, "fall in love", and get married. Rather, the families select what they deem a suitable spouse and believe that love will develop for the couple as they build their life together. In these arranged marriages neither the bride nor the groom has much of a say in the arrangement even if they don't agree with their family's choice. In some cases, the man would be permitted to marry a second wife of his choosing, as long as he doesn't divorce his first wife. Divorce is not an option for either husband or wife, and it is usually a very binding and difficult agreement to break. For the wife, even if she is unhappy in her marriage, she is typically afraid to voice her objections or go against her husband's decision as doing so would disgrace her family.

This marriage culture causes many women to feel helpless and hopeless. This predicament coupled with lack of access to education and work opportunities, results in some women feeling as though they are forcibly molded into a "superwoman" who merely produces and raises children and obeys her husband's wishes.

The Mien culture in the U.S. today, however, is evolving as increasing numbers of women have the opportunity for education. The rapidly growing number of female Mien students in higher education programs has created hope for the future in the minds of younger generations. Mien women have, for the most part, now liberated themselves from domestic confinement and are instead pursuing individual career choices, making them more equal participants in society. Although some Mien women still marry before completing high school, they often still pursue higher education and their own careers. Of course, they simultaneously fulfill their responsibilities of nurturing their families.

While the educational and career landscape has evolved, Mien women still have to cope with certain cultural assumptions. As mentioned above, for instance, some Mien girls still feel the pressure to marry while they are youthful and beautiful. Others fear that they will have a harder time finding a mate if they pursue higher education as in the Mien culture most men prefer to marry a woman with a lesser degree of education than them. They believe that the highly educated women represent a powerful force for social change and that their success would make them too independent and more reluctant to follow the husband as the sole head-of-household. Tradition-minded men don't want to relinquish the control and decision-making power traditionally awarded to them, thus making them less inclined to choose a woman of such stature.

Love and Sex

The term 'love' usually denotes the emotions connected with "falling in love." The experience includes the ecstatic feeling that one's aloneness has ended, that one has found a soul mate, and that this elation will last forever. Traditionally, love meant wedding bells and a happy ending, according to Collins.

Research shows that men approach relationships primarily with sex in mind, while women downplay the element of sex and emphasize emotional attachment and intimacy. Men often become cynical about emotional attachment and regard it as a trick used to get sex from women. When men fall in love, they tend to over-romanticize and idealize their women. The woman they love becomes an idol, to be protected from the world. She is someone whose favor they seek out mightily; once she has been won, she should be safely stored away. This attitude seems to please and attract women.

The family always involves sex (Collins). Ferree noted that in the division of labor and roles, power, relationships, personality, behavior attributes, and self-concepts are assigned on the basis of sex. Furthermore, the individuals' biological and socio-cultural characteristics have jointly contributed to human development and behavior. Physiological and hormonal variations between males and females and their complementary roles in reproduction are biological sex differences. Contemporary research has also suggested that there may be variations in aggression and brain structure between the genders (Gladure, Rossi). Gender, on the other hand, is socially and culturally constructed rather than a biological given (Arcus et al).

Traditionally, Mien people view love and sex slightly different from the way they are viewed in modern Western society. Sex can be a controversial and taboo topic among the older generational Mien. Mentioning sex is viewed by the colder generation as being in bad tasted. Love and sex are considered as *"suangx-ndiev sic"*, meaning "under the blanket issues" and are not to be discussed in public or shared with anyone outside of a married. Furthermore, the Mien people believe that a real true love is to be revealed through services, hard work, royalty, and faithfulness in a relationship and not a subject that one should be inquired or taught by parents or family members. Sex is considered as taboo and it is a shameful topic to discuss with anyone, including the married couple. Therefore, the gap of communication barrier becomes wider not only for the spouses but also between the parents and their children as well. Having said this, one important question arises, *"What then does a married couple do when they encounter a sexual problem?"*

Normally, when a couple experiences unbalanced love or sexual issue within their marriage, they would keep it among themselves and try to avoid shame and embarrassment. If the problem is made known to the family and or the elders, it would create an embarrassing situation for both the children and the parents. It would be a disgusting topic for the children to know and a humiliating matter for the parents or grandparents to hear. The couple would most likely be scolded by the elders for concentrating on such an unimportant issue. What matter most is food, shelter and health for the family and any other need is secondary and should not be a big deal. Furthermore, the couple could be condemned as un-human, as it has been said that, "Only animals do not feel shameful about their sexuality and that sex is not as important as daily foods" or in Mien, *"Maiv zeiz hnaangx-donx."*

Couples with sexual problem would usually refrain themselves from seeking for professional help or a solution outside of their marriage. For those who were willing to step outside of their cultural box to get some help, but because of their poverty and far distance from any kind of medical or professional assistance center, it would be almost impossible to receive any form of information or assistance as needed. Again, the importance of keeping the family name and reputation from any form of disgraceful situation, the individual or couple would most likely keep the matter under the blanket and try to endure the issue as long as they could.

Therefore, the cultural aspect has generated a huge communication breakdown between spouses, especially for those who still hold strongly to the traditional belief and cultural expectation.

Sexual activity was not highly valued in the isolated Mien agricultural society, nor was it strongly valued as sacred within the traditional marriage setting. Although sexual relationships outside of marriage were not condoned, they were not considered a transgression for husbands who possessed great wealth or power in the community. Since the Mien society valued men above women, sexual activity outside the marriage was unacceptable for the wives. Men and women had different views and interpretations about sex. Women normally viewed procreation as the reason for sex, and once they had borne enough children, practiced it less in their marriages. To some women marital sex has been seen as an obligation to fulfill or a service to their husbands, rather than something pleasurable for themselves. The men, on the contrary, treated sex more as pleasure than for procreation. Having the ability to produce children was necessary in the intensive labor based work environment where the mortality rate was high. Infidelity and fornication were very common then and still are.

Marriage and Divorce

In the traditional Mien culture, a marriage is a life-time commitment and a person is to carefully select his or her mate. It is commonly believed that the first mate chosen for marriage is the most important and the right choice. It is unlike buying clothes or shoes from a department store wherein one can take all the necessary time to choose from different colors, sizes, and brands. After the item is purchased, taken home and tried on again for size, it can be returned (even without a receipt) for any reason. The Mien have a saying they preach to their daughters, that "*Cuotv maengx gaengh mbaeqv aiv, bieqc maengx gaengh mbaeqv hlang*" which translates as "the door step is low upon leaving and the doorstep is high upon returning."

When a woman is married she devotes her entire life to her husband and his family with very few opportunities to return home to her own. The steep bride price paid by her husband and his parents seals the commitment and serves as an agreement to remain married to her husband and support his parents for life. A common saying in Mien is, "*Zoux mbuangz zoux taux zuangz*", meaning "to be a daughter-in-law, is to do it for life." The only possibility for her to return to live with her biological parents is when her husband passes away. However, even in that case, her father-in-law has the right to remarry her to another man and ask for a bride price equal to the amount he paid for her, if she is still young. Her bride price would be even higher if she has children born from her late husband. In this situation, the Mien say that the bride price is pre-determined by the number of "heads" (*i.e.*, the mother and her children).

In the traditional Mien society, divorce was very rare, if at all. Marital conflicts are typically handled by both the husband and wife's parents. Should the husband give his consent for divorce, the wife could choose to return to her parents or live by herself or with her children. If the divorce is initiated by the husband, she does not have to pay back the bride price. By initiating, he is relinquishing the bride price, the engagement bracelets, and all other wedding expenses. However, if the wife leaves or initiates or causes the divorce, including through committing adultery, she and her parents are bound by the "two-one" (*sung-gouv*) marital code to pay back double her bride price and all of the wedding expenses. As such, very few women could afford to divorce their husbands. A knowledgeable researcher of a longitudinal study on Mien people in Thailand, Chop, proclaimed, "I would like to note that since I studied the Yao (Mien) tradition, I have never known of any case of divorce among Yao (Mien) people. However, I have seen one case of 'separation', I would like to call it". (Her studies of the Mien people in Thailand included eight major provinces: Chiangmai, Chiangrai, Phayao, Nan, Lamphang, Sukhothai, Phetchabun and Kamphaeng Phet.)

Reviewing data from several national surveys on happiness and satisfaction of marriages, Campbell identified the following groups as the 'most unhappy' people in American society during the period of 1957-1978. These groups include the unemployed, the separated and widowed, the socially isolated, the physically disabled, blacks with low incomes, and unmarried mothers. Campbell also reported that the happiest people in America were young married women without children and married men with grown children. "Poor people today ordinarily do have higher divorce rates than rich people. But by taking the comparison a little further back into the past few centuries, we find that, historically, rich people had most of the divorces, poor people just couldn't afford them" (Collins).

Parents and Children

Mien children traditionally are not raised to be independent or selfish thinkers unlike American parents who encourage their children from an early age to think for themselves and make their own decisions. In the U.S., children are encouraged by their parents, teachers, and society to believe in themselves and to decide for themselves what they want and what they should do. While in the Mien culture, by contrast, children are conditioned to consider the will of the family as the main priority. A child is accountable for his behavior to not only his or her family members but also to the community as well.

For Mien parents in the U.S., raising their children with dual cultural expectations can be a great challenge. Their traditional parenting methods and discipline styles often work against them in the U.S. Children that were born and raised in the U.S. often do not accept or understand their parents' non-linear communication style. Many children become confused and misinterpret the meaning of their parents' teaching methods that are not complementary to what they learn in school, or see in the homes of their peers, the media and their neighbors. At the same time, Mien parents who are accustomed to their traditional communication style and are unfamiliar with Western parenting techniques face significant barriers to developing healthy relationships with their children.

The contradicting methods of communication and parenting styles create an intergenerational gap between Mien parents and their children. Children are told to hide their feelings during a conversation; this is especially true when being disciplined. Parents generally do not give positive comments, praise, or express their appreciation and gratitude when their children are doing well. Most attention is given when a child has done something wrong. The frustrated parents often use a high voice and angry body language and hurtful or critical words are expressed. Children who are not accustomed to this type of parenting style can easily become discouraged and rebellious. They become greatly puzzled by the messages their parents are conveying. Some children cannot tolerate the seemingly illogical parenting style and turn against their parents.

Inappropriate punishment is reported as one of the most damaging parenting techniques used. Regular negative, punitive, or ridiculing of children's normative behavior can cause children to withdraw from taking risks to learn or try new activities or to express their desires and concerns (Lewis and Feiring). By contrast, children form and maintain healthy, secure relationships with parents who respond sensitively and appropriately to their children's signals and needs.

In the Mien and other Asian cultures, the family is central to the children's economic and social resources and provides a primary framework for their cognitive and social development. In the family context, children engage in activities either alone, with siblings, parents or grandparents that foster intelligence and academic skills. They learn how to think critically and creatively from the role models inside and outside of the home. Their home and community environment fosters their social and intellectual skills so that they may understand how to evaluate their own thought processes, develop positive interaction skills to initiate and maintain relationships, and acquire the ability to avoid or resolve social conflict. Children who lack adequate economic and social resources often demonstrate a negative impact to their social, cultural, intellectual and/or spiritual growth.

Marital Issues

For the Mien people in Laos and Thailand, the major marital issues that emerged were usually infidelity, problems with in-laws, physical and emotional spousal abuse or alcohol, gambling, or opium addiction. Let us first take a look at the in-law issues that can arise for Mien women. As stated previously, wives have multiple family roles and obligations in the Mien society. In addition to being a mother and submissive wife, she is also expected to respect, obey and cook for her husband's family. When the roosters crow in the morning she is expected to get up and prepare warm water over an open fire with split wood for her in-laws to wash their faces and brush their teeth.

Once the morning meal is prepared, she would politely call her in-laws to the table to eat breakfast together. She should prepare meals daily with sufficient ingredients, such as salt and chili peppers which must be seasoned just right. The rice also should not be too soft or too hard. She would be criticized for meals that are not well prepared to their tastes. As a show of respect, during meals she is not to sit down, but to squat when her father-in-law is present in the room. Worse yet, in addition to her father-in-law, she is also to respect all of her husband's older brothers by squatting when they are present in the room, regardless of her physical condition, even if she may be pregnant or nursing a baby. She is still expected to show respect and honor her father-in-law and brother-in-law, under the cultural code of "*ngamv ong-buoc, ngamv baeqv*". She can stand but cannot sit on a chair or stool. If she fails to obey this silent cultural rule, it would be considered as impolite and highly offensive. This kind of behavior would bring a great disgrace to her husband and the family.

When guests are staying in the house from another village, she is to prepare meals for them and be as polite and respectful as she possibly can while at the same time trying to manage her children, and tend livestock. She is not to eat together with her husband and the guests. Her husband, father-in-law and other adult males would eat first and she and her children would get to eat last. In some cases there would be very little or no food left for her to eat. When there is some or a little left over she would make sure that her children get to eat before she does. In some cases she would go to bed with an empty stomach after all the hard work that she had done. The belief is that a wife going to bed without any food in her stomach is better than a guest going hungry.

She is also told to hold her tongue when being lectured by her in-laws whenever a mistake is made or at any disappointment that she has caused. Without the full support and protection of her husband, her married life would be miserable. Because it is one of her main roles in the family, if she is unable to have children, she does not receive much love or favor from her in-laws. It should be noted, that in this culture 'being able to have children' means having at least one boy. In some cases when the wife could not bear children, she would have to grant permission for her husband to have a second wife. In other cases, the husband and wife and other family members would reach an agreement to adopt a child or children.

Another sign of respect and obedience is that when a wife speaks to her parents-in-law she is not to have eye contact. Eye contact was traditionally considered to be offensive and impolite in the Mien culture. Mien people only make eye contact with their enemies or those they are intentionally offending. Likewise, during a conflict, the wife is to be attentive to her husband or parent-in-laws. Conversation becomes a one-way communication.

Traditionally, Mien spouses did not have major conflicts over their finances. There was nothing much to discuss. Their ultimate goal in life was to produce sufficient food supplies for their family and to avoid hunger and starvation. Physiologically, people develop the idea that they need to work hard, be benevolent to others and show respect to their elders. Survival depended mainly on the family's ability to fill up their rice barns and corn sheds, as opposed to worrying about earning a high income, investments, keeping budgets or balancing a checkbook, as is the case in modern American society. Money was necessary to purchase fabrics to make clothes for the family, or to exchange for cooking oil, salt, silverware, or cooking utensils. With the exception of these necessities, Mien couples did not have monthly bills to pay or budgets to balance as demanded in the modern U.S. In the regions inhabited by the Mien, there were no stores or malls for people to shop, nor credit cards, nor bank accounts. The only major debt couples had to worry about were the bride prices they owe to their in-laws.

Today marital issues have broadened to include religious differences, financial worry, long-term unemployment, sexual problems, physical and mental illness, abuse, alcoholism and substance abuse, gambling, etc. Different facets of these and other issues can hinder or promote growth in any family relationship. The impact is largest for those with less education that lack the tools and know-how to resolve conflict. Due to their lack of education, they are unable to apply the reasoning skills needed to assess the issues and make necessary corrections. As a result, for many couples, small challenges can become impenetrable barriers in their relationship.

In the Mien culture, there are also certain expectations not only for one's biological children, but for sons—and daughters-in law as well. The specific expectations are dependent upon the position one holds in the family.

For the son-in-law, when he returns home with his new wife after the wedding, he begins to play the role of a husband. He is, however, not to forget that he still has the role of son to fulfill as well, especially while he and his wife are still living under his parents roof. Their marriage and other family matters are still guided and corrected by his parents.

Typically, the husband's mother becomes the nanny and marriage expert for his wife. The mother is expected to intervene into their personal and family matters. She provides guidance on being "a good husband and wife" in order to avoid behaviors that would bring shame to the family. Once they have their first child, she also teaches them how to be "a good father and mother." The mother, who is considered as the most experienced and knowledgeable about life and family, is to be respected and appreciated by both the son and the daughter-in-law.

Despite his objections, she is still his mother, and he needs to give her the freedom to intervene whenever she feels necessary. By any means, if the son ignores the instructions of his mother or father, the parents will consider him disrespectful, disobedient, and may demand that he repay the money they spent on the wedding and on his wife's bride price. Again, however, it is important to note that treatment of children in the Mien society varies from household to household as in any society and cannot be generalized to cover all Mien parents.

In the Mien and many other Asian cultures, daughter-in-laws have the most complicated and challenging role to play in family. The daughter-in-law is given most crucial and difficult responsibilities of anyone in the entire family. She wears multiple hats and different shoes inside and outside of the home.

As a wife, she is to love, please, and be obedient to her husband. She is to give him love, affection, attention, clean his clothes, patch or repair his clothes, prepare his food, and work along side of him when possible. She is also to bear him children, especially a son.

As a mother, she is to nurse the babies, care for her children, and hand-embroider and sew their clothing,. At night she sleeps between her husband and their baby. Since there was no diapers available in the remote villages in the past, when the baby wets one side of the bed, she is to turn him over to the other side. When both sides of the bed are wet, the baby is to sleep on her stomach. During the day, she is to carry her baby on her back while she works in the home pounding rice, grinding corn, and preparing meals for the family and the domestic animals. Depending on the size of the family and the number of pigs and chickens, she may work from sunrise to sunset and yet not be able to complete all of the housework. In addition, she is also responsible for organizing the home, preparing meals for her in-laws, tending to the livestock, and she is expected to work in the fields with her husband and other family members whenever possible.

As a daughter-in-law, she is to respect her in-laws and please them with her cooking and diligent attention to her chores. It is not acceptable for her to argue, talk back or disagree with her in-laws. Since they spent a lot of money on the wedding and bride price, she is to demonstrate her worthiness to the family in her daily performance. She is to carefully receive their orders and fulfill them satisfactorily. (This cultural norm has resulted in many women viewing themselves as property that can be bought or sold.)

Today, as many Mien people are now living in the U.S., they have become educated in many social and academic arenas, and have begun to study and question their traditional family values and norms. While some still preserve the traditional cultural behaviors and patterns, others have assimilated completely into the fast-paced Western society and have very little interest in Mien history or tradition.

Types of Family Structure

Researchers have explored different types of family structure. Collins identified three distinct family structures. They are: the patriarch, the Victorian and the egalitarian family.

In the first type, the patriarch, children are subjective to their father. The father is the leader of the family in a position of dominance and decision-making power.

The second type is known as the Victorian Family. In this family structure, the women are to be loved, cherished, and nurtured for their beauty, charm, and sweetness. They ought not struggle as men do. Women's tender attributes need full protection. The most delightful thing the world can offer women is their ideal of womanhood—being the women of the world.

The third type is the egalitarian family. In this family structure, both men and women have equal rights and are considered equals or partners in raising their children and making decisions. The relevant laws in the U.S., based on the Equal Rights Amendment of 1972 give all males and females equality of respect, dignity and opportunities in life.

Regardless of the different types of structure, "the family has always been an important part of society, and it continues to be so today. The basic unit of stratification is not the individual so much as the family" (Collins).

The Mien family structure can be classified under the first family type, the patriarch. In the patriarch family structure, the children and wives are subject to the father's leadership. For an unmarried female, she needs to obey her father and older brothers. Once married, she is subject to her husband. When widowed, she needs to respect and obey her sons. A woman must never be independent unless she has no children, parents or other male relatives. She must never separate herself from her parents before married, her husband after she's married, or her sons when widowed or divorced as leaving any of them would make both families contemptible.

Although the Mien come from a patriarchal society, parents and children love and respect each other, albeit demonstrated in a culturally specific way, nonetheless. Children find meaning in life through reliance on their parents while the parents control their children, teach them the necessary knowledge to thrive in life, pass on the family values and survival skills, and guide them in moral character development.

The traditional Mien patriarchal family operates under the following eight principles.

1. The ideology with respect to men results in gender inequality. Mien households are generally organized along corporate lines, usually centered on the conjugal relationship where the husband is the head of the entire family unit. This form of patriarchy has created gender inequality within the family, especially for the wives and female children. The Mien family, kinship and gender relations were organized and in patterns of male economic activity. Kinship structures are predominantly patrilineal where the descent is traced and property transmitted through the male members. Women tend to marry outside their kin and often outside their village community, leaving their own homes at marriage to join their husband's family. Households are organized along highly corporate lines, with strong conjugal bonds and cultural rules that emphasize male responsibility for protecting and provisioning women and

children. Household resources and income are pooled under the management and control of the male patriarch. The payment of bride price by the groom's family to the bride is the norm.

Household inequality: There are basic inequalities in gender relations within the family or the household, which can take many different forms. Family usually pays more attention and values sons higher than their daughters. Traditionally, family thinks that girls are less capable or less worthy of investment in terms of education since girls are physically, emotionally, and intellectually weaker than boys. Family expects future support and stability from sons more than from daughters. This form of unbalanced belief is largely developed through the fact that when boys get married, they will bring home their wives to support and strengthen the family needs; whereas, girls would leave their parents to form a new home with their husbands.

The family arrangements can be quite unequal in terms of sharing the burden of housework and child care. Men are believed to work naturally outside the home, and women are to handle household matters in caring for the children, tending livestock, preparing meals, and sewing or patching family clothing. The reach of this inequality includes not only unequal relations within the family, but also derivative inequalities in employment and recognition in the inside and outside world.

2. Today, legal marriage is either pronounced by a shaman, modern pastor, priest, or a judge. Traditional marriage was acknowledged by a shaman or *saikung* and witnessed by the family, relatives, friends, and neighbors. This forms the basic constituent of a Mien family. Non-legal marriages do not generate the same parental and spousal rights and responsibilities. In a Mien marriage, the husbands usually hold stronger and higher rights and responsibilities than the wives. Mien marriages involve a bride price, in some cases where the bride price was too high, it created a great financial barrier for some couples to get married. For married couples, divorce was rarely an option for the wives regardless of the marriage situation. Under any conditions, when a husband decides to divorce his wife, he shall

do so with the support of his family members without any legal restrictions or boundaries. However, when a wife chooses to divorce her husband for any reason, she is expected to repay her husband and his parents, doubling the bride price as previously discussed. In most cases, the financial limitation created an impossible route for any married woman to take or consider.
3. Household and family members are treated as a congruous or well-adapted and appropriate. Within a Mien family dynamic, the wellness of the family outweighs the desire of an individual. Parents are accountable for their children's actions as discussed earlier in this chapter. Likewise, older siblings are held accountable for their younger sibling's actions and behaviors when their parents are not present.
4. The family household is treated as a single unit with the father and/or grandfather being at the top of the pyramid. Fathers and grandfathers are the backbones of the family. When a grandfather reaches his senior years and is unable to take on any physical labor, he instead provides emotional and intellectual guidance to his sons and grandchildren.
5. The husband is the sole bread-winner and is responsible for the financial well-being of the family. The children and elderly are financial dependents on the husband and his wife. The weight of the family falls on the husband. He must do all that he can to sustain the physical, emotional and spiritual needs of his family. Failure to do so will bring disappointment, shame, embarrassment, and the loss of respect to the family.
6. The wife is given the role of providing care and services to the family members in need.
7. In the traditional Mien communities in Laos and Thailand, strong support was provided by the community for families in need. On the other hand, there was no public assistance available of any kind to support families in need. When a parent is missing for whatever reason, the children are cared for by the remaining parent. When both parents are absent, usually the grandparents or another relative would adopt them. Orphaned children would not be left alone by themselves.
8. Family members have always been economically interconnected. There are intergenerational and intra-generational transfers that

routinely take place within families. A family goes through both good times and bad times together as one. When a good time comes, the family rejoices, celebrates, and laughs together. When a tough time comes, the father and mother are at the frontline protecting their children. When food becomes scarce, the children eat first and the parents eat last, from the youngest to the oldest. Parents' primary concern is the safety and wellness of their children. The more children a couple have, the harder they must work and the more they have to prepare themselves for more hardships (known as *guaax hnyouv camv* in the Mien language).

Sadly, these rich family values have become depreciated by many children who are born and/or raised in the Western culture. For many Mien that have grown up in the new land of wealth and opportunity, they have not recognized the true love, hardships and suffering that their parents or grandparents endured in Laos or Thailand in order to bring their families to safety and freedom in the U.S. This generation of American-born and raised Mien youth, therefore, cannot comprehend or maintain these core family values. The traditional family structure has become a strange concept to the newer generations of Mien people in the U.S. The Western culture does not promote interdependence among family members but rather independency in self-worth, self-value and individualism within the family and society. Interdependence within the family circle has been viewed by Western culture as a sign of weakness, laziness or incompetence (*mau, lueic, maiv maaih banh zeic* in Mien language).

The longer Mien families live in the U.S., the smaller the size of families. For example, during the late seventies and early eighties, when Mien families began to immigrate to the U.S., Canada, and France, everyone from multiple generations lived together under one roof as they had in Laos or Thailand, regardless of the size of the family. For example, my family of six people lived together in a small one-bedroom apartment. Later, after I got married, my wife came to join our family and we had seven people living together. The kitchen was so small that my wife and mother couldn't cook together. They had to take turns in preparing meals for the family. Since the bedroom only had enough space for my parents, two younger brothers and a younger sister, my wife and I slept at the entrance of the bedroom. As long as we were able to be together, we did not complain about the tight living situation. Being together and building the security among family members was an important part of family life.

Other Mien families lived together in the same apartment building. Many apartment buildings were filled with Mien and other refugee families from different parts of Asia. Children were able to play together inside and outside of the apartment buildings, and adults were able to socialize among themselves within the different apartments. While the children enjoyed themselves on the playground, their elders shared foods and exchanged stories about their lives. Families were able to benefit from mutual resources developed by and for the community and that created more security and happiness for everyone. However, the image of family being "together" has changed. Today, the Mien are learning English, pursuing higher education and ambitious careers and, as a result, have greater financial means than ever before. They are, therefore, able to live in larger homes, though family sizes are shrinking at the same time. After high school completion, some youth become full-time students and move out to a college dormitory, and others may get married and move out of their parents' homes to start their own lives. Mien children in America differ from Mien children living in less affluent societies, such as those from small villages in Laos, Thailand, Vietnam or China, in their desire for personal space, privacy, and independence.

Chapter 3

Mien Families in America

Major Turning Points for Mien Family Life and the Generational Groups

Mien people living in the U.S. can be classified into four different groups. They are the nomadic, the sojourner, the pathfinder and the millennial. The nomadic generation includes parents or grandparents who were born between 1920 and 1962. The first group consists of parents who were born overseas in Laos or Thailand, got married and had children overseas, and brought their family to the U.S. as young adults. The second group is the sojourners who were born between 1963 and 1978. The sojourner group includes individuals and couples, who were born overseas in Laos or Thailand, got married overseas, as well as those who came here as young adults, got married in the U.S., and their children were born in America. The third group is the pathfinder group encompassing singles and married couples who were born from 1979 to 2000. This group has parents who were born and raised in the U.S. and started their own families here. The fourth group is the millennial group, which includes people who were born and grew up in the U.S. from 2001 up to the present.

First generation parents not only have different educational and occupational backgrounds as the other generations, but they also have gone through life experiences and challenges that lead them to raise their children and grandchildren differently than modern society. These parents came from a primitive lifestyle where their survival mainly depended on the grace and goodness of nature to provide them the heat and rain needed to grow their crops. They have adopted parenting skills, child-rearing techniques, and cultural values not from reading textbooks, attending seminars, or from experts on TV, but mainly from their parents, grandparents and other neighboring families.

The sojourner parents have similar life experiences and hold similar cultural values as the nomadic generation parents. Both of these generations came from an agricultural background and went through the recruitment of adult males into wars, fighting during the different wars in Laos, and migrating from one region to another for safety. Some people in the sojourner generation may have had some limited education in the Laotian educational system. Those who were able to attend some grade schools in Laos were able to acquire some Laotian literacy skills, but had their education significantly interrupted by constant relocations. Families in this generation lived in war zones, constantly fearing for their lives. At an early age, they learned not to trust anyone outside their immediate family. So many people had their trust broken not only by the government but by their fellow countrymen as well. In addition to their life betraying experiences, they had to uproot their families and leave their homeland where they faced real dangers of life and death fleeing to Thailand. They encountered so many unimaginable hardships prior to leaving Laos, during the journey to freedom, in the refugee camps in Thailand, and through post-migration traumatic stress after they resettled in the U.S.

The third generation of Mien living in the U.S. is the pathfinder group. These are people who migrated to the U.S. from Laos or Thailand and those individuals born in America between 1980 and 2000. Those who arrived either as young children or grown adults not only discovered themselves to be the new strangers in a new land, but experienced cultural shock and language barriers. Mien people described themselves as "fish living on land and cats taken out of sacks." While the adults had to undergo many shameful and embarrassing moments because of not speaking the language and not understanding the cultural norms and expectations, and racial tensions, many young people encountered the societal influences of cultural assimilation and acculturation. Identity crises emerged to challenge the young adults requiring them to redefine their personal goals and interests, family values, social acceptance and societal expectations.

The pathfinders who received extensive formal educational training in the U.S. have become the bridge builders and messengers defining the gaps between themselves and other generations. They have some very crucial roles and responsibilities to fulfill not only within their family but also within their community. They are the amphibians who not only can walk on a dry land within the dynamic of their family circle, but they also can swim in the surrounding ocean. They have no choice but to quickly adapt and function well in their new roles and duties, for their family and friends rely on them as language and culture brokers. They are also known as the bridge-builders between the other three generations and particularly for the nomadic generation. They serve as messengers or interpreters between the older generation of parents and grandparents and the younger generation of their children and grandchildren. In addition, they become the connection for the older generation between their traditional and modern worlds.

The fourth group of Mien people in the U.S. is the millennial. This generation includes individuals who were born and raised in this country from 2001 to the present. At the present time they are not parents, yet they serve as the future Mien. These are the young bodies, souls and spirits of Mien people for future generations. The strengths and weaknesses of Mien cultural values and traditions depend on this generational group. There many factors and societal influences that can impact the future generations of Mien, not only in America but in many parts of the world.

There are clear distinctions between the millennial generation Mien and the other generations, including survival skills, the knowledge and access of technology, traditional versus modern worldviews, personal and family values, and societal pressures. For physical needs, today's Mien children are unlike their parents and grandparents whose survival skills were mainly dependent on intensive labor in order to put food on the table for the family. They do not need to get up every morning, seven days a week, before dawn to sharpen their knives and axes to cultivate the field. Instead, they only need to pick up a pen or pencil to write or hold the knowledge to operate a computer. For intellectual growth, there are both public and private schools available for people to gain the best and highest education in the land. There are a wide variety of choices, options, and support services for people to become educated in almost any profession.

For spiritual needs, the millennial Mien have limited or no former knowledge about the ancestral worship or traditional religion of their parents or ancestors. They are born and raised in a society where churches exist in every city and town. Public schools and available textbooks do not teach a Mien student how preserve his or her traditional religion. Instead, individuals are being exposed in the public school system to knowledge about global religions, beliefs, and making independent choices for one's spiritual health. Therefore, today's Mien children and youths are being bombarded with all kinds of mixed messages between the home, the church, the school and the world of media. The different and confusing complexities presented to them have led many young people to isolate themselves from participating in any particular religion or belief. The free agent form of individualist life style definite has created a generation gap between the millennial and the sojourner and nomadic generations. At the present time, there is no solution to bridge this gap. It has become wider and deeper as time passes.

The differences between the millennial and the other generations are many. Young people are very technology savvy, constantly on the go and changing rapidly. They are involved with so many activities that the older generations not only cannot comprehend what is going on in the lives of their children, but cannot accept them as appropriate social norms in the Mien community. These changes include dress codes, body language, behavior, hair style, body piercing or tattooing, peers, after school and on the weekend activities, and time spent on the internet and telephones. Some of these activities require parental involvement, participation and financial support. For academically challenged children who have extra-curricular activities after school, such as sports, music or an early start program at a local community college, parents need to support their children in order for them to be successful. This kind of parental involvement is necessary but it also causes limitations on their personal or family time.

The millennial group of Mien value optimism and diversity differently from their parents. The traditional collectivism that is being valued and preserved by the older generations can be a dividing factor with the millennial generation. The minds of the millennial see America as a multicultural and multilingual nation. Children begin their education from grade school to college with very little foundation of the traditional family and cultural values of their parents and ancestors. Their minds have been filled and refilled with broad and mixed messages from today's technology world and expectations. Parents try to instill in their children one set of personal and family values, while the media and technology offer them different deals that are hard to refuse. As we all know people are attracted to bigger and better things in life. Therefore, modern society has captured the attention and interest of today's young people much more rapidly and effectively than their parents.

Since children have been taught to be open-minded to accept and appreciate diversity, they begin to do so by opening their minds, hearts and bodies and exposing themselves to the big and wide world. Being taught to appreciate diversity is an important part of our personal social developmental process. However, the sad part comes when people leave their minds open all the time and do not have any limitation, boundary or digression to what is appropriate or inappropriate, healthy or harmful, valuable or invaluable, or constructive or destructive form of information, behaviors or life sustaining ingredients. When a person's mind is being constantly opened, that person's mind will be filled with anything and everything that comes into it. Not everything is good or necessary for the mind; there has to be a certain parameter to the information that comes in and goes out of the mind. The "open-minded" concept has caused today's young adults to create conflicts with their parents and the older generations, especially in the areas of socializing, dating and intermarriages. The turning points of Mien family life and generational groups are summarized in the following table.

Table 1. Turning Points in Mien Family Life

TURNING POINTS IN MIEN FAMILY LIFE		
GENERATION	YEAR OF BIRTH	CHARACTERISTICS
Nomadic	1920-1956	Primitive lifestyle Life depended on the goodness of the nature
Sojourner	1957-1978	Being recruited into war Constant migrating for safety Live lives full of fear, mistrust and betrayed Family uprooted, dispersed Encountered hunger, starvation, diseases and death Refugee camp experience of neglect, abuses, rapes, tortures, diseases
Pathfinder	1978-2000	New strangers in a strange land Cultural shock, language barrier, fish living on land, "cats taken out of sacks" Searching for identity and belonging Racial and discrimination issues Assimilation and acculturation pressures
Millennial	2001-present	Technological savvy Constant on the go and change Being involved in many activities Value optimism and diversity Independent and self-centered Government is the cause of today's problems

In the typical Mien home, parents expect their children to achieve high academic performance and at the same time assist with household chores, take care of younger siblings, and earn income to support themselves, their family and those who are unable to obtain employment whenever possible. The older children are responsible for providing transportation, translation and interpretation for the family and relatives, especially for their elders.

Girls have more household responsibilities than boys. They are often called to prepare meals, do laundry and babysit. They have more restrictions than their brothers.

It is not unusual that the older children become tutors for their younger siblings if their parents are not literate in English. The older children are also held accountable for their younger siblings' actions when the parents are not present. These responsibilities put the older children in the position of acting as parents to their younger siblings. They automatically become the authoritative figures to discipline their younger siblings for inappropriate or dangerous behaviors. By granting such authorities to watch over, care for and discipline, the older children need to perform their assigned roles and duties or they will have to explain themselves upon the parents' return.

Younger children are expected to respect their older siblings and honor their parents. If they harm their parents, they are being warned of generational curses or being struck by thunder (*mba'ong piqv*). The Mien people have a saying that, "*Jae-dorn da'lueix da'lueix seix nzipc seix, jae-nyeiz ndongx-ndueih luonh taux meih*." It simply translates, "as chicks become chickens and children become parents, what you do to your parents will be done unto you." This profound statement echoes a loud and clear message to the children and adults on how they should love, obey, respect, and care for their parents in a manner in which they would expect the same treatment from their children. This golden rule informs the children that every action you take creates a reaction. Depending on the type of reaction they prefer to receive, they would need to act accordingly. Since everyone desires the best behavior from their children, parents often remind their children of this golden rule.

Children are always expected to respect their parents, older siblings, elders, grandparents, teachers, and authority, for the Mien culture teaches "the older you are, the more wisdom you have accumulated, for you have seen the sun first." Although this may be a common belief for many elders, the statement is no longer valid for the younger generation as they receive more education in the U.S. The younger generation tends to view knowledge and wisdom differently than the older generation.

Religious Points of View on Marriage

As mentioned in earlier chapters, the Mien religion is known as ancestor worship, Taoist or animism. Traditional Mien sacred texts or religious ceremonial books do not discuss any particular guidelines as to how a couple should conduct a marriage or live out their married life. The texts provide basic information on spiritual ancestors, their ranks and positions, and how they are supposed to be honored, remembered and worshipped. None of the moral values are instituted in any of the religious text books. Generally speaking, the religious points-of-view on marriage have been studied and reported that, "from the middle ages to the early part of the twentieth century, marital disharmony has occurred in a social context strongly supportive of the institution of Christian marriage. The few remedies offered ranged from the church's admonition to formal discipline in rebuke or penance, or pastoral counsel supporting the members of the family, and neighborly intervention. For the deserted wife and children, there might be support from extended family or friends or from the operation of the poor law, or from charitable funds" (Her Majesty's Stationary Office).

Religious point-of-view on marriage has also been studied by many researchers. Eichler stated that religions play an important role on what are 'good' or 'bad' families, especially sexuality. Public morality is associated with human sexual behaviors and it should be regulated through families. Each individual in the society plays an important role within the larger society. The way we conduct ourselves and our marriage lives stem from our own personal experiences, level of education and religious beliefs. Wilcox reported that the cultural content of particular religious activities, beliefs, and practices, then, can matter for family behavior. Variations in religious strength, the religious logic of practice, and family-related ideologies and norms may be associated with distinctive levels of familial involvements and patterns of familial interaction. Religious institutions that have a substantial measure of religious vitality, distinctive congregational practices and style of religious worship, and a countercultural family worldview are especially likely to have a distinctive effect on the family life of their members. In turn, individuals who identify with the religious and family related into the life of that institution will probably be more influenced in their family behavior by the cultural content of their religion.

The response to marriage issues differs from culture to culture, state to state and nation to nation. As a society becomes more individualistic and less collectivist, traditional family core values become weakened, less valued and gradually disintegrate. Men and women are now free to marry, to manage their relationships, to determine the size and spacing of their family, to determine their marriage and increasingly to re-marry if desired. Within the Mien communities in the U.S., it is believed by the majority of leaders and elders that the divorce rate among non-Christians are higher than among the Christians. The general view of this topic has been studied and reported by W. Bradford Wilcox, a sociologist at the University of Virginia. In his study, Wilcox explores how American Protestantism shapes the behavior of husbands and fathers. He examines the familial behaviors of evangelical men with different religious practices as shown in three large-scale surveys taken in the early 1990s. The surveys found that active evangelicals spend more time on parenting and working to fulfill the emotional needs of their wives and children than do nominal evangelicals. Wilcox argues that 'religious community' culture 'domesticates' men, making them more attentive to the emotional needs of their wives and children.

He concludes, "My findings indicate that the wives of both conservative and mainline Protestant family men are more likely to report happiness with the love and affection they receive from their husbands, compared to wives of unaffiliated men. The wives of active conservative and mainline Protestants are more likely than their nominal counterparts to report of happiness with the love and affection they receive from their husbands". Although the study does not focus on the Mien people in the U.S., the findings yield similar results to my own observations as an educator, ordained minister, and counselor.

The changing of family value systems, communication styles, the meaning of love and forgiveness, and being faithful to each other before God and humans are some of the important concepts that exist between these two groups of Mien in the U.S.

Mien Christians and non-Christians have different views and interpretations on love and forgiveness. I have asked Mien shamans, *saikungs*, and elders about any ceremonial texts which define the meaning of love in Mien, and none are known. Through my discovery, people normally define "love" as a strong affection between two people. Love creates a very deep emotional and physical feeling of like, acceptance, approval, and enjoyment within a person and the one he or she is attached to. In the Mien traditional culture, love is revealed silently through hard work, being responsible, obedience, sharing goods, and living together under one roof. Although love is not being expressed verbally, Mien couples and family members love each other inwardly in a silent way.

According to the American Heritage Dictionary, love is defined as a "strong affection for or attachment to another person based on regard or share experiences or interests." Webster's Unabridged Dictionary says, "[l]ove is pleased with; to regard with affection on account of some qualities which excite pleasing sensations, or desire of gratification." A more modern version of Webster states "[l]ove is a feeling of warm personal attachment or deep affection." In either instance, love is defined in general terms with criteria and conditions.

Conditional love relies on performance. One can only love the other when the expectations are met and the meanings of love are similar. It is like, "I have a love box. (I am the only one who knows the shape, size, and depth of this box). If you love me, you should fill it with the right pieces of "love ornaments." Love exists depending on whether or not the gratification is maintained. As long as one person can generate the warm, fuzzy feelings in another, love prevails, but when events interfere with or eliminate the fuzzy feelings, love disappears. And that is the point—for many people, love is just a feeling, sometimes maintained over a period of time, sometimes quite temporary. In other words, it is the feeling that is loved, not the person. The focus of love is on the feeling instead of the person whom they are joining their life with. If the relationship interferes with one's pursuits in other areas, it can be isolated and removed.

Authentic love, genuine love, real love, true love or abiding love is unlike feeling love. It comes from a higher calling and has a deeper meaning. It has a sense of commitment, a feeling of responsibility to the other person, and a willingness to work out problems. The problem of conditional love is very apparent in Mien marriages in the U.S. In our current American culture, marriage is frequently a union of two independent people, sometimes fiercely independent, which turns into a power struggle, each of them asserting their respective "identities" and "rights." Love is related to the performance of the other person. Each seeks to achieve his or her goals with little emphasis on common goals.

Many Christian Mien married couples and families are taught the different views and interpretations of love and forgiveness by their pastors, Sunday school teachers, and the Bible. Those who have been taught and have accepted the teaching of the Bible have a different understanding of the meaning of love. The Bible describes love from a biblical perspective that a real love is sacrificial love. True love is an altruistic love that comes with forgiveness and every lasting love. Love is defined by the Bible as patient, kind, not envy, does not boast, does not proud, not rude, not self-seeking, not easily angered, keeps no record of wrong, not delight in evil, but rejoices with truth, endures hardship, always trust, always hope, always perseveres, and never fails (I Corinthians, Chapter 13). According to this profound meaning of love, couples, families, and individuals who have adopted this principle can create a healthy and meaningful relationship within their marriages.

The altruistic or amazing love of God is so different from the kind of love most of people have known. Real Love is caring about the happiness of another person through Godly and moral lenses without any thought for what we might get for ourselves. It is necessary to understand that unconditional love does not mean permissive love. Unconditional love needs to be viewed and determined through Godly, moral and ethical perspectives. If not, God's unconditional love could be incorrectly misinterpreted and applied in permissive or promiscuous ways. We can be certain that we're receiving Real Love only when we make mistakes, when we fail to do what other people want, when we fail to meet people's expectations, and even when we get in their way, they are willing to forgive, accept and correct us for our wrong doings. That is Real Love (true unconditional love), and that love alone has the power to reconcile conflicts, heal all wounds, bind people together, and create relationships quite beyond our present capacity to imagine.

Permissive love believes that showing one's love and feelings, in return, is the ultimate goal in a relationship. Permissive love tends to avoid conflict at any cost. Discipline and limits are often missing from the permissive love. Permissive spouses do love each other and are highly bonded to one and another. They believe the key to their spouse's heart is to relate to their spouse as a peer instead of as a spouse. Rules, if they exist at all, are inconsistent at best. Rules developed by fallible humans are meant to be broken sooner or later, in one way or the other without any lifetime guarantees. If a permissive spouse needs to act on a rule or expectation, often times that spouse will use any means necessary including bribery, gifts, food, services and other motivators to gain their spouse's compliance.

One of the problems with permissive love is that spouses need healthy limits and expectations not only to learn appropriate behavior for functioning as a member of a family or society, but also to feel valued and cared for. Often, over time, spouses in a permission love relationship suffer a loss in self esteem because there is no check and balance on their actions or behaviors in a relationship. Likewise, spouses feel like an important part of a marriage relationship when they are held to a higher standard and are required to be part of that functional family. Permissive love, in their desire to be everything for each other, often times miss the target entirely and have very little to offer in marriage relationship. Permissive love in a marriage relationship does not have a strong inner sense of boundary or discipline, or a sense of connectedness with each other. Permissive love does not work in a marriage relationship or either other relationships. Applying God's altruistic love with human's real love and affection is a healthy part of a marriage and family relationship.

In the environment where love comes with certain conditions, love may only exist between two or more people when the terms and expectations are being met. For some people love is revealed through physical beauty or attraction, and for others it is demonstrated through good deeds, kindness, hospitality, generosity, and emotional connection. When love comes with terms and conditions, love is destined to fail or end when the actual realities do not match the expectations. Therefore, disappointments, despairs and consequences occur when people do not receive what they have hoped to get. People normally react according to their present state of mind, emotion, understanding, and expectations. The presuppositions one has developed about oneself and the society become a driven force to how a person reactions toward life circumstances.

Changes in Mien Marriages and Families in the U.S.

Since the turn of the century, families and society have undergone several major upheavals, including wars, migrations, a great depression, and a modern recession, which is, to all intents and purposes, another great depression. In the U.S., Mien people reside mainly in the states of Washington, Oregon, and California in both large and small community settings depending on their employment, housing availability, accessibility to natural and community resources, relatives and individual trusted and respected community leaders. Mien refugees from Laos and Thailand have had their lives shaped and reshaped from their past isolated, disadvantaged and primitive environments. Today they are living in a highly technological society where they experience unfamiliar cultural systems. The Mien have been known for their diligent agricultural and strong family values. Living in remote villages they practiced slash-and-burn agriculture. Resources were formed from nuclear and extended families, relatives and individuals villagers.

In the Mien traditional relationship between boyfriend and girlfriend (*gorngv-waac mienh or ja'zeih auv ja'zeih nqox*) and husband or wife, affection toward one another was always performed in the dark, known as "*Love grows in the dark.*" After dinner darkness quickly surrounded the village and provided the villagers secret and private intimacy settings. With flash lights (for those who could afford ones) or with dried bamboo sticks, tied up in bundles, there was sufficient light and for boys to discover ways to meet or visit girls in their homes, usually in their bedrooms. (Mien people in Laos and Thailand used to sleep on bamboo or wooded beds, unlike the soft and comfortable western mattresses). For unmarried individuals intimacy began in the dark. For married couples, intimacy developed and grew from the dark as well. Affection of any form between lovers was to be concealed during the day but could be freely revealed at night when no one could see. In many cases, lovers could not even see each other's faces. Love connected through kinesthetic sense. To put in a simple form, "Love was not by sight but by talking, touching and feeling."

In the isolated villages in Laos and Thailand where Mien people used to live and many still reside today, people usually work from sunrise to sunset. When the sun rises, public affection disappears. True love is to remain and be cherished inwardly until the sun goes down until daylight appears again. Gifts, presents, love letters or notes were never delivered in person between two unmarried lovers. Married couples did not exchange or present their love or gifts to each other in public either. This cultural norm poses a great relationship barrier to many Mien couples in the U.S. As couples have lived and assimilated into American society, expectations and perceptions of family, love and marriage have changed. Those that have been acculturated now believe that sincere love and appreciation are expected to be revealed in public as well as in the homes. It is not considered as a form of pride. There are several occasions and holidays in the U.S. that couples expect their spouses to be familiar with and apply them in their marriage relationship, such as, Valentine's Day, Mother's Day, Father's Day, birthdays and anniversaries.

Traditionally, none of these occasions existed in the Mien culture, except for rare birthday celebrations for parents and elders. In the U.S., Valentine's Day marks a significant event for couples to reveal their love and appreciation to each other through roses, gifts, love letters, poems, greeting cards, romantic dinners, movies and other romantic activities or get always. Love letters, poems, greeting cards are strange concepts to Mien elderly couples, especially after marriage. Many Mien find themselves facing one strange concept after another. It is almost like peeling an onion where one would find layer after layer of newly revealed practices or customs.

In my volunteer counseling service at a local church in Tukwila, Washington and with many years of contacts with Mien, Hmong and Lao communities in the U.S., I have seen many individuals and couples express their frustration and unhappiness toward their spouses for not being romantic or thoughtful during these special holidays. Some women have expressed their disappointment when their husbands failed to celebrate one or more of these special days. Some wives even are upset when their husbands for gaving them inappropriate gifts or presents for the occasions (as defined my modern society). These disappointments due to cultural differences can often lead to resentment. Wives view their husbands as being unloving, inconsiderate, or uncaring. The cultural changes and unparallel knowledge and expectations put many spouses in difficult and challenging positions. Many husbands, especially those from the older generations, are confused about the meanings of the different holidays and events throughout the year. While the younger generational spouses are well familiar with these cultural systems and value them greatly, there are those who do not understand the social changes, and are therefore placed in a catch twenty-two type of situation. On the one hand, these husbands know that they will be in trouble with their wives if they don't celebrate the occasion, but on the other hand, it might be worse if they produce the wrong present. Cultural differences such as these new and confusing American customs have created barriers and issues for Mien spouses as they assimilate into western society. Most women have special preferences when it comes to gifts and presents from their husbands. To avoid some of these pitfalls, it is crucial for the husbands to know their wives' favorite colors, styles and desires, and know their sizes, shapes and brand names they prefer.

On the contrary, the older or less acculturated spouses become confused and astonished when they received unexpected gifts, flowers, letters, cards, romantic dinners or getaways. Some couples can be greatly embarrassed when their spouses show public affection, such as holding their hands, giving hugs, or presenting gifts or roses to them in front of their children, friends, relatives or co-workers. The most westernized and thoughtful husbands would take extra steps to take their wives out for special candlelight dinners or romantic activities. Some organize special events to reveal their loves for their wives through songs, poems, and entertainment. The religious groups often organize special programs or services at their churches to celebrate the different holidays. For those who have been exposed to the new cultural practices, they have gradually learned to accept and participate in these activities. Despite the "traditionally inappropriateness" activities, some elderly and the less-acculturated couples have come to enjoy themselves during the celebrations. Some become great supporters and encouragers to the different cultural system while others are offended and will not participate in these types of romantic functions again.

Retreats for married couples and love celebrations for Mien people are also new ideas since they did not exist in Laos or Thailand. The first

Mien Couple's Retreat started in 1997 in the Northwest organized by the Seattle and Portland Mien churches. Now, the retreat has grown and branched out to Mien churches and community members in California, with participants coming from many different states and Canada. It has become an eye-opening event to draw couples together for relaxation, fellowship, learning new ways to strengthen their families and marriages and solving marital conflicts by incorporating Biblical principles and Western family management styles. Every year, couples' lives have been changed and local couple's retreats and workshops have developed within many local churches as they become more popular.

The more couples and families become familiar with the U.S. cultural norms, the more receptive they are in terms of revealing their affection and appreciation to their spouses. As people are exposed to the different sets of cultural values, the more they are willing to accept new concepts or ideas. Understanding the meaning, value, and rewards of appreciating one's spouse, parents and grandparents have been taught through the teaching and preaching of pastors and Christian teachers. Sunday school teachers also emphasize the important of honoring and respecting one's parents and elders. Appreciation of gifts, presents, letters, greeting cards, and embracement are given from children to parents and grandparents. Anniversary and birthday celebrations are becoming customary with gifts and cakes made by non-Mien people given to commemorate the special occasions.

For the non-Christian Mien, birthday celebrations involve a big feast with live bands to entertain people by creating an atmosphere for spouses to publically display their affection and appreciation on a dance floor. Couples dance together and with other spouses or friends, enjoying the fun and relaxation. Families and friends are requested to be present from different cities and states. Locally and nationally known Mien musicians and singers are invited to celebrate and perform during these special occasions. Many of these celebrations involve the butchering of a pig or a cow in order to provide plentiful food for all the quests. While the interested couples and individuals enjoy themselves on the dance floor, grandparents and elders keep watch over the young ones and their grandchildren at home. Many elderly people have come to accept the new social and cultural changes after numerous cultural shocks in learning the customs of western culture. After many years of effort trying to preserve the traditional cultural norms and values, many elderly parents and grandparents stop trying and gradually begin to accept them as they are. It becomes clear that many have adopted the concept of "If you can't overcome them, it would be better for you to join them."

Family Matters

Even though the father is the head of the house and makes the final decisions for all family matters, there are some issues that require advice and feedback from the whole family (parents, grandparents) or the community, such as the community leaders or other knowledgeable or wise family members. The Mien think and believe that a group consensus is often the wisest and best solution to problem solving. In some situations, despite the individual's concerns or interests about the issue, he or she would normally agree with the decision made by the group.

In the U.S. Mien-American-born and educated individuals have different views on individual decision-making and group decision-making. When a decision is to be made by a group, the most assimilated individuals are usually expected to be able to express their opinions and to exert fair influence when the decision is made. To fulfill the individual's expectations, he or she can be quite concerned about matters of procedure. The main concern is for the purpose of ensuring fairness where the members of a group in a decision making can make logical and suitable decisions for themselves. According to cultural expectations, males are more matter-of-fact and achievement-oriented, while females are necessarily more warm, emotional, and expressive or verbal. These roles are seen as mutually reinforcing one another, making up a mutually beneficial system.

Today Mien marriages and families have different sets of social, cultural and religious values that govern their new lives in a new land. They are no longer living under the traditional family norms, values and expectations, but are free to choose whatever lifestyles they desire. Being Mien in America, individuals and families are not only encouraged by the society to make their own choices, but are given different sets of moral, social and family values to choose. There are so many choices to choose from, and in many cases these choices become overwhelmed for the individuals and families. Unfortunately, people who cannot make their own choices shouldn't worry because society will decide for them. Before they become fully aware of it, the matter may have already been settled.

Mien marriages and families in the U.S. have different sets of challenges and family issues. Their marital and family issues have been broadened to include religious differences, financial problems, child-rearing issues, prolonged unemployment, communication failures, sexual problems, physical and emotional illness, physical and emotional spouse abuse, alcoholism and drug abuse, gambling addiction, dual career problems, issues of power and control, and the loss of love and passion compared to those living in Asian countries. In terms of religion, Mien in Asian countries worship ancestors or practice animism and have limited exposure to Christianity or other religions as those who are in the U.S. There are fewer idealistic conflicts between spouses on religion differences simply because the options weren't available. Children or family members could not make their own choices to worship any religion they desired. Since religion plays a major part in a person's life, making a personal choice in conflict with the norm would have to be approved by the family and sometimes by the whole clan.

Financial limitations are another big issue facing marriages and families. Families with low or insufficient income to meet the family's needs and demands can be forced to work in multiple employment and/ or odd work schedules preventing them from cultivating their family relationship and having quality family time. With various other reasons, financial burdens have created many challenges for family members to grow as a single unit, because they are often fragmented into different parts. Children from a low income family often are pressured to gain employment as soon as possible in order to supplement the family needs and expenses. While some children are able to complete high school, others may be required to drop out of high school as soon as they are able to find a job to help the family. Therefore, it either delays or prevents them from going to university where they can earn a higher degree and advance their careers. This topic is further discussed later in this chapter. As discussed in Chapter Three, religion plays a major part in the Mien people's lives in the U.S., especially in marriages, but there are other dilemmas that emerge in people's homes, as follows.

The Results of Unhealthy Communication

Unhealthy communication often leads spouses and family members into abusive relationships. Spousal abuse is believed to exist in every country and every culture. There are many forms and degrees of spousal abuse within marriage and in families. However, not every spousal abuse or domestic violence is reported or known to the public. In certain cultures, family and spousal problems are not to be shared or known by anyone outside the family. It is considered as embarrassment, shameful, and degrading for outsiders to know about the family's issues. Within the Mien culture there is a closed door policy, that is, family matters are to be kept private. Poor communication or ineffective conversations can gradually develop into verbal abuse, physical abuse, sexual abuse, emotional abuse, economic abuse, and spiritual abuse within the marriage and family unit.

Marital conflict is unavoidable. When each partner brings his or her own perspective into the relationship, which is influenced by gender, family and religious backgrounds, and life experiences, most marriages encounter disagreement and profound differences of opinions. In healthy communication relationship, most disagreements are resolved in a nondestructive manner, with each partner learning how to work through their conflicts in a way that allows discussion and understanding in a controlled and respectful manner. When communication breaks down, it can create frustration and disappointment, leading to arguments, accusations, defensiveness, and poor choice of words and hurtful tones that often lead people to become verbally abusive. Verbal abuse in any marriage or relationship is very destructive. Physical and verbal abuses are two major prevalent marital issues resulting from unhealthy communication within the marriages and families. These issues are more severe for couples in Laos and Thailand than the Mien in the U.S. In my seven years of counseling services, I have met many Mien women who related their emotional and psychological wounds and pains from the verbal attacks by their husbands. In the U.S., there are laws and law enforcement officials to protect women and children from the abuse of their husbands and fathers. So, physical abuse is less frequent for the Mien living in the U.S. than those still living in Laos and Thailand. There are protective service agencies, such as Child Protective Service and Adult Protective Service, who intervene when abuse is reported. The accessibility to telephone usage in making reports to law enforcement and making contact with service providers helps to alleviate some of the domestic violence within the families, whereas in Laos and Thailand, many individuals and families live in remote areas, have little or no access to make contact with the government officials, and the culture provides very little support to abusive or abused individuals and families. Since educational service was very limited in Laos and Thailand, there were no counseling programs or support services for the victims. In addition, the abusers do not receive any form of treatments or counseling services for their psychological and anger problems.

I had several opportunities to conduct Mien Marriage Conferences in Chiangmai and Chiangrai, Thailand in December of 2006, 2009, and 2012. The conference conducted in 2006 was the first Mien marriage conference held in Thailand, and it marked an eye opening event to all the participants. Since such an event had never taken place in the history of Mien. Couples were thrilled with and astonished by the information they received. The data gathered from the personal interviews, surveys and breakout sessions revealed several major marital problems within the Mien marriages and families in Thailand. The three predominant marital issues were physical abuse, verbal abuse, and sexual abuse.

Domestic violence has become the largest marital problem with villagers, compared to those who live in the city or suburban areas. More than ninety-seven percent of the victims are women and children. Within a male dominant society, women and children have very little power or right to go against their male-chauvinist and abusive husband or father. The concept of men paying the "bride price" for their wives causes men to place themselves as superiors to their wives. Being the fathers, they gain the authoritative figures to take charge of their families. Therefore, wives and children become submissive to the headman of the family. An example of how abusive some men can be is from a testimony given by one of the conference participants. The day before the conference ended, a man's wife approached me as I was making my way to the cafeteria for lunch.

A soft voice behind me called for my attention. I turned around and a woman with an unhappy face called out, "*Fin-saeng youz aac, yie tov caux meih gorngv joux waac oc*" meaning, "Young teacher, may I have a word with you." I turned around and saw a woman standing beside one of the women from our church. Before she could begin to say a word, tears were flowing from her eyes. I knew that she was heavy-hearted. I waited for her to catch her breath so that she could tell her story. After learning that she had been living with a very abusive husband, I asked of her husband's identity and background. Later in the evening, after my workshops and sermon were over, I asked to meet with her and husband. The couple met with me from late evening until early in the next morning. They both shared with me some of their marital issues. After I gathered some pertinent background information from both of them, I provided them some counseling skills to resolve their family matters. We had to end our meeting to get ready for the morning service, but when the morning came, people were given the opportunity to share what they learned from the conference. Many men and women came forward to share their life-changing experiences. Surprisingly, the final person was the husband I had talked to the previous night. He spoke the following words:

> "My fellow friends and relatives, the words that I am about to say are not something that you should take home with you. What I am going to tell you is something that you should not copy. In my life, I don't have any good examples for anyone to follow. My first wife, I beat her and she ran away. My second wife, I beat her and she ran away. My third wife, I beat her and she ran away. Now, the woman I am married to is my fourth wife. I have learned so much from this conference. It is my hope that God will help me to become a better husband for my wife. I am a weak man

and I need a lot of help from God. Please pray for me, thank you."

The man's public acknowledgement of himself and the confession of his wrongs were so shocking to the audience, because this was a man who had never admitted any weaknesses or mistakes. For their years of marriage, his wife had never heard him accept any of his wrong doings. She was so thankful and hopeful that her husband would stop beating her or degrading her.

The story above is just one of many unknown cases of marital abuse. Physical, sexual, emotional, and spiritual abuses exist within the Mien marriages and families. However, the majority of abusers do not want to admit their negative or destructive behaviors, and the abused individuals often just accept their abusive situation as a way of life, and do not know how to escape from the relationship. In many cases, the victims are better off staying in their relationship then leaving their abusive husbands, because in a society where women and children's primary needs are solely depended on the head of the household, they have nowhere else to turn, like in the U.S. These individuals have to learn how to endure pain and move on with their lives. As we know, an abusive relationship creates a destructive life pattern not only for the abusers, but for their victims as well. If there is no way to stop the abusive life style, it can, and in many cases, will continue to flow down the generational lines, which was the case for the man whom I alluded to earlier. After asking him some personal and historical questions, I discovered that he too came from an abusive home where he was constantly being beaten by his father. He had also witnessed many years of physical abuse by his father on his mother. Therefore, he did not realize how much his father's abusive behaviors had affected him and created a pattern of abusive relationships.

The above story serves as one of the many hidden personal and marital issues within Mien people in the U.S. The "face saving" concept has prevented many individuals and couples from seeking professional help. Therefore, the emotional and psychological problems that one has built up from their past are not being made known to the individuals, their family members and other concerned people in the community.

How Achieving the "American Dream" can Help or Hurt Mien Marriages and Families?

The longer one tries to hide negative life experiences and not take necessary procedures to receive the proper knowledge and resources to deal with them, the more harm it can cause to the person and those individuals around him or her. This seems to be one of the major barriers for many Mien adults or elders not only in Thailand or Laos, but for those living in the U.S. as well.

It is an undeniable claim that people coming to America have a certain level of expectation or hope for a better life for themselves and their families. For some, life in the U.S. is like living in a paradise, while for others life is not as convenient or familiar as their home countries. Not everyone living in the U.S. has equal or similar educational or socio-economical backgrounds where they can simply transition into an advanced technological society. Those who have solid formal educational backgrounds have more advantages than those who do not possess any forms of education to help pave the way in achieving the America dreams. They do not hold the necessary skills or tools to accomplish the goals they have for their families. Thus, in order for them to accomplish the American dreams, it means that they have to put in more effort than those who know the language, culture, system and have the money power and information.

It is true that those who hold knowledge and information possess certain levels of power and control. The less fortunate or less educated ones would have to strive much harder to get the resources and knowledge they need. As mentioned earlier that the Mien did not come to the U.S. with the expectations to achieve any of the "American Dreams." The ultimate reason for these people to come to America was to be alive and free from political persecutions. The concept of achieving the "American Dreams" did not exist in their minds at all. They had no clues or dreams about the nature of America prior to their arrival. Through the process of striving to become productive individuals in the U.S. and working hard to provide for their families, they somehow found themselves living an American dream. While for some people the American dream is achievable through luck and good fortune, for others it may take years of diligence, strong determination, and sacrificial work. For some, no matter how hard they try, luck and fortune never come. Sadly speaking, in the process of becoming successful and productive to achieve the American dreams, many marriages and families have been greatly impacted by their pursuit.

In my counseling practices, I have worked with couples and families whose relationships were at the verge of separation and/or termination. The husbands, being the sole providers for their families, sensed the financial pressure to work long hours at one job or in some cases two or three jobs in order to earn sufficient income for their families. Since the majority of Mien families have between two and six children, a single income is not often enough to cover all monthly expenses. In those situations, both parents are required to work. Depending on the ages of the children, who usually are still young, childcare poses another financial challenge for the family. Couples who do not have parents or in-laws available to care for their children are left with no options but to work on alternating schedules. While one spouse works during the day to tend and care for the children, the other spouse works at night. The conflicting work schedules not only gradually distance the parents, but also unconsciously push the caring parents away from their children and each other. The longer the couples stay at their jobs, the more they are away from each other. The family relationship becomes weaker and more distant.

Once someone has developed certain life-routine and does not recognize the negative impact that these routines pose for the family, positive resolutions to correct the problems can be hard to accept. In many instances, the family relationships become gradually weaker and sadly end. Due to the family's financial issues and living situation, often families find themselves with limited options. The spouses either keep their jobs, maintain the conflicting schedules in order to have a roof over their head, put food on the tables, buy clothes for their children, pay auto insurance, maintain the monthly car payment, and cover the older children's educational expenses, or they have to change jobs or quit one of the of the jobs to spend more time with the family, leading to staying in a rut and not being able to afford a nicer home to live and nicer cars to drive. For many young married couples and older families, chasing after the American dream has placed them into very difficult financial and legal situations that can lead to separation, divorce or other destructive behaviors in the families because of the pressures and added stress.

For children who only get to see one or both of their parents a couple times during the weekdays and few hours on the weekend, the parent-child relationship only grows colder and farther apart. At the end it breaks the hearts of both the parents and the children. It creates a "lose-lose" situation for the family. Children who are not being raised by two parents in the home have more behavioral problems. The children's negative behaviors can easily be seen in schools and public places. As a teacher, I have also worked with students in different levels. Sometimes I learned about the family problems through student writings, comments made in the class with other students, and the behaviors they reveal in class.

In my counseling practices, I also discovered that the conflicting work schedules and the demands of some employers have created great burdens and pressures for them to be away from their spouses and children. Some employers require their employees to work long hours, overtime, on the weekends, and maintain rigid work schedules. Some of these employers provide some financial help for the family, and yet at the same time hurt the family structure and relationship. Some children have developed social and emotional distance from their parents due to the family's conflicting home, school activities and work schedules. The conflicting work schedules prevent parents from participating in their children's education, social events, and extra-curricular activities, such as sports and music lessons. Rigid or inflexible work schedules have also become an issue for families who hold strong value in regular church attendance. Attending church on Sundays is very important for many, especially for those who hold leadership roles and positions in the church.

The pursuing of the American dream of owning a nice house and expensive vehicles has also destroyed some marriages. For an example, the seasonal fishermen would spend four to six months on a fishing boat to catch fish in Alaska. These husbands would be physically and emotionally detached from the wives for a period as long as half year. While they were away working and earning money to support their families, their wives and children were alone at home. Emotionally, when two people are deeply in love and have to be separated for such long periods of time, the spouse left behind faces isolation and loneliness. Humanly speaking, people need companionship and connections with other human beings. Everyone has his or her emotional needs. When these social and emotional needs are not being fulfilled, some people would seek outside or different alternatives to meet their needs. Thus, the situation creates opportunities for spouses to be unfaithful to their marriages. Infidelity sometime occurs at the most unexpected situations. When an extra-marital relationship is established and the infidelity is discovered by the other spouse or as Mien people say, "*Wuom nzang la'bieiv cuotv*" meaning "You can see the rock when the water becomes clear," then the marriage is at risk. Depending on the couple's problem solving skills and their moral principles, the marriage can be repaired or broken at this point. Usually, when a marriage relationship is broken, people's hopes and dreams are shattered. In many cases, achieving the American dream is not as difficult as keeping it. While some have only experienced a small part of their dreams, others are able to maintain them and enjoy them.

There are couples who have tried and tried so hard and yet not been able to achieve their American dream. Once they have exhausted all the resources available to them, and are still not able to fulfill their family's dream, some spouses turn themselves to other fast and easy ways to make money. I have worked with some husbands who felt so compelled to fulfill their roles as the head of the family, the providers and protectors, to meet the needs of their families in any possible way because it is considered a great failure to not be able to provide for your family. The cultural pressures force the husbands and fathers to become competitive with other successful men. When a husband is unable to achieve the American dream like his siblings, relatives and friends have, he often begins to sense a personal failure. Some men become heavy gamblers without knowing the odds of losing and causing more financial hardship on their families. When the addiction becomes too great to end, it breaks the family. Some men end up destroying their own marriage relationships in the process of trying to earn quick and easy money to buy their families nice cars and or a big home. Their final results end up hurting their families more than helping them. At the end, these men not only lose their money, but they lose their self-value, families and children as well.

In addition, when a spouse is not available to carry on the family roles and responsibilities, the house chores and duties can become a huge burden and overwhelming to the staying home spouse, especially if the children are young. Even with older children, there are still many educational activities that happen during school hours, school and on the weekends. When the family's needs become too great for one spouse to manage, an emotional breakdown can occur. Thus, the frustrations and disappointments cause the spouses to have miscommunications eventually leading into major relationship crises.

Chapter 4

Different Mien Groups in the United States

The Mien people in the United States view themselves and the western cultures in two groups: the Christians and non-Christians. The readers will notice that family matters are being viewed and handled in a slightly different manner between the Christian and non-Christian homes. Christian Mien parents have certain moral principles; family and individual values for themselves and their children, siblings, relatives, and others. These moral values exist based on the levels of knowledge within their religious beliefs and standards. In order to understand Mien marriage and family communication, it is necessary to get a clear view of the different spiritual groups of Mien in the U.S. The Mien in the U.S. can be classified into two major groups; the Christian and the Traditional Religion, the ancestral worship.

Approximately sixty years ago virtually all Mien lived in the borderlands of Southern China and the Northern parts of Southeast Asia (Vietnam, Laos, and Thailand). Their religion was comprised of both animistic and Taoist elements, animism dealing with lower level beliefs and rituals and Taoism, adopted from the Chinese many centuries before, and directing the larger or major ceremonies through qualified priests. Beginning in the early to middle 1950s, however, some Mien became Christians, first in Thailand and then spreading back into Laos. Mr. C.W. and his wife Lois Callaway, from Vallejo, California, were the first missionaries to bring the Gospel to Mien people in remote areas in Thailand.

This adoption of Christianity by a small number of Mien beginning in the 1950s caused a significant cleavage in Mien culture between the majority of traditional Taoists and the minority of Christians. Over the years, the initial tension over religion has subsided somewhat, particularly in North America where Christians now number roughly 15% of the Mien population and where members of both communities have been able to put aside differences in order to cooperate in a number of community-wide projects. However, this original two-way distinction in religious affiliation has become more complex in North America because of the variety of religious beliefs and secular value systems the Mien have come into contact with.

On the Christian side, the exposure into different denominations has, at least superficially, divided Mien Christians into Baptists, Independents, Nazarenes, Church of Christ, Pentecostal, Mormons, etc. Nevertheless, there are basic beliefs which override denominational distinctiveness and help to keep most Mien Christians together in their beliefs. However, the formerly single Taoist side has divided into three distinct subgroups; the traditional, the integrator, and the contemporary.

The Non-Christian Mien

Of the non-Christian Mien, there are three distinct subgroups; *the traditional* group, those who still worship their ancestors (also known as the animists or Taoists), *the integrator*, those who have accepted other forms of religions outside the ancestral worship, such as a female angel *"Jiem-Yiem Muangz"*, and *the contemporary*, or those who do not hold any particular religious viewpoints. More detail on these three groups is provided herein:

1. **The traditional group.** This group consists mostly of the elders who were born, raised and educated with the traditional forms of spiritual worship and healing practices from their homeland in Laos or Thailand. The two well-known and accepted methods of healing for any health related issues were Shamanism and Herbal medicines. While Shamanism provided spiritual and psychological healings, the Herbalists provided treatment for physical ailments. Both the spiritual and physical healers were highly respected, acknowledged and very much needed in an environment where scientific medical facilities and providers were not available. Their skills and knowledge were usually passed down through the generations. These two groups of healers had to go through years of hands-on training before they could perform their earned roles and responsibilities of Shaman or Herbalist.

Most Shamans believed once they fully immerse themselves to become ceremonially trained Shaman, that they would commit their lives to worship and practice their religion without compromise. Thus, wherever these individuals live, they will continue to hold steadfast to their trainings, teachings and beliefs. They continue to practice the skills and knowledge they acquired through the generations. Likewise, their children and grandchildren are expected to carry on the family tradition. There are still dozens of traditional Mien spiritual healers or Shamans in the U.S. Mien temples are built to teach the younger generation to become Shamans and to preserve the ancestral worship as practiced in Laos and Thailand. Some of the ancestral temples can be found in Sacramento and Richmond, California where there are larger groups of Mien communities. However, very few young adults have the passion or desire to learn about this traditional form of spiritual practice. Mien children and young adults are mostly concentrating on their education and future careers in the U.S. They want to complete their high school studies and continue on to two and four year colleges. The differences in priorities and expectations have created communication barriers. Parents and grandparents who view the traditional religion as a crucial component of both physical and spiritual life, have tried to convince or demand that their children and grandchildren study Chinese so they can understand the sacred religious texts written in Chinese. In order to perform the ritual ceremonies, it is necessary for an individual to be able to read and understand the sacred texts.

The expectation to be literate in both English and the spirit language has become one of the greatest disagreements that these traditional families struggle with. As the parents age, they sometimes strongly demand that their children study both Chinese and English so that they can become proficient in both cultures. There are many children who do not share the same expectations of their parents. The youth who want to choose their own future careers and to achieve the "American dream", will often end up disappointing their parents and creating major communication gaps. In some cases they cause permanent rifts between family members. Perhaps this is because of the belief that parents need their children to send money and food to them in the spirit world after they die, in the form of ritual ceremonies.

Parents are afraid they will be abandoned after they die. The younger generation does not understand or share this belief because they are focused on the here-and-now of the "American dream." Some parents are able to find a common ground to reestablish the family relationship, but for others it becomes a permanent dividing wall. Major disappointment, frustration, anger and shame develop in the hearts and souls of many individuals and families. There have been many cases in which family relationships were completely disconnected, where the parents disowned their children and the children disclaimed their parents. Thus, the determination to uphold the ancestral traditions in family relationships has created many layers of emotional pains in the hearts and minds of the parents, grandparents and children. A ripple effect then passes on to other immediate family members, this is a typical norm of the Mien culture.

There are very few children who are able to fulfill both their personal goals and the expectations of their parents and grandparents. However, such tasks are not simple. An individual has to be able to go to school six or seven days a week in order to keep up the pace with their public school and private schools. Monday through Friday children spend attending classes in public school then Saturday and Sunday they devote to private lessons studying the Chinese language. Depending on the individual's age, grade levels and intellectual abilities, the work from both schools can be overwhelming. The majority of these students are usually between the middle school and high school ages. A person has to have a strong desire and be fully committed in order to accomplish such tasks and responsibilities. Many teenagers are not willing to give up their social lives to become devoted to this kind of demanding schedule. This kind of pressure and demand places a child in a "sink or swim" situation, and it takes a skillful and dedicated person to develop such talents and skills.

Not every child growing up in a highly technological and scientific society sees the need to organize their lives around an "unknown or unseen" spirit world. Many of these young people are traveling on highways and freeways while their parents and grandparents are still finding their ways around on trails and streets. When family members do not share the same belief systems or worldviews, a breakdown in communication and perspectives are bound to occur. Unfortunately, this issue has become prevalent to the Mien people in the U.S.

2. **The integrator group.** The second group of non-Christian Mien is classified as the integrated group. This group is comprised of those who were born and raised in Laos or Thailand. They gained a certain level of knowledge in the traditional ancestral worship and grew up being educated in the U.S. These individuals are not Shaman or Saikung. They are not capable of performing any spiritual healings or ceremonies. However, they have been exposed to many of the ritual events and can seek assistance from qualified spiritual healers to perform spiritual ceremonies when needed. They have connections with spiritual healers, who know how to prepare for the ritual ceremony, and they are capable of preserving the family tradition with the help of other experienced elders in the community. For example, an individual needs to know how to select the appropriate animal (a chicken or pig), male or female, how to clean and cut the animal into certain proportions, how to place the animal in the appropriate position for a ceremony, how much (self-made) paper money is needed, the quality and style of the paper money, the number and size of cups to be filled with wine and much more. (I only mentioned a few items that are necessary for any ritual ceremony. Some types of ceremonies involve more items and have more detailed procedures than others.) Essentially, a person needs to know all the details necessary when preparing for a ritual ceremony because some involve days and months of advanced preparation. It is believed that the spirits of ancestors are very critical and selective "*mienv huv haic* or *la'nyauv haic*". When they become offended, the spirits of ancestors can cause major harm to a family. In many cases, sudden deaths have occurred. Whereas in another case the entire family lost their lives. It is said that these curses and disasters continue to flow down the generational line and have affected the whole clan, from parents to children and grandchildren. Farms animals and domestic animals have died without particular sicknesses or diseases while others were being attacked by wild animals, because the ancestors "did not protect" the people or their property.

Many of the people in this group have gained sufficient knowledge about ancestral worship and continue to practice it in the U.S. They rely on the guidance of the knowledgeable Shaman, Saikung or spiritual healers for the different forms of spiritual and physical healings. However, this second group of people are not as devoted to their beliefs as the traditional group. They are more receptive to other cultural and spiritual beliefs. Some people have stepped out of the spiritual circle to explore other moral principles and spiritual powers. Some have even incorporated other forms of religions into their traditional one. Worshipping a "Female Angel" or in Mien known as *"Jiem-Yiem Muangz"* becomes a new form of belief system for Mien people in many states. At first, there were only a few Mien families in Sacramento and the Bay Areas of California who adopted this form of angelic worshipping, but now families in other states have begun to follow this spiritual power. *Jiem-Yiem Muangz* is believed to be a very attractive and holy angel who brings joy and happiness into the lives of people. Her mission is to bring blessing upon the people and to preserve life; therefore, she does not eat meat she eats only fruits and vegetables. Due to the nature of her radiant beauty and kindness, everywhere she goes, she brings hope and joy to help people in need. She is also known as a "good-hearted" angel. She does not possess any form of wickedness or trouble and does not judge anyone for their behaviors. Her roles are not to punish people for their wrong doings, but to deliver hope and healthy blessings to those who worship her faithfully. Therefore, anyone who worships her needs to provide an alter in their home with burning incense, regular offerings of fruits and vegetables, and not eat meat on the first day of each month. In addition, they need to be faithful and royal to her while doing good deeds to their communities. By doing so, she will bless them and protect them from potential harms and other forms of life tragedies. Their lives then will yield the fruits of happiness and love in beauty as she is. So, there are families who not only encourage their children to preserve their traditional religion, but also to adopt others, the "better or more powerful one". The idea of mixing one's traditional religion with another comes from the belief that "the more you have the more power and benefits to you." Of course, not all Mien share the same ideology.

In addition, the integrated group unconsciously has developed a dual standard for their children and grandchildren. On one hand they emphasize the importance of cultural preservation through worshipping one's traditional religion, but on the other hand, they combine their belief principles with others that are considered as "better or more powerful." The mixture of religions has created confusion not only for the younger generation but also for the older generation. When interviewing some of the children whose parents have incorporated other forms of spiritual beliefs, they are uncertain as 'to which religion their parents are actually worshipping. There are no written texts in English that they can read to gain the in-depth knowledge in order to know the difference. They know that they are not to go against the requirements or recommendations of their parents, and yet they cannot go against their own conscience. Some of these young people's emotions are being torn in two by what is making sense to them through the modern culture and by what their parents expect them to follow and practice.

Individuals within the integrated non-Christian Mien have different challenges. Many are neither literate in their indigenous language nor English. When they were in Laos or Thailand, they did not have the opportunity to attend school. Most of their lives were interrupted by wars and suffering in the refugee camps in Thailand. Upon their arrival in the U.S., they did not meet the age requirement to attend grade schools. Those interested in getting an education also lacked the English proficiency to be accepted into a community college. Some were placed into adult educational programs where the teachers and school administrators were not fully prepared to help them with their educational needs. These individuals were placed between two different worlds of the traditional and modern cultures. Mien people identify themselves as, "*sung-zaux caaiv sung-mbaih*", meaning the challenges brought by the two cultures are like when a person tries to cross a river with two rafts; the left foot on one raft and the right foot on the other.

After living in the U.S. for several years, some people become familiar with the Western culture and gradually acquire enough English language skills to attend two-year and four-year colleges. They receive a wide range of educational and employment to fulfill needs. Individuals in the integrative group often become mediators between the traditional group and the contemporary group. The communication pattern of these people is slightly different from the traditional group. Due to their bicultural and bilingual skills, they are able to relate and communicate more effectively between the traditional and contemporary groups. These individuals have become acculturated into western culture while maintaining their traditional culture. They have cross-cultural communication skills, whereas the traditional and contemporary groups lack this skill. They can understand and make a better connection among the people of their generation and the older generations. They know what communication style to use when conversing between the older and younger generations.

3. **The contemporary group.** The contemporary non-Christian Mien refers to the younger or second and third generations, the individuals who were born and raised in the U.S. These individuals were born in western hospitals, treated by western healthcare providers, educated by western educators, entertained by modern media and culture, and housed and cared for by their integrated parents. Many forms of social and cultural training influence their thinking, decision making and daily lifestyle. At home, their parents have certain cultural guidelines and expectations for them to fulfill and at school they are given other sets of curricula, dress codes, classroom rules, expectations, safety rules and guidelines to follow. Their worldly view of family, authority, school, work, religion, sports, hobbies and entertainment is far beyond what their parents expect or can comprehend.

These children grow up in an environment where they are surrounded by television, radio, wireless telephones, emails, instant text messaging, twittering and endless electronic games and videos. Their lives are being shaped and formed by what they see and hear inside and outside their homes. The family's traditional values and beliefs become new concepts and strange ideas for them. They cannot relate to their parents and vice versa. At schools they are being educated in English about the U.S. history, economy, politics, freedom of choices, religions, philosophies, independency, and much more. Their parents cannot even begin to understand some of these concepts because of the language barrier, and are unable to correlate or educate them at home. Therefore, these children receive conflicting teachings of information from the schools, home and community. Due to the overwhelming sources of education presented to them, many of the second and third generation Mien children have difficulty sorting out the truth. Many of the contemporary young adults today cannot identify themselves in any particular belief system. While some cannot comprehend the complexities of the traditional Mien religion and cultural norms, others do not see the need to seek spiritual healing for physical or emotional problems when there is advanced medical science available to cure most diseases and illnesses.

Those individuals who have become educated and are financially secure do not hold the same views as the traditional or integrated groups. Some even take further steps, believing that since they are not living in Laos or Thailand, they don't need to follow the traditional ways of life or even see the need to be literate in Mien. Some hold the belief that worshipping one's ancestors is only necessary for people who live in a disadvantaged society. When these families or individuals receive balanced health, flourishing business and whose everyday needs are being met; they don't see the need to rely on the blessings, guidance, or protections of their ancestors.

The communication skills of the contemporary group are very contrary to the traditional form of communication. The thought and behavior patterns compared to their parents or grandparents are like night and day. The younger generation children and adults are often confused by the ways their parents and grandparents communicate. The traditional communication style is a non-linear communication pattern that can create great confusion. The younger generation learns from the modern culture that in order to be an effective communicator, the speaker needs to be assertive and speak directly to the point. Speaking to the point or being direct is considered an unprofessional and uneducated form of communication according to the traditional communication style. This, in turn, causes a large rift between the younger and the older generation.

The Christian Mien

Within the Christian circle, there are as many different spiritual groups of Mien as there are non-Christian Mien. Mien Christians do not all hold the same Biblical worldviews or beliefs about God and humanity. Those who attended Bible colleges, seminaries, or have other Bible training have a deeper understanding of the Bible and live their lives with different principles and moral standards than those who have limited or no biblical background. A person's education level and the knowledge of the Bible differentiate him or her greatly from those who have little or no formal educational foundation. Mien Christians in the U.S. can be classified into three sub-groups: the nominal, marginal and the conservative groups.

1. **The Nominal Group.** The first group is comprised of individuals or families who have converted into Christianity with limited knowledge of the Bible. These people have a weak foundational Christian faith and doctrine. Once they become Christians, they still preserve and practice their traditional ancestral worship while supplanting another religion into their belief system. The individuals and families in this category may define religion or Christianity as a ritual. Serving or worshipping God means to follow a certain procedure, standard or routine instead of having on-going relationships through prayer and reading the Bible, since this is what they were accustomed to in their traditional ancestral worship. Their reasons to become Christians are based on many factors other than receiving salvation. Some of these reasons include: wanting to be set free from the oppression of the spirits (demons or bad spirits) '*biaux mienv*' in Mien, to receive social acceptance and or financial support from the church, to gain trust or approval from the potential soul mate and his or her parents, to escape generational curse, or to retaliate against one's parents or family members for personal reasons.

The three common reasons for Mien people to become Christians are:

    1.) to be free from the oppression of the spirits (demons or evil spirits)

2.) to gain the approval of the parents to marry a Christian person
3.) to receive social or financial support from their sponsors or community members.

The first and most common reason is to be freed from the influence, attack or oppression of their ancestors. As discussed in previous chapters, Mien people follow a religion that is full of fear, uncertainty and anxiety. Ancestral worship (or animism), teaches that a person's body inherits ten souls; three rest on the head and seven on the body. Whenever one or more of the souls are frightened, the souls will leave a person's body and sickness occurs. In addition, the religion teaches that numerous spirits dwell on different places and objects. They include tall and strong trees, rocks, mountains, oceans, lakes, rivers and houses. Whether it is intentional or not, when these spirits get offended, they can cause illness, disaster or even death to one person and/or their whole family. Young boys and girls need to have their heads covered with beautiful handmade hats to avoid being touched by passing spirits. It is believed that when children are playing outside, the spirits are roaming from place to place, and when they see young children playing outside of their homes, they like to pat their heads as parents or adults do to their young ones. When a child's head is touched by any spirit other than their own ancestors', a health problem will occur since one or more of the spirits has been frightened. Thus, the family has to pay for a Shaman or Saikung to call back the frightened soul(s) that have been left inside the child's body. Every time a Shaman is involved there is also a live animal, (usually a chicken) and money involved. Depending on the degree and severity of the sickness, sometimes animals as large as pigs and cows are required to be butchered and sacrificed to the spirit in order to recall the soul. For families who are poor and lack resources, these kinds of "common" ceremonies can become expensive and are often considered to be heavy burdens.

The second reason Mien people embracing Christianity is to gain the approval for marriage. Gaining the approval of both sets of parents is a very crucial process prior to uniting two people in marriage, mainly between a Christian and a non-Christian family. The conservative Christians believe that their sons and daughters become spiritual children of God. As good and evil cannot equally co-exist to bring peace and harmony, so as a couple with different beliefs cannot be healthy and happy in their life-long marriage. Usually the Christian parents hold a strong objection to allow their daughters to marry non-Christian sons. In some cases, Christian parents make special exceptions to allow their sons to marry non-Christian daughters in the hopes that the daughters-in-law would become Christians once they are married. As in the Mien culture, after marriage, sons usually bring their wives to live with their parents; however, in the U.S. children sometimes can choose to live on their own. In either case, the daughters-in-law are expected to take on the beliefs and expectations of their husbands and or the parents-in-law. Because of the cultural tradition, conservative Mien Christian parents often refuse to let their daughters marry non-Christian men.

While many Mien Christian parents object to allow their children to be married to non-Christian children, they still expect and wish their children to marry Mien instead of other ethnicities in order to preserve Mien language and culture. The two highest expectations most Mien Christian parents have for their children are: 1) to marry someone who is Christian and 2) to marry someone who is Mien, preferably a Christian Mien. Likewise, the objections of different belief systems also exist within the traditional non-Christians. Some Mien traditional parents refuse to let their sons or daughters marry someone who is a Christian Mien if they knew that their son-in-law or daughter-in-law would not reconvert to worship their ancestors. In some cases, the equally yoked expectation has created social and cultural divisive between the ancestral worshippers and Christian parents and children in the U.S.

The third common reason for Mien people to become Christians is to receive social, emotional and/or financial support from the mother church. When families run out of resources within their immediate families, they would seek assistance from a local church. Most Mien churches in the U.S. have some form of charity funds to support the members for emergency needs. The fund is designed mainly to cover funeral and burial expenses. This is a very necessary line of social and financial assistance for families with limited resources. Whenever a member of the church dies, all of the members of the church would be notified and a collection of donations and love offerings would be sent to the family to help cover the expenses. Families and church members would step in to assist the family. When a family member is deceased, there are many detailed procedures that need to be done. For non-Christian families, there are many complicated and crucial ceremonial rituals that are required to take place prior to the final stage of burial service. The length of the funeral service can be anywhere from three to seven days. Clans, relatives, friends and neighbors would be joining the family throughout the entire service. This type of ceremonial ritual can be very costly, on an average of $5,000 to $15,000. This cost does not include the fees of transportation, lodging and number of days that family members and friends would take off from their work. Therefore, some individuals and families have become Christians solely in order to receive this kind of support services.

The nominal group has a slightly different view of salvation than the conservative group. The conservative Christians view the primary reason to become a Christian is to receive salvation of eternal life in heaven, not just to be freed from the bondage of the dark spirits. Conservative Christians view Christianity as receiving God's free gift of eternal salvation in heaven while we are living our lives on this sinful world. Christianity is about faith and the relationship between human beings and God. It is unlike worshipping the deceased ancestors or other gods. The people who fall under this classification are still very confused about Christianity and the traditional ancestral worship. They often mix their new religion with the old belief systems. For example, when a family member becomes ill, the individual or parents (in the case of a child), pray to God for heavenly power and seek spiritual healings from a Shaman or Saikung to restore the soul of the sick person. They believe that the more sources of spiritual power one can acquire, the quicker the healing process. They view religion as a source of energy from the spirits. They develop misconceptions about the real meaning of Christianity. Therefore, these people will place themselves in a new "spirit world" by relying on one's past religion, the protection of the ancestors, and the blessing from God for their present and future needs.

On the same line, the nominal Christian Mien is typically not very serious about his/her spiritual life due to one or more of the reasons discussed above. These people tend to focus on their immediate needs. They place their faith in the things that can be seen and touched. They sometimes would incorporate other belief principles into the ones they have already developed. Sometimes these people live their lives under heavy guilt and shame. They feel guilty for abandoning their ancestors by becoming Christians. Their ancestral worshipping family members often remind them about the betrayal of their ancestors. It is believed that when the children of the deceased stop worshipping them by regularly providing them food and money, they would have to wonder around from place to place eating the morning dews. This form of belief places heavy guilt on individuals and families who have accepted a new religion. They feel that they owe it to their ancestors to worship them and provide for them as much as they can. They believe that by becoming Christians that it now means they cannot continue to have an altar in the home to provide regular offerings, annual offerings, nor call on them for any spiritual matters. They feel like they have not only neglected their own parents or grandparents who were mainly depending on them for needs in the spirit world, but totally isolated themselves from their protection and blessing. Since their biblical foundation has not taken strong root in the word of God but are on shallow ground, they are very vulnerable to pressure or harassment from their non-Christian friends and family members. In some instances, the family and community pressure them to revert back to their traditional religion; this type of pressure can be very intense. For example, when my family first became Christians in a Thailand refugee camp, my father's siblings and relatives were so unhappy that they called a meeting to persuade our family to reconsider our decision. As my father reluctantly refused to accept the majority's choice, people were very disappointed and some began to verbally criticize and attack our family. Because my father was not only a community leader, but also a spiritual healer, to them this was a major issue. This was considered a loss to them. In the community point of view, they were no longer able to depend on him for spiritual matters. In the personal side, my father's leadership, honor, and respect as a spiritual healer gradually diminished. Therefore, nominal Christians who are not knowledgeable in facts concerning Biblical studies cannot clearly distinguish as to what religious aspects or principles to preserve and which to let go. Their misconceptions about the Bible have created a sense of confusion that leads to frustration and ultimately results in discouragement. Some families even reverted back into animists or ancestral worship.

Literacy plays a crucial role for individuals and their families to develop their own knowledge of the Bible. Since the majority of Mien people did not receive a solid formal education when they were in Laos or Thailand, it hinders their intellectual abilities to read and understand the Bible. Most of them receive their biblical knowledge through a verbal form of education when being preached to or taught in churches. While the majority receives their Christian education through sermons delivered on Sundays, others are being educated from Sunday school or mid-week Bible studies. Most Mien churches in the U.S. have small group ministries for older and younger adults. Some of these sub-ministries are men's, women's, couple's, and single's groups. Depending on their personal commitment and motivation to learn, many churches provide different learning opportunities for their church members. Some churches even teach Mien literacy classes for their church members and other members of the community so they can learn how to read and write in the Mien language. Of the Mien Bible, only the New Testament hadn't become available for people to read until 1990 for those individuals who were not able to read in English but could read in the Mien language. The complete Bible of both the New and Old Testament was not completed until the summer of 2009.

Despite all the different learning opportunities provided by the local churches, the nominal Christian group are interested the least in learning. They do not take advantage of the resources available to them because they do not see the need as being important or necessary for their spiritual growth as the moderate and conservative groups do. These individuals attend church services or activities as an obligation for Christians. Nominal Christians touch their Bibles maybe once a week when they attend church on Sunday. Once they leave the church, their Bibles are placed on a shelf, in a car, or in some safe place. The Bible is not being read or used at home. The Bibles are only opened during the sermon times. Aside from that, their Bible is kept safe, cleaned, or misplaced. Thus, these individuals not only have very minimal knowledge in the word of God or in the Bible, but they also do not share the same spiritual views as the moderate and conservative people do.

In addition, their involvement and participation in the church activities are limited. They do not support the church very well in means of volunteering or financial offerings. Another term for these individuals is event-Christians. They usually are present during special programs or events that provide special activities or foods. They tend to find out the schedule ahead of time and just show up when the meal is ready. Once their mission is accomplished, they do not return until the next major event. The nominal Christians normally attend church when they have special needs or prayer requests. If they are doing well physically, spiritually and financially, they do not see the need to attend church. Regular church attendance and activities are viewed as social events, not as a necessity for spiritual growth. Therefore, their spiritual lives are weak, and they do not live their lives under the same principles and guidelines of the Bible. Many may combine their beliefs with other sound doctrines or belief principles. They can easily be persuaded into other religious beliefs.

2. **The marginal group.** The marginal group of Mien Christians refers to those who hold more religious knowledge and have stronger beliefs than the nominal group. Some of the major doctrines of belief include the following:

   a. Marginalized Mien Christians believe that Jesus is the Savior of the world and that He does not judge those outside this realm as eternally lost. They reserve the belief that God is both generous as well as gracious with love and accepts people as they are. Therefore, an individual can live his or her life according to his or her own desires. Once a person has sinned against God, that person can just request that God grant them forgiveness and God will automatically pardon their sins. Therefore, God is viewed as a loving and forgiving God who overlooks of the wrong doings of the people.
   b. They preserve the belief that God is willing to pardon people of their sins if they sincerely confess them and ask for forgiveness.

Therefore, a person can continue to sin and then just go ask God for forgiveness whenever needed.
c. They recognize the faithfulness of other people who may belong to other faiths, and view such as "alternative faiths" rather than calling them "cults." They do not accept anything someone else has to say as truth. They may view that there is no absolute truth and everything is relativism.
d. They believe that men and women, who are attracted to the same sex, deserve the basic human rights as those attracted to the opposite sex. They put this human right above any individual's views or questions regarding their sexual practices in their own personal lives.
e. They think that the way we treat one another and other people surpasses doctrinal issues.
f. They believe hell means *Sheol*, the grave separation from God and is not a literal eternal place of tormenting fire.
g. They see themselves as Christians, but believe they can balance between good deeds and spiritual guidelines without any major spiritual consequences.

In a nutshell, we can see that marginalized Mien Christians are those who begin their faith and believe with an open mind but have been indoctrinated with deceptive and erroneous opinions presented as beliefs. They see problems, have concerns, and want to resolve them. They associate with only the church teachings that suit their purposes and consider the rest as being too improbable to believe. Since they are without a set of systematic beliefs, they are open to accept whatever is personally fulfilling. They commonly grasp that of which is pleasing to people and develop as humanists. They have departed from faith in the authentic teachings of the church or have rejected one or more teachings of the church as not being worthy of belief. They have more concern for the values of this life than for the values of eternal life.

3. **The conservative group.** The conservative Mien Christians are those who either have adopted or have converted from their ancestral worship to accept the Bible as the word of God given to human beings. They believe that the Bible provides a basic instruction for people to receive eternal salvation from God through the redemptive

work of God's one and only Son, Christ Jesus. The Word of God serves as the road map for people to live in love and harmony while they are living in this earthly world. They believe that the entire truth is contained in what they have been taught either by their parents, siblings, relatives, friends, Sunday school teachers, pastors or other instructors during their formative years. They believe and stand firm on the biblical knowledge they acquired through a Bible college or from Sunday school. They accept the content of what they have been taught as being an unchangeable and irrefutable truth.

They hold unswervingly to what they understand as being the teachings of the church or church authorities. Mien religious conservatives seek to preserve their spiritual truth and core values. They provide support services to their fellow sister churches that they are affiliated with_or have become members within the fellowship. Sometimes the leaders and pastors may find themselves at odds with their fellow Mien Christians and non-Christians when the culture contradicts their beliefs or viewpoints. On the extreme side there are individual believers and church leaders who have developed certain spiritual principles and boundaries that they would not cross and thus separate themselves even further from the other conservative Mien Christians.

There are two key points that led the conservative individuals and families to have uncompromising spiritual worldviews. First, they came to a realization that God is the one they should worship since He is the creator of their physical and spiritual lives. As human beings, we are all sinners and cannot save ourselves from our own sins. He is the one who loves sinners so much that He was willing to send His Son to die on the cross to pay for all of our sins. Therefore, they believe that they should recognize this gracious God and gladly accept his amazing love and forgiveness. By becoming children of God they have nothing to lose and everything to gain. The second point is that the Bible commands all believers to worship no other gods. In order to abide by God's word and follow his commandments, these people chose to worship the living God instead of their deceased ancestors. It is important to understand that one of the main reasons that these people chose to come into Christianity is because of the many years of negative experiences they had in worshipping their ancestors. People normally do not reject something that is helpful or beneficial to them. Since religion plays a major part of a person or group's culture, there has to be something dramatic that took place in these peoples' lives in order for them to reach such a strong conviction to leave their traditional belief.

Individuals and families who fall in this category experience the most pressures from their non-Christian relatives and friends. In many cases, due to their deep knowledge and firm belief of the commandments of the Bible, they would draw certain boundaries that can create major communication barriers between their immediate and extended family members. The two major divisive and controversial issues have to do with religious practices. As I have briefly discussed earlier in this chapter that Mien people came from an ancestral worshipping or animism background, it is a part of the religion for a family to sacrifice a domestic animal to their ancestors or other form of spirits as a part of the healing practices. Whenever a ritual ceremony is given, a Shaman or Saikung would be called to offer an animal to the spirits. In some cases, scrolls filled with red and black painting of Taoist gods are displayed in the room. These sacred scrolls are meant to be opened by qualified individuals and at an appropriate setting. Therefore, when a ritual ceremony takes place, family members are called to participate during the entire process.

Mien conservative individuals and their families usually have two boundaries that they would never cross. The first is to avoid playing any role in the religious ceremony, and the second is not to partake with any kind of foods offered to idols, as commanded by the Bible. Traditionally speaking, when someone becomes ill, it involves the entire family to seek resources and solutions to cure that individual. When a Shaman is called, a domestic animal is needed to be killed for sacrifice. Butchering, cleaning and cooking a pig or cow may involve many of the family members. Once the sacrificial ceremony is completed, cooks are needed to prepare the meals. When the meal is ready, the family is called and they are expected to gather together. Conservative Christians usually do not participate in the preparation of a ritual ceremony or eat the foods sacrificed to an idol.

These boundaries can become very divisive depending on the individual's and family's spiritual convictions. Individuals or families with moderate education and broader multicultural knowledge from the U.S. are more open minded and become less offended by this form of boundary. However, individuals and their families who are very traditional and have limited religious worldviews tend to become highly offended. These boundaries have created communication gaps for family members who are conservative Christians. The core values these people develop in their new religion have created many different levels of misunderstanding that led to poor communication. In some severe instances, family members become disconnected or segregated. Differences in beliefs usually disintegrate people from family members instead of uniting them into a harmonious family unit.

The conservative Christians are being placed in some levels of challenging and awkward positions. As a mediator and family counselor, I have seen and witnessed some family members being caught in between the circles of a new faith and an old belief. While there is a small grey area between these two circles for some families, for others they become black and white with no connection in between. The vast majority of the conservative Christians hold some levels of leadership at their church, such as Sunday school teachers, deacon or deaconesses, or the elders. These individuals are expected to live above the reproach of their Christian lives. They have high leadership and spiritual standards to conduct themselves in private and public. They are being viewed as the "role models" for those who are in the nominal and marginal groups. The leaders in this category cannot compromise their spiritual faith or doctrine; otherwise they may become stumbling blocks to their followers. Individuals who cannot or would not compromise their new faith with the old tradition usually are being viewed as too rigid or in Mien *"sienx duqv muonc haic"* by their family, relatives and friends. The situation becomes the worst when it involves parents and children or spouses.

Chapter 5

Survey Construction

This chapter provides a detailed discussion of the construction, distribution and content of the survey used for this study. The proceeding chapter discusses the results from the study.

Survey Construction

The survey was specially designed to focus on the variables that strengthen or weaken Mien marriages and families in the U.S., for both cultural and linguistic reasons. Since this study uniquely emphasizes the Mien ethnic minority, I took a cautious approach in drafting the questionnaires. The questions were critiqued by knowledgeable professors on the subject, colleagues of mine, prominent community leaders, and fellow pastors who all provided valuable input and suggestions regarding the content of the questionnaire. After making several rounds of revisions, the survey was field-tested with a small group of sixteen couples at a regular couple's gathering. It was then finalized and implemented through a six-month study.

Distribution of the Survey

One hundred completed surveys were collected from fifty married Christian couples and fifty non-Christian or traditional ancestral worship couples. One hundred twenty-five surveys were distributed in total; fifty were collected from the Christian couples at the fifth annual Mien Christian Couple's Retreat of the Northwest which was comprised of participants from Washington, Oregon and California and from a monthly couple's meeting at the Mien Evangelical Church, located in Tukwila, Washington. The remaining fifty from the non-Christian couples were completed by interview. I personally coordinated and conducted both sets of surveys. Since the majority of the Mien Christian married couples could read and write English,

I was able to gather sufficient information without any major language barrier. The other half of the study was completed through interviews at the participants' residences, except for six couples who completed their interviews by telephone due to scheduling conflicts.

The participants found the process of gathering the data to be pleasant and rewarding, and I was pleased with the valuable information and comments I was able to gain from the questionnaires. The participants were grateful to take part in the study. The participants and many community members expressed their gratitude and offered their best wishes for the successful completion of the study. Many community leaders expressed their deep gratitude to me for being a pioneer researcher in the field of Mien marriage and family. As Chairman of the Mien Christian Mission Fellowship, a Sunday school teacher, family counselor, former couples' group leader at Mien Evangelical Church, and a speaker in the Mien community, I had the great privilege to work with both the Christian and non-Christian communities. The couples were cooperative and delightful to work with. I was grateful and honored to share my hopes, goals and the research purposes with the participants. Through this research process, I was able to learn more about their needs and struggles, and received input valuable to the successful completion of this study.

Content of the Survey

The first section of the survey deals with demographic information. It contains questions on the participants' age, gender, current religious preference, length of time living in the U.S., place of birth, educational background, age when first married, place of marriage, and length of marriage.

Section B consists of eight questions regarding each individual's decision-making abilities within their marriage (and family) in regard to child-rearing, disciplining, family finances, relationships inside and outside of the family, and perception on their marriage communication.

Section C deals with resolving conflicts within a marriage. There are six questions under this section and they focus on how participants normally resolve conflicts within their marriage: who do they seek help from when they cannot reach a mutual agreement on family matters; who takes initiative to resolve problems within the family; who do participants share their problems with; and who do they seek help from when they have personal problems.

Section D tackles communication within the marriage. This is the lengthiest section, consisting of 32 questions. Some of the questions are in regards to communicating individual needs or issues to their spouses and children, expressing love, revealing appreciation, expressing gratitude, complimenting, communicating goals, plans, feelings, frustrations, needs or expectations, expressing physical and emotional needs, sharing happiness and good news, honesty with their spouses, satisfaction in marriage communication, frequency of communication barriers and conflicts, and being good communicators and listeners.

Section E, the last segment of the survey consists of four questions. It contains questions on participants' satisfaction in their marriages, perceptions on major problems facing both the Christian and non-Christian married couples, and the major causes of divorce and frequency of the occurrence of divorce.

Under the background information section, there were fifty males and fifty females with ages ranging from 18-64 years old. The couples married youngest in the study were 15-17 years old. Two women married at the age of 15, three men at 16, eleven women at 16, nine men at 17, and nine women at 17 years old. There were thirteen men and seven women married at the age of 18. Seventeen of them married between the ages of 19-21 and the rest of the eight people were between 30-64 years old. There were only two religious preferences for all the participants: animists, or 'traditional ancestral worshippers', and Christians. Per survey design, there are equal numbers of Christians who believe in God, Jesus and the Holy Spirit, and animists who worship their ancestors. Ninety percent of the Christian participants originally came from traditional ancestral worship. Only three individuals were born in the U.S. from parents who converted to Christianity after they immigrated here.

The participants' length of residency in the U.S. ranges from 6-25 years. Five individuals have lived in the U.S. from 6-11 years, twenty people between 12-17 years, and the remainder between 18-25 years.

Under 'highest educational achievement level,' six participants completed junior or middle school, twenty-nine individuals obtained a high school diploma, five people achieved an Associate's or two-year college degree, two people obtained Bachelor's Degrees, seven people are participating in a vocational training program, and the remaining informants do not have any formal education. A small portion of these individuals have participated in some form of language development program in the U.S. with local community colleges or English as a second language (ESL) classes.

Sixty-three people expressed that their reason to get married was their own choice, 29 percent from parental pressures, 4 percent from family pressure and 4 percent from environmental pressure.

The last two questions ask about the country of their marriage and the length of time they have been married. Fifty six percent of the participants were married in the U.S., 28 percent in Thailand and 26 percent in Laos. The newlywed couple had been married for one month. The majority of them, 77 percent, have been married between 1-15 years. Thirteen percent are between 10-15 years. The rest of the 8 percent have been married from 16-28 years.

Section B deals with household decision-making. There are eight questions about marriage and family decision-making. The first question asks, "Who is the decision maker in your marriage?" 44 percent are the husbands, 16 percent are the wives, and 30 percent are joint decision-makers.

The second question involves who is the decision maker in the family, 78 percent are the husbands, 22 percent are the wives and 2 percent are the parents.

The third question asks, "Who decides how you should discipline your children?" 81 percent indicated that both parents combine their effort to discipline the children while the children's father alone corrected 19 percent.

The fourth question deals with who takes the initiative to discipline the children. According to the participants' responses, 72 percent of the fathers initiated the children's discipline and 28 percent was by the mothers. In most homes, the fathers hold family authority. The children are trained, guided, loved, cared for and disciplined by the fathers more than the mothers.

The fifth question deals with who makes decisions on finances. Eighty-eight percent of the household finances were managed jointly, 16 percent by just the husbands and 6 percent by just the wives.

Question six involves making decisions outside of family matters. Eighty percent reported that the husbands are the ones making the decisions outside of the family, 15 percent by both spouses and 5 percent by the wives.

Question seven deals with who makes the decisions for household matters. Interestingly, the wives make 40 percent of the decisions within the house, 50 percent are made by both spouses and 10 percent by the husband.

The eighth question asks how participants feel about their communication in their marriages. Forty-two percent said they are satisfied, 43 are semi-satisfied, and 15 percent are unsatisfied.

Section C deals with conflict resolution within participants' marriages and families.

Question nine asks, "When there is a conflict within your marriage, how do you normally resolve it?" Eighty-six percent of the participants talk about their problems with their spouse, 8 percent consult with their parents and 6 percent seek advice from friends or family members.

Question ten asks, "When you and your spouse cannot reach a mutual agreement to your family matters, whom do you consult with?" Forty-six percent would consult with their parents, 34 would consult with a trusted community leader, 20 percent would consult with friends or relatives, and 10 percent would seek God's help through prayer.

Question eleven asks, "When you and your spouse cannot come to an agreement on an issue within your marriage, whom do you consult?" Sixty-nine percent would seek help from their parents, 34 percent from a community leader or pastor, 20 percent from friends or relatives and 10 percent from God.

Question twelve asks, "When there is a problem in your family, who makes the initiative to resolve it?" Sixty-three percent responded that the husbands do, 38 percent said both spouses, and 9 percent reported the wives. The husbands in this study seemed to take more initiative and responsibility to resolve issues existing within their family. In some families, the wives are the ones wearing both "pants and skirts" in the home because their husbands are irresponsible and unreliable to resolve family issues. Some women have higher education and acquire more skills in managing and dealing with household matters then their husbands.

Question thirteen asks, "When you have a personal problem, whom do you share your problem with?" Forty-nine percent would share their personal problems with their spouses, and 27 would share their personal issues with their friends or close family members. It is not a surprise that 24 percent would discuss their personal problems with their pastors and God in prayer as more people are developing their hope and trust in God. Having mentioned that half of the population in the survey is Christian, it should not be a surprise that there are many individuals who put their faith in God for solutions to life situations.

Question fourteen asks, "When you have problems, who do you seek help from?" Only a small portion of the participants seek assistance from their spouse. Twenty-seven percent would go to get help from their other loved ones. Twenty-four percent felt comfortable in seeking help from their pastor or church members. The remaining 49 percent would seek help from their friends and close family members. The responses from this question indicate that there were some trust issues, problem solving skills and unparallel communication.

The fourth section in the questionnaire deals with communication styles and expectations within their marriages and families.

Question fifteen addresses the question, "How do you communicate your needs or issues to your spouse?" Seventy-nine percent indicated that they usually reveal their needs to their spouse directly without framing them in analogy, unlike what their parents modeled when they were young. Twenty-one percent stated that they still expect their mates to know their needs without being direct, since they have been married for a lengthy amount of time. These individuals were born and raised in Laos and Thailand. They believe that their family's expectations of common needs should automatically known by their spouses. They should not have to repeat themselves since their spouses are "adults and no longer are children." The hidden expectations and indirect communication styles create confusion and unhealthy relationships for these couples and their families. Many of these parents are creating deeper gaps with their children—especially those who are born and raised in the U.S. Spouses who do not practice straight talk often have communication barriers in their relationships. Thus far there are still many individuals who are accustomed to the traditional indirect communication style.

Section D further addresses communication. This is the lengthiest section in the survey. It contains thirty-two questions regarding family and marriage communication.

Question sixteen asks, "How do you usually communicate to your child or children?" Eighty-five percent indicated that they would talk to their children directly. Unsurprisingly, 8 percent reported they are still applying the traditional communication medium with their children through different forms of analogy both intentionally and unintentionally. They do not know how ineffective their communication style is to their children. They had not thought about it, nor has anyone ever told them. The questions of effective communication between parent and child challenged some couples to pause and reflect on their daily communication patterns. Some parents realized that their children are very direct communicators. Many times these parents are shocked by the ways their children express their feelings or their minds. Some parents become very frustrated when their children talk back when there is an issue or when they are being disciplined. Seven percent of the parents expect their children to know their point without being direct. A common form of teaching or discipline is through making comparisons to other children to get their point across to their children. Through this, confusion can easily result.

The seventeenth item on the survey deals with how participants express their love to their spouses. Twenty-seven percent typically show their love to their spouse through gifts, helping out with household chores and caring for their children. Thirteen percent expect their mates to sense their love without having to tell them directly. Sixty percent of the participants indicated that they are assertive and direct in revealing their love to their spouses.

Question eighteen asks participants to reflect on how they usually reveal their appreciation to their spouse. This question received similar answers to question eighteen. Twenty-one percent stated that they make their appreciation known to their spouses through gifts and assistance in the home. 39 percent would not make any comments regarding their appreciation to their spouse and expect them to know their appreciation without having to verbalize it.

Question nineteen deals with how spouses express their gratitude toward their mates. 79 individuals express their gratitude directly to their spouses. Twelve people expect their mates to acknowledge their gratitude without having to tell them in words. Nine do not directly verbalize.

Question twenty asks the participants to evaluate how they complement their spouse. Eighty-five percent tell their spouses directly and 15 percent do not give verbal complements. It is not something that they are comfortable with or feel necessary. Sometimes in this culture complements can cause embarrassment to the giver or receiver.

Question twenty-one asks, "How do you communicate your goals, plans, feelings, frustration, needs or expectations to your spouse?" Eighty-three percent tell their spouses directly, 12 percent communicate through hidden agenda where they do not show, but expect that their spouses already know. There were also 5 percent who communicate through different forms of expressions.

The twenty-second item in the survey assessed participants on how they would reveal their physical needs to their spouses. Again, the respondents reported similar responses as in the previous question. That is, 92 percent would be assertive in letting their spouses know their physical needs while 8 percent still expect their spouses to understand their needs without having to mention them. As one woman put it, "My needs should be ingrained in my husband's brain. We have been married for over ten years and have raised four children together. He knows everything about me. For me to tell him or remind him of what I want him to do around the house is like talking to a young child. He is a grown up and I expect him to be an adult."

Question twenty-three asks, "How do you express your emotional needs to your spouse?" This question yields a higher and closer result to the typical or traditional Mien culture. Sixty-seven percent stated that they usually reveal their emotional needs to their partners. Many of the respondents concluded that their spouses, usually the wives, do not understand or meet their emotional needs, especially intimacy. They feel frustrated and angry at being neglected by their wives for not sensing their emotional and physical needs. This is an important issue in most marriages. Vice versa, spouses whose emotional and physical needs were being ignored by their husbands would tend to fulfill their missing spots elsewhere. Thus, many Mien couples are facing this physical intimacy issue. Incongruence of personal and cultural expectations can lead couples into marriage disaster.

Question twenty-four asks, "When you are happy, whom do you share your happiness with?" Disturbingly, a large portion, approximately 25 percent of the participants felt closer to their friends than their spouses. Ten percent share their happiness with their children while 65 percent share with their spouses. One would expect a higher percentage in sharing their happiness with their spouses; however, the result reveals an alarming problem in today's Mien relationships.

The answers for question twenty-five are exactly the same as question twenty-four. The question asks, "When you receive good news, whom do you share it with?"

The next question, twenty-six, deals with a person's honesty and integrity with their spouse. In responding to the question, "Are you always honest when you reveal your concerns and needs to your spouse?" some participants paused for a couple of seconds before providing their responses. Eighty-five percent said they were honest in making their concerns and needs be known to their spouses while 15 percent are not always being truthful. There are different reasons why some spouses were not always being honest. Some reasons include that they were disappointed with their spouses for some past issues and, thus, keep the feelings to themselves, or that their spouses were not trustworthy.

Question twenty-seven asks, "To what extent can you count on your spouse to give you honest feedback?" Only 73 percent can truly count on their spouses to give them honest feedback to their needs and feelings. A large portion, 27 percent were not able to trust their spouse for sincere and honest feedback. The responses given in this question helps us to better understand the answers from the following question: "Are you satisfied with your marriage communication?" Only 56 percent are satisfied while 34 percent are somewhat satisfied and 15 percent were unsatisfied.

The twenty-ninth question deals with how relaxed or peaceful one is when the spouse is away from the home. Eight percent would be very relaxed and peaceful, 12 percent would be a bit relaxed, 29 percent would be a little relaxed and 51 percent will not be able to relax or have peace when their spouse is away from the home.

Question thirty asks, "How much would you miss your spouse if you could not talk or see each other for a week?" Fifty-one percent would miss their spouses very much, 29 percent quite a bit, 12 percent would miss their spouse a little, and 8 percent would not miss their spouse at all.

Question thirty-one asks, "How much would you miss your spouse if you could not talk or see each other for a month?" Ninety percent would miss their spouse very much, 7 percent quite a bit, and 3 percent would miss their spouse a little.

Question thirty-two involves the frequency of participants' ability to communicate with their spouses about their anger. Nineteen responded that they are able to communicate with their spouses on a weekly basis, 23 discuss with their spouses about his or her anger issue monthly, 58 percent are able to talk with their spouses once in a while regarding their anger or frustration.

The thirty-third question of the survey asks the respondents how often they have an argument with their spouse. Twenty-five indicated that they argue weekly, 65 people argue once a month and 5 percent argue only once in a while.

Question thirty-four asks, "How often does your spouse make your feel angry?" Ten percent revealed that their spouse makes them angry two to three times a week, 88 get angry weekly with their spouses, and only two people said an argument happens once a month.

Question thirty-five asks, "How often do you and your spouse engage in conflict?" Ten percent reported in having conflict two to three times a week, 70 percent involved in weekly conflict, 7 percent engaged in monthly conflict, and 2 percent once in awhile.

Question thirty-six deals with the frequency of one spouse trying to control the other's communication. Fifteen percent reported this occurrence two to three times a week, 24 percent weekly, and 61 percent regularly.

Question thirty-seven requests feedback from respondents on how often they get angry or frustrated when unable to communicate their point clearly to their spouse, without interruption. Seventeen individuals reported that they are interrupted by their spouse on a weekly basis, 45 percent said this happens 'most of the time' and 38 percent said it occurs 'once in a while'.

Question thirty-eight seeks answers on how often the informants have open communication with their spouses. Ten percent indicated having open communication two-three times a week, 22 percent on a weekly basis, and 68 percent have open communication once in a while.

Question thirty-nine deals with how often the couples have to give in to their spouse. Thirty-four percent of the respondents revealed that they have to give in on a weekly basis while 66 percent give in most of the time.

Question forty asks, "How often does your spouse make you feel guilty?" Fifteen percent said on a monthly basis, and 10 percent said once in a while.

Question forty-one deals with the frequency of communication barriers between spouses. Twenty-five percent responded two to three times a week, 58 percent on a weekly basis, and 27 responded once in a while.

Question forty-two is, "How often does your spouse ignore you?" Seventy-nine percent indicated regularly while 21 percent indicated once in a while.

Question forty-three asks the participants, "How often does your spouse complain about your communication?" Thirty-five percent reported that their spouses complained about their communication regularly while 65 stated once in a while.

Question forty-four asks, "Do you consider your spouse a good listener?" Thirteen percent said yes, 10 percent said no, and 77 indicated sometimes.

When asked on question forty-five, "Do you consider your spouse a good communicator?" Twelve people responded they do, 38 percent admitted that they are not good communicators, 50 percent sometimes claimed to be good communicators. "Do you feel valued or respected by your spouse when you communicate?" is question forty-six. 15

percent said no, 45 percent said yes, and 40 percent indicated that their spouses sometimes respect them.

Question forty-seven deals with the question on "Are you satisfied with your marriage? 42 percent are satisfied, 43 percent as somewhat satisfied, while 15 percent are unsatisfied with their marriage.

Question forty-eight deals with the question of, "What do you think are the major problems facing both the Christian and non-Christian Iu-Mien married couples in the U.S.?" Eighty-eight percent believed that there are many variables, but some of the major areas are poor communication, limited education and resources in the marriage, ineffective parenting techniques, inability resolving conflicts, lacking moral principles and values, financial insecurity, and independency imposed by the western culture.

Question forty-nine asks, "What do you think are the major causes of divorce for Iu-Mien couples in the U.S.?" The responses were ineffective communication styles, spouses not being able to meet each other's emotional and physical needs, lacking sincere love and respect, infidelity, gambling, alcohol and drug addiction, and inability to cope with societal pressures regarding beauty, physical attraction, and love.

The final question deals with participants' opinions on the divorce rate of Mien people in the U.S. The majority of them voiced their opinions on the Mien divorce rate to be between 10-20 percent. The responses provided by these individuals pose a great concern about the stability of Mien families and marriages in the U.S.

Further detail on the survey results is discussed in the following chapter and the results of the research analysis, evaluation, and recommendations are presented in the final chapter of this book.

Chapter 6

Results of Questionnaire Survey

This chapter contains the data that has been collected, analyzed and summarized from a lengthy research questionnaire. The results of this study serve as the primary source of information for this book. The construction, formulation, and detailed data analysis of the questionnaire is available in Appendix One for review. The survey was specially created to focus on the study of factors and variables that strengthen or weaken Mien marriages and families in the U.S. for both cultural and linguistic reasons.

Questionnaires were carefully constructed to gather a broad range of data from the participants and have been categorized into five areas of concentration, including participant demographics, household decision-making, conflict resolution, methods of communication, and personal opinions. The questions were formulated to assess the directly measurable aspects (quantitative) and the opinion aspects (qualitative) from the participant responses and the author's own observations and insight into the Mien culture in general.

In order to ensure that the content of the questionnaire was appropriate and addressed the main issues faced by the Mien, knowledgeable colleagues, community leaders, and pastors were asked to provide valuable input by examining and critiquing each question. The survey was field-tested prior to the implementation during a six-month period.

Questionnaire Survey Results

The data collected from the surveys has been categorized, analyzed and summarized as follows: the data reveals several key variables in the success and failure of Mien marriages and family stability in the U.S. This research provides readers with a deeper focus into the Mien people and their culture in general, in addition to presenting some intriguing observations about their strengths and weaknesses. The analysis of the data suggests five major factors that impact the success or failure of Mien marriage and family development in the U.S.:

1. Educational achievement
2. Religious belief systems
3. Intercultural communication
4. Conflict management
5. Love and respect

1. Educational Achievement

The majority of the Mien population do not have strong academic backgrounds as discussed previously. At the time of this study, participants had limited formal education. Only two percent had obtained a four year college degree, five percent had completed two-year college, and 27 percent had finished high school. Seven individuals had completed some form of vocational training with or without any prior schooling, while 53 percent had no formal schooling or training, even in their own indigenous language. In addition we found that their parents and grandparents had not obtained any form of formal schooling.

The data reveals that 42 percent of the people surveyed described their marriage relationship as satisfactory. Researchers know that education provides a link to the development of social, economical, and relationship ties. In the U.S., being literate in English creates a career pathway individuals need to gain new knowledge and skills for personal growth and enhancement of their relationships. There are conferences, workshops, classes or books available to improve one's personal, social, and professional skills as needed. Participants with limited education lack the western parenting and relationship developmental skills needed to communicate effectively with their families. Spouses with a strong literacy background are able to adjust more rapidly into today's multilingual, multicultural and complex technological society. They can also acquire new strategies to deal with their marriage and family issues.

Individuals with some level of higher education tend to be more romantic with each other and are often more receptive to adopting new ideas to enlighten their marriages. They adopt western social appearances and personalities much more rapidly than those who have less western education. In most cases, individuals with limited education tend to rely more heavily on their own personal experiences and cultural knowledge acquired from their homeland. Thus, they are applying many of the previously learned principles or belief systems into their daily lives, which can be either supportive or destructive to their modern lifestyles. In some cases their traditional principles generate a culture 'clash theory' between themselves and the individuals around them.

Although educational achievement is not the only issue confronting today's Mien marriages and families, it is an obstacle blocking many individuals from acquiring the necessary skills needed to improve their problems. There are other areas that contribute to the success or failure of a relationship. Data indicates that people with some level of solid educational foundation are better able to create stronger relationships than those with less of an educational foundation. They are able to observe each other's strengths, weaknesses, and can understand and accept the differences. Thus, they have healthier relationships with their family members. They can appreciate each other's differences and seek new knowledge to enhance their marriage and family relationships from outsiders. Lack of knowledge and resources limits many people from seeking outside help or from utilizing the resources available to them in the community. The more education and higher level of education a person has achieved, the more they are aware of and can utilize a broader set of support services to help themselves and their family members when needed.

Education is the real key to realize and understand the world. True education serves as a pair of glasses for people to see things clearly as they are and to walk on their path safely without endangering themselves or others. Education also serves as a hearing aide to assist people to understand what they hear and provide appropriate responses. Education is a road map, a compass and navigator that enables a person to find his or her way around this complex world and to reach his or her destination as safely and quickly as possible. Valuable education serves as a firm and unbiased bridge for people to cross from one location to another without demanding any unnecessary tolls or compromising of one's personal values and principles. Real education brings life, help, hope, healing and restoration for individuals and families in both good and bad times.

2. Religious Belief Systems

The results of this survey have revealed an interesting factor leading to the wellness of a family relationship. Religion or a belief system plays a crucial role in one's daily personal and family life. Currently, approximately 80 percent of Mien worship ancestors or other forms of gods, and 20 percent are Christians. Out of the estimated twenty-eight thousand Mien in the U.S., there are approximately five thousand who believe in God and/or are Christians. Thirty-eight out of the forty-two participants who indicated they had healthy marriages and relationships reported that they were Christians, except for one couple whose wife believed in ancestral worship and the husband believed in God. The remaining eight Christian couples report that they experience some communication difficulty in their marriage. These couples all do not possess a strong educational background and have some literacy limitations.

The exact Mien population in the U.S. is unknown; however, Table 2 below offers a quick glance into where Mien people reside throughout the U.S., divided by Mien Christians and non-Christians.

Table 2: Mien Christians and Non-Christians in the U.S.

	Families	Individuals	Christians	Non-Christians
Washington	480	2,800	410	2,790
Oregon	450	2,600	490	2,110
California	4,700	28,000	5,600	22,400
Illinois	10	70	60	10
Alabama, Miss.	12	85	22	63
Alaska	45	230	70	160
Total	**5,697**	**33,785**	**6,652**	**27,533**

Figure 1: Mien Christians and non-Christians in Washington, Oregon and California states.

Mien Christians and Non-Christians in WA, OR and CA

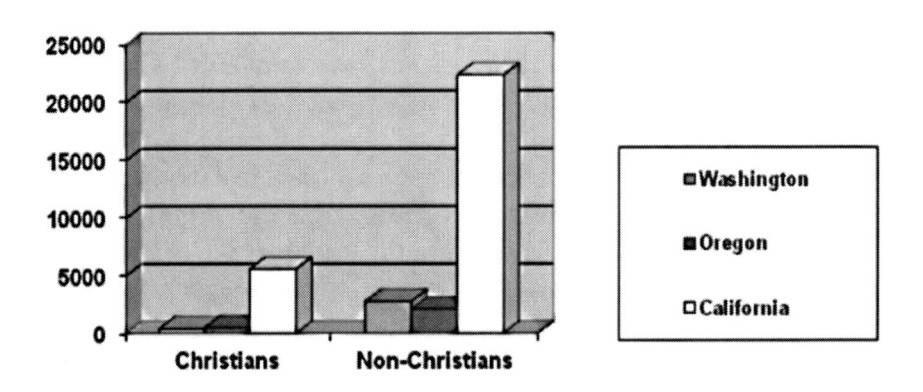

The following chart presents the population breakdown of Mien Christians and non-Christians in the U.S.

Figure 2: Mien Christians and non-Christians in the U.S.

Mien Christians and non-Christians in the U.S.

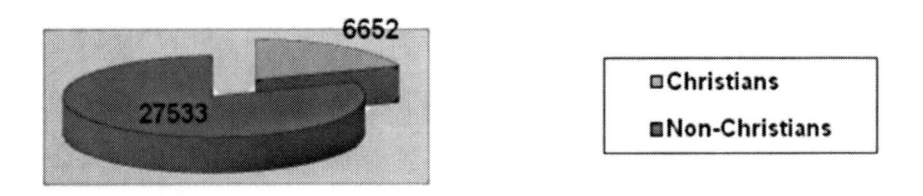

The forty-two successfully married couples in this study demonstrated a strong commitment to their beliefs, values and moral principles. They reported that they are faithful Christians who attend church regularly, participate in their local church activities and events, and have strong connections to the church. They offer their skills, gifts and talents to the church with gratitude. They enjoy serving God through helping their fellow Christian brothers and sisters. They volunteer many hours of service and donate financial support to the church. They see the church as an important place for them to receive not only biblical training, but to be strengthened by the weekly preaching and teaching of the Word of God, and are being encouraged and supported by the pastors, elders and church members. To them, church is a healthy and resourceful environment for the whole family and community members. Their children attend the weekly Sunday school programs in multi-grade levels: K-1st, 2nd-3rd grade, 4th-5th grade, 6th-8th grade, 9th-12th grade, while the adults can choose to attend the young adult class, new believer's class, or any other three adult Sunday school classes at Mien Evangelical Church, located in Tukwila, Washington.

Throughout the years the church, in cooperation with other churches in the states of Washington, Oregon and California, has organized annual children's Vacation Bible School, children's camps, youth camps, family camps, couple retreats and leadership trainings. There are many opportunities for church members to be educated with different skills and the knowledge necessary to establish healthy and fruitful marriages and families. There are scholarships and support programs for individuals who are unable to attend national conferences and workshops due to financial hardship. Both adults and children have many opportunities to meet together as families and participate in many well-structured and nurtured activities throughout the year. This environment provides family unity in loving, caring, and supporting materials. In some cases both the husbands and wives serve together as teammates. The couple's monthly meetings and activities bring them together to share and learn new skills that are applicable to marriage and family development. Couples are now attending local and national marriage and family conferences and workshops. The majority of the services are free of charge to members and non-members of the church. When a marriage or family conflict arises, the family can seek help from the pastor, elders, lay pastors or church counselor at no cost. The more individuals and families are committed to attend church on a regular basis, the more they are being exposed to both English and

Mien language through the teaching, reading, writing of the weekly lessons and the preaching from the pastor.

On the contrary, individuals and couples who are not Christians are missing the support services mentioned above. Although the church welcomes and invites their non-Christian relatives and friends to participate with the church regular and annual programs and activities, very few people take advantage of these support services. Due to the different belief systems, most people feel reluctant to attend church organized events often feeling alienated. Religion plays a crucial role in their daily life. While at the same time religion promotes high family and moral values, it creates division for some families. The traditional and modern Christian believers have different sets of principles and moral standards. In most cases, their core life-governed principles draw families together in some amazing ways through forgiveness, repentance, and restoration. Admitting one's mistakes or weaknesses to one's wife, children and others is a challenging concept for Mien men to undertake. Sometimes pulling a tooth is easier than for a man to admit his mistakes. This factor is especially true for those who are in the leadership positions. In the traditional Mien culture, there is an instilled philosophy of a man losing face and leadership power when he admits his weaknesses or faults.

Religion sometimes segregates family members from regular visitations or meetings. It can be a high cost for some families when they are visited by a Christian family member or relative. Many ancestral worshipers still practice the religious concept of "*siangx mienv*" or "ancestor notification" to inform them that someone other than an immediate family member is visiting, and that they are not to be offended or to cause any illness or harm to the family. The host family members who are not Christians can become ill if the ancestors are being offended by the intruders. Animal sacrifice is required to avoid any physical and spiritual disturbance. The family needs to make an immediate animal sacrifice by a shaman to their ancestors. For example, several years ago my wife and I visited one of her sister's families in California for the first time in seven years. The moment we entered the house, the family provided us with a warm welcome. After we greeted each other, the family quickly began to prepare lunch for us. Prior to enjoying the meal, as we were very hungry from the fifteen-hour driving trip, I requested permission to offer a prayer for the meal. The husband, the head of the family, quickly granted the request. Shortly afterward, we discovered that two chicken's lives were lost due to our presence and the offensive prayer. A shaman was contacted to offer the chickens as a form of apology to the family's ancestors for having Christian guests, asking them not to cause any physical or spiritual harm to the guests and the family members. Finding live chickens and an available shaman to perform such an urgent ceremony can be a great challenge. Money, time and extra effort are always involved.

The problem did not end there. A domino effect occurred at the same time. When the shaman finished the offering, the family began to prepare lunch for us. As we began to eat some people from our church began to question which dish contained food that was sacrificed to idols. The individuals from our church had been taught from the Bible that Christians should not eat foods offered to any form of idol. Since the chickens were already offered to the family's ancestors or some form of spirits, and there were no other choices, some people just ate the rice. Therefore, by not eating the foods provided by the family, it created another problem for the family. We learned that we have not just offended the family's ancestors, but the whole family for rejecting their food. We faced the dichotomy of two different belief systems—the traditional ancestral worship and the Christianity belief. These different beliefs put two groups of people into a very awkward position. We, the Christians, were put into the position of having to decide whether we should practice the traditional Mien 'face saving' by eating the foods, or to 'lose our own face' and keep our consciences clear by refusing to eat the foods that had been sacrificed to an idol. It was a very uncomfortable situation for everyone. A nice family visit suddenly turned into a very sensitive religious conflict.

Since sharing a meal with loved ones is an important cultural dynamic within the Mien family, many individuals find themselves in the difficult situation of either enjoying the meal to please their family members, or standing firm in their biblical beliefs of not eating foods offered to "*mienv*," the devils or demons, which could be detrimental to a family relationship. In extreme cases a couple's belief system or religion can help or hurt their marriage relationship. This is especially true in the case where one spouse is a traditional ancestral worshipper and the other is a Christian. The traditional Mien expectations for a wife to be submissive, respectful and loyal to her husband and in-laws poses a great challenge to couples who do not share a common set of belief values. Because divorce within the Mien community is not encouraged, some wives find their marriage relationship very difficult. A non-Christian husband is often expected by his parents, clan members or family members to preserve the family tradition, and meet the high expectations or standards of religious principles set for him by the Mien culture. Thus, differences in religious beliefs between a couple can strengthen or weaken a family relationship.

Despite some of the negative impact that religion has brought forth within a marriage setting, many researchers report great benefits. Religion can serve as a protective factor with regard to health status. Epidemiologic studies have indicated that religiosity is inversely related to adult mortality rates, reported by Levin and McCullough, Hoyt, Larson, Koenig, and Thoresen. There is also a strong correlation between religion among individuals and reduced substance abuse. The fifty Christian couples who participated in this study had strong religious connections and their views on the use of alcohol, tobacco usage, and other illegal drugs, seen as harmful to a person's physical and spiritual body. They reported that they refrain themselves and prevent their children from using these harmful substances because of their belief in the Bible which states that the body is the temple of the Holy Spirit. Therefore, they are instructed by the Bible to keep their bodies from being contaminated by harmful chemicals or substances. There is less alcohol and drug usage within the Christian couples and families. These parents discourage their children from introducing chemicals or elements into the body as well.

Religiosity is also a tool that can be used to measure a family's support and use of problem-solving skills. Dubow and Tisak showed that religiosity reduces the effect of life stress on outcomes such as adjustment and academic achievement. Individuals who have hope in God are able to handle their stress better than those who don't. Besides bringing one's petitions to God in prayer, the individual can seek assistance from church members or the pastor. The individual is not confronting life challenges alone, and can get extra support from the church members. The more an individual or couple attends Sunday school and church services, the more they will learn from the teacher, pastor and other church members about problem-solving skills. When a problem exists within a family or couple, the pastor, church counselor or elders can step in to help resolve the issues. Parenting classes and marriage building skills are also being taught at the church for its members.

Lastly, religion affects attitudes and values within a marriage and family domain. Committed and faithful individuals perceive religion as meaningful and purposeful in their lives. Pargament and Wills & Hirky reported that religiosity may influence the way people tend to cope with problems and their perceptions about the coping functions of substance use. This claim is supported by the results of this current study described herein. The 50 couples practicing Christianity in their daily lives are not in favor of substance use. They even refrain themselves from participating in non-religious activities where alcohol or other substances are served. The traditional believers view alcohol usage as normal and acceptable for individuals who choose to use them. It does not create any contradiction to their belief system. Alcoholic beverages are expected to be served during special ceremonies or activities, such as birthday cerebrations, new years, weddings, special feasts, or other religious events.

The Christian individuals believe that the Bible provides clear guidelines for individuals to live a productive lifestyle and for couples to form their family life-union in love, understanding, supporting, encouraging, helping, caring, forgiving and accepting one another as different in physical forms and personalities, and yet being in perfect union spiritually under the Lordship of Christ Jesus. They are two different beings and yet viewed as "oneness" in the spirit. This belief is a very strange concept to Mien individuals who are not Christians or do not understand because it contradicts the original teaching of a Mien culture where the husband is the head of the family, and he is fully in charge of his wife and children, not "one" with his wife. The Christian Mien can understand and yield to the Lordship of a supreme God, but non-Christian Mien cannot relate to this concept. Thus, religion plays an integral role within a marriage. Religious beliefs can help or hinder the social and spiritual growth of a marriage and family relationship. Couples with the same moral and spiritual principles have a stronger marriage foundation than those married couples and family members who hold different views about human conditions and relationship development.

3. Intercultural Communication

The third and most important component that contributes to a healthy relationship is **intercultural communication** as mentioned in Chapter Seven. In addition to males and females speaking different languages of love, the new culture and communication style in the U.S. adds another barrier for Mien couples and individuals who are standing between the two worlds, the traditional culture and the new culture. Depending on a person's acculturation and assimilation level, the linear and circular communication styles can enhance or hinder a marriage relationship. Those who are attempting to mutually understand each other in their communication enjoy their marriage and family relationships more than the traditional communicators. One significant perception in the communication process between a man and woman is that the man is more affected by the negative words or responses he receives from his spouse than those who are outside of the marriage. He has more tolerance for negativism or criticism from his peers or co-workers than his own beloved wife. The woman on the contrary, is more sensitive to negative words or actions given by those who are outside of the family. Generally speaking, women also have higher tolerance from outsiders than their own husbands.

Within the marriage there are different languages of love. One uncommonly spoken language in the Mien culture is the intimate style of communication. Sexual intimacy has contributed greatly to some of the major factors impacting Mien marriages. Through my regular contacts with Mien leaders and community members in f Washington, Oregon and California where most Mien people reside, and from the participants' reports through the marriage survey, sexual intimacy is one of the major contributing factors to marriage problems and the divorce rate in the U.S. There are also many unreported cases of separations, divorce, and domestic issues within the Mien communities. Communication barriers in sexual intimacy have caused many unresolved issues between couples. Spouses have left their mates to pursue another more gratifying sexual relationship. The language of love is important in all marriages, not only to the Mien families. However, due to cultural issues where Mien couples do not discuss their sexual problems outside of their marriage, the issues never become public information. Through this survey, some individuals admitted they knew many divorced couples separated due to sexual communication barriers. They even reported knowing families who are currently facing a similar communication breakdown. Despite the sexual communication problems the couples have, they refrain from getting outside counseling services due to their cultural beliefs.

Mien people treat sexuality differently than the westerners as discussed previously. Sexual activity varies enormously from one culture to the other. In the traditional and even in modernized society, many view sexual acts as shameful and disgusting. Pornography was never an issue because it never existed in an agrarian society such as the Mien culture. Intimate language was not taught or used around children. Parents usually avoided discussing or giving information about human sexuality, just as much as children did. Sexual topics are considered embarrassing and should be avoided within a family circle. Culturally sensitive issues have created wider communication gaps for both couples and their children.

Since sex education was not available for the Mien parents who got married in Laos or Thailand, they have very limited knowledge today about sexual communication. Couples living in the U.S. who are trying to apply the communication style they brought from their native countries, find that this style does not bring the best results to their marriages. In the traditional form of communication where children were not able to openly receive sexual education from their parents, curiosity would lead them to personal experience. Many of the participants, through their discoveries of sexuality, ended up of getting married at young ages or becoming single mothers.

The 42 percent of participants reported having healthy marriage relationships are bilingual, bicultural and are more acculturated than others. Their understanding and acceptance of the western world-view and communication style are at different levels. They are able to adjust well to the demands and expectations of the modern society. They communicate in linear form and practice less circular communication styles. These individuals are classified by the traditional group of Mien parents and elders as "*ziux zaaqc mba'zorngh gorngv waac*" meaning the "straight nose communicators."

Couples reporting high marriage satisfaction reveal an open and mutual communication. They tend to have regular communication with their spouses and children. They voice their needs, concerns, and interests to each other on regular basis. When confrontations occur, they usually do not speak in idioms, analogies, or talk around the subject. They communicate assertively instead of being passive communicators. They practice more physical affection than the traditional spouses. Within their homes and marriages they are more verbal in comparison to spouses who were born, raised and grew up in Laos and Thailand.

The modern married couples have adopted a western style of communication. They take vacations together as couples or families, date each other, plan and attend family activities such as picnicking, camping, bowling, having barbecues at the parks, fishing or hunting. Both Christian and non-Christian Mien families have been gradually adopting western holidays, such as Valentine's Day, Mother's Day and Father's Day as special occasions to reveal their love and appreciation to one and another. Some non-Christian Mien communities across the states of Washington, Oregon and California organize live band events to share their memories of the past, their happiness in the present and hope for the future. People get together to socialize and exchange gifts, share food and dance with each other's spouses or the spouses of their acquaintances. The live bands present special songs from their homelands or other modern songs reminding each other about their struggles in the past and the success or happiness in their new lives.

The Christian couples, however, celebrate the same holidays in a slightly different format. They normally celebrate a special event with songs of worship and praise, and followed with a special message presented by the pastor, other church leaders or a special guest speaker relating to the theme of the occasion. There is always an educational lesson or message taught by someone at Christian gatherings. For example, a Valentine dinner is organized by the church members to celebrate the love they receive from God and their spouses. The event usually begins with songs of praise and worship to prepare people's hearts, minds and spirit for the message. They conclude the event with a romantic dinner where couples share their personal life stories or testimonies. Some individuals dedicate special love songs to their spouses. In many occasions, silence and happy tears fill the room when couples admit their mistakes of wrong doings, ask their mates for forgiveness, or express their happiness through songs or poems. Great healing and reconciliation can take place over a small event that brings hope and encouragement to the couples and the audience as a whole.

One major difference between Christian and non-Christian Mien in any community event or social gathering is the concept of God-centered versus people-centered. Individuals who become committed Christians place God as their central point of meet and greet, and the non-Christian emphasize the status and culturally appropriate form in their social gathering. The Christian Mien acknowledge themselves as sinners, saved by the grace of God, with the need to be empowered or strengthened not by man, but by the work of the Holy Spirit. Man needs to learn the word of God and to apply it to their daily lives. Thus, songs of worship and praise are always present in addition to a special message taught by the pastor. The non-Christian Mien normally gather together to acknowledge certain key community leaders or individuals for being successful, educated, talented, or task accomplishments. Music, songs and performances occur to entertain each others. Alcohol beverages are served for social networking and personal enjoyment. Romantic songs as well as sad songs are played or sung for entertainment. People enjoy themselves while trying to please their acquaintances, honored guests, or respected individuals by buying them expensive drinks and paying for special or dedicated songs for the quests to dance with their spouses, known as "*maux nzung*," a borrowed Lao and Thai word. In addition, some people would "*maux sieqv*," meaning to reserve a particular girl to dance with the honored quests. The higher the fee an individual paid to reserve a particular girl, the higher respect or honor is given to that individual.

There is also a slight change in the communication patterns between the Christian and non-Christian Mien. The Christians avoid using terminology or phrases that are related to spiritual language. Mien people have three different forms of language communication. One is known as the *spirit language*. Spirit language or "*ziec-waac*" in Mien, is mainly used by shaman or *saikung* to make sacrificial offerings of animals, such as chickens, pigs or cows to the ancestors. The second style of language or communication is "*nzung-waac*" or *song language*. This form of communication was very famous in the traditional village settings. Individuals would express their happiness or sorrow through songs while working in their rice or cornfields. In the evening, knowledgeable individuals would read their testimonies or other textbooks written in Chinese characters out loud for the family members and neighbors to hear. In other special occasions, young men and women often discovered their soul mates through the all night long exchanging of words and knowledge through their songs.

The third form of common communication is *oral language* since the Mien writing system is still new to many people. Today there are few Christian Mien leaders in the U.S. who are able to communicate via letters and emails with their fellow Christians overseas. Both Mien Christians and non-Christians in the U.S. have acquired different forms of skills since their resettlement. Today they are adopting western instruments, lyrics, and musical communication styles. Learning how to play guitar, piano, bass guitar, keyboard, flute, trumpet, writing and singing modern songs are some of the newly acquired skills.

4. Conflict Management

The fourth variable that contributes to the growth of marriage or family relationships is **conflict management**. Conflict in marriage is inevitable, and its presence is neither good nor bad. It does not necessarily mean a marriage is failing or determined to fail. In order to successfully manage conflict, marriage partners must be committed to work on the differences in bringing success to their marriage, to improve their communication skills, and to adopt productive problem solving techniques that are culturally relevant and practical. Conflict can be successfully managed if both partners are sincere and committed to make a change that brings a win-win resolution to the relationship. Major conflicts do not normally occur without any causes. Whenever they appear on the surface, there are some levels of roots that have been taken place underneath them. Therefore, whenever a minor or a major conflict appears in a marriage relationship, it requires both spouses to take the ownership or accountability to resolve it as soon as possible without causing any further injury. A successful conflict management involves the effort and energy from both spouses.

Conflict is a normal part of marriage, but most couples have not been taught a healthy pattern of handling it. The word "conflict" means, "to strike together." Each person is unique and what he or she brings to the marriage is also unique. Thus, it would be difficult to avoid conflicts in marriage when two people are living together. Mien people say that, "*Hnangv nyaah caux mbietc juangc sung nzuih yiem zungv maaih qiangx ngaatc zuqc doic, hmuangv doic juangc norm biauv yiem zungv simv maiv cuotv haih zoux bun doic,*" which means "As teeth and tongue are jointed together under one roof and occasionally attack each other, it is not possible for a couple and family members living together in one house to avoid having any problems." There are times when the tongue and cheek have been bitten by the teeth in very painful ways, and yet they still live together despite of their strengths and weaknesses. Regardless of the position they form or are assigned, they need each other, and each part has an important role in the body to play. Only through cooperation of the tongue and teeth, do they allow the mouth to fully function in its' designated role and duty. One would be insufficient and incapable without the other. Yet, when a problem occurs, whether with the teeth or tongue, it affects the whole mouth. As conflicts are impossible to avoid in any relationship, healthy conflict management allows couples to learn more about each other and model what they want their children to learn. Couples should not try to avoid conflict, but rather manage it in a healthy and productive manner when conflicts happen.

Why Conflict Develops

Conflicts develop throughout many different conditions in life and for many different reasons. One is the struggle to understand each other as human beings and yet remain different in the way they communicate their needs, wants, expectations, love, and feelings. Men and women use different languages communicating with each other. Men's goals in using language tend to be about getting things done, whereas women's tend to be about making connections to other people. Men express themselves more about things and facts, whereas women communicate more about people, relationships and feelings. Men's way of using language is competitive, reflecting their general interest in acquiring and maintaining status; women's use of language is cooperative, reflecting their preference for equality and harmony. These differences routinely lead to "miscommunication" in a marriage relationship.

Conflict develops as married couples struggle to know and understand one another. It is the result of their desire to develop healthy relationships in their day-to-day lives. If anyone tries to avoid having any form of relational differences, the only way is not to be in a relationship. However, by avoiding other human beings, one needs to ask the question "Is this the best way for me to avoid having conflicts in this world?" As humans are created by God for relational purposes, it is not possible for any active and functional body not to be involved in some form of physical, social, emotional, or spiritual relationship with people or God. People of all ages, creeds and cultures need to have two relational connections—a horizontal relationship with other human beings, and a vertical relationship with the Creator God. Both are equally important and they need to be balanced. This topic is discussed further in the following chapter.

Conflict is the result of differences in taste, background, temperament and unmet needs. Conflict also results when two people compete for control. The methods of gaining control may differ from person to person. Some people may be demanding, dominating and confrontational. Others may complain, withdraw or hold grudges through non-compliance. Both want control and they seek it in different ways. Conflict is the result of not knowing the facts, making assumptions, and creating unfulfilled expectations. Most couples enter marriage with the feeling that their hopes and dreams have not yet been completely fulfilled. They are then attracted to a person of the opposite sex, who appears to have skills and insights that they lack. The expectation is that the mate would somehow fill the void that contributes to their own discontent. Moreover, conflict usually exists from unparalleled communication patterns. When two people cannot understand each other's communication style, frustration and misunderstanding can easily take place. Lastly, conflict is the result of poor listening skills. Many people tend to be self-absorbed and self-centered, much less concerned about the viewpoint of a spouse than our own viewpoint. In general, people are quick to pinpoint the mistakes, wrongs and weaknesses of others, but often fail to recognize these flaws in themselves.

Many times we are blinded by our own ignorance and stupidity to fully understand ourselves and others in a clear sense. Couples with imbalanced cultural viewpoints encounter more communication barriers and marital conflicts than couples who share similar cultural perspectives and expectations. From the result of the study, these couples can be classified into three groups: the traditional, marginal, and modernized, as presented in Chapter One.

Under the **traditional group**, couples were born, raised, and educated or grew up in Laos or Thailand. They were taught by their parents, grandparents or relatives to use passive and indirect communication. There are certain cultural and religious values for individuals to adopt according to the unwritten norms of the clan or community setting. Individuals were taught to carefully observe the cultural patterns and examples of conflict management established by their village leaders. The leaders resolved conflicts that were not settled by the individual parties. Some of the common strategies to ensure victory in any dispute were 1) to have friends, family members and relatives who could argue aggressively through power or logical reasoning, 2) to make threats or harm through physical or spiritual power or, 3) to bribe the leaders who served as mediators or judges and the witnesses.

Conflicts within the family were usually handled differently than issues with people from outside of the family. The wives and children usually submitted to the decisions made by the husband, the head of the family. They seldom challenged his authority or decision. Physical abuse was common among the traditional group of families, where the husband usually applied his authoritarian power over his wife and children. Corporal punishment was also a common practice by parents in Laos and Thailand. Minor punishments included twisting or flicking the ear, pinching the body, or knuckling the head. Major discipline or punishment could be quite severe and harmful to the mind, body and soul. These included whipping with a stick, firewood, or a fire log where bruises and cuts on the skin occurred; or punching, kicking, hanging the person upside down with ropes on the ceiling while inhaling the smoke from the burning of dried chili or dried grass underneath. In other cases, the victim was starved or forced to perform some physically intensive labor.

The wives and children of the traditional group were usually the victims under the dictatorship of their husbands just as they were taught to be. Communication was one-way; the father or husband usually dominated the conversation. Disagreements could lead to a physical confrontation and the husbands or fathers would normally win. Some men treated their spouses as objects since they had to pay a high bride price to the wife's parents. In some cases the parents of the wives asked for a very high bride price, and it took the couple many years of sacrifice and physical labor to pay back the money owed. The high bride price can place the wife in a difficult position if she chooses to leave her husband when conflicts become overwhelming within her marriage. In order for her family to accept her back, they would have to repay her husband double the bride price it cost him. Children, especially boys, growing up in this type of environment may develop a false ideology that men are the kings of the jungle and abuses are normal within the culture. This circle of destructive behavior continues as children get married and form their own families. As the Mien say, "*Jae-dorn da'lueix da'lueix seix nzipc seix*" meaning "baby chicks will become chickens and act accordingly," as discussed earlier.

On the contrary, women who came from an abusive marriage environment for either personal or cultural reasons, once they have resettled and become well situated in the U.S., often begin to resist and fight back with their husbands and or the family. Many wives have turned themselves from being tolerant into intolerant. They no longer continue to be submissive in an abusive relationship. Some women compared their abusive and controlling life to birds being kept in a cage. In any prolonged abusive environment, the wives felt like they were being treated as slaves under the mercy of their owners, who were their husbands and their in-laws. Worse yet, in order to prevent the birds from getting out of the cage and flying away, the owners also had their wings clipped. Therefore, the birds' freedom to fly, to enjoy themselves and the world have totally been eliminated. As birds are only able to move around within the limited space of the cage, many wives were placed in a restricted marriage relationship where they were under the total authority and control of their husbands and the in-laws.

Women also know well that not all cages are the same size. Some cages are bigger, wider, and taller, and some cages are very narrow and small. Married women in any culture seek equal right, opportunity, love, respect, and honor from their husbands and the society. Many women who came from any type of social and relational abusive environment would do whatever it takes to free themselves from further hurt and harm. In some cases, the wives would take their children and leave their husbands for good. While some women made the decision to remain single for the rest of their lives, others may remarry with someone from a totally different culture. For example, my mother-in-law, became single at the age of thirty two with five young children. She promised herself and her children that in order for her and her children to be freed from any potential abusive relationship and hostile environment, she would remain single for the rest of her life—and she has kept her word ever since.

This resistance does not only happen to married women, but also to the younger generation of girls. During my regular contacts with Mien young adults for many years as a youth counselor at an annual Mien Christian Youth Camp in California and other visits with Mien youths in Thailand and Laos, I have learned that many young women who had personally experienced their mother's spousal abuse decided not to position themselves in that type of relationship. In order to free themselves from the traumatic family circle, some made the decision not to marry a Mien man from a particular clan, and others would choose to marry someone from a different race.

Polygamy and infidelity were common within the traditional cultural norm. Men with high power, status and wealth would usually take two or more wives and they would all live together under one roof. In many cases the wives had very little power to stop their husbands from committing adultery or polygamy. The husbands normally played the aggressive role while the wives and children were placed in passive roles. This cultural phenomenon applied to many couples and families; however, it did not take place across the board. Just as in any culture, there are those who live at extremes while the others live in peace and more balanced lives. An individual or family life experience in the past can become life-long lessons for the younger generation.

The traditional group of families living in the U.S. is making slow progress in the development of marriage and family relationships. They approach and resolve conflicts by bringing in family members from both sides. If a resolution cannot be reached within a 'closed door' family discussion setting, then the matter will be brought into the attention of the clan leader or community leader before the case goes to court for a final judgment. This traditional conflict management technique is not very popular or deemed appropriate by the modernized group, as discussed further in this chapter. This matter has become one of the dividing factors between the traditional and modernized groups. As we are already aware, changes take time. There is no quick fix for cultural issues and changes. However, it is necessary for people to make the appropriate adjustments that are beneficial to the growth and wellness of marriage and family. This research study revealed that the Mien traditional group of marriages and families are more reluctant to adopt new forms of marriage and family communication or parenting styles that are different from the traditional ways then the other groups.

The second group, the **marginal couples**, are those who stand between two worlds, the modern and old. In their marriages they strive to reach their life goals, like trying to cross a river with one foot on one raft and the other foot on another raft, known in Mien as "*Sung-zaux nzaeng sung-mbaih or yietc jieqv zaux caaiv yietc norm mbaih.*" One has to fight for balance, speed and control against the current and other pressures. The person rafting represents the marriage, and the two rafts represent the two different people forming their lives and souls together into "oneness." One spouse is from the traditional culture and the other is from the modernized culture. Married couples in this group have to work the hardest in their marriage and family relationship. In addition to understanding each individual's differences, of which there are many, the couple needs to overcome the cross-cultural communication and expectations between the new and the old cultures. The challenges for this group are many since they often play the roles of mediators between the older generation and the younger generation. They are the ones who can understand and relate well between the traditional and the modern groups. However, there are two major areas that they need to acknowledge and overcome in order to acquire the conflict management skills that are relevant to their present life circumstances and family situation.

First, there is the need to identify one's personal beliefs and values between the old and the new cultures. The stronger connection one has with either the new or the old family value system, the easier one can relate to that culture and the harder to transition into the other culture. One's perception and identification with the new culture plays an important role in determining the communication and conflict management styles that one would apply into his or her marriage and family relationship. For those who value and practice traditional conflict management style over the modern one or vice versa would most likely have communication issues with their spouses who hold different cultural views. Problem solving strategies are like mechanical tools. As specific tools are designed to perform certain tasks, a problem solving skill that works well in one cultural setting may not be applicable for all settings. A great or useful conflict management style is also like a good medication; when used appropriately it becomes a wonderful cure. However, when a great medication is used for the wrong illness, it can create more harm than good. When people from different cultures continue to practice their traditional styles of conflict resolution, they often find them to be counterproductive in the new society. This issue has become a great challenge for many Mien individuals and families in the U.S.

Second, there is the challenge in choosing which traditional cultural values to preserve and which to let go. Many individuals and couples in this group face the dilemma to either preserve the cultural values that please their parents and elders or to adopt the new ones that are suitable and helpful to them and their family. Conflict management skills for individuals and families in this group may include both the traditional and the modern styles. As discussed earlier, the traditional form of conflict management in a marriage involves both sides of the families. When the issue could not be settled with both sides of the family members, then the matter would be presented to a village headman or a community leader for resolution. Marital disputes of any kind usually kept low and quiet within the family to avoid the potential of shaming the individuals or immediate family members. Couples were taught to keep all their personal and marital differences underneath the blanket, which meant that the couple had to keep their problems secret and only discuss them when their children and other people could not hear them. If the opportunity was not available to discuss the issues during the day, they had to discuss them while they are in bed in order to prevent others from knowing them.

When a matter was brought before a village headman or community leader, it would no longer be a secret. Others would quickly learn about the matter, and the couple's reputation will soon be known to everyone. The more people knew about a couple's marital conflicts, the less respect the couple would receive from the village or community. People would perceive one or both spouses differently according to the rumors they heard. Any dispute resolution handled by a community leader or a mediator comes with a price. The person who loses the case only has to compensate the mediator for his time and knowledge to resolve the matter, but also to offer a meal to conclude the case. The meal usually involves a live chicken, rice, wine, and money to pay for the damage or offense done to the other party known as "washing away the shame" or "*nziaaux hmien*" in the Mien language. In most cases, the losing party is poorer or less educated than the winning party. Individuals with great wealth or high knowledge normally do not lose their cases. The cases were usually won by bribing the mediator, through logical reasoning, paying someone to be false witnesses, or threatening them with harm or retaliation. Individuals or families with great resources, wealth, spiritual knowledge or military power had less to fear in losing a case against those who lives in disadvantage social and economical conditions.

As a young child, I remember seeing people offering bribes to my father, who was not only a clan leader, but was also a head leader of many leaders, ("*da'saengx*" a Laotian word adopted by Mien people), to help them win their cases. An example—one early morning, I saw a man came to our front door and ask if my father was home. He was holding a live rooster and a bottle of homemade wine. My father invited him to come into the house, and immediately he knelt down on the ground and began to bow several times before my father before he made the request for help. After he finished telling my father the issue, he reached into his pocket and pulled some cash and presented it to my father along with the rooster and wine. My father did not want me to be involved, so gestured for me to go and play with the neighbor kids outside. Later, I insisted my mother tell me about the money and chicken. I did not care much about the wine, but I wanted to know if I would be able to eat some of the chicken and use the money to buy something for the family, since we were poor and did not have much food to eat.

Some people in the marginal group cease to practice or accept the traditional way of handling problems. They notice the weakness or injustice form of resolving conflicts and move away from it. Thus, their negative view on the traditional conflict management has led them to rely on the western judicial system to resolve issues within the family or community. As stated earlier, individuals and couples in this group encounter more cultural issues than the traditional or modern groups. Whichever circle they choose to be in, there have to prepare themselves to justification and criticism. Since they are the ones who stand between the traditional and modern circles, they are vulnerable to condemned by the traditional group to have neglected and abandoned their traditional cultural values or by the modernized group as being too traditional and old fashioned. In order to have a healthy marriage relationship, the couple has to learn, understand, adapt, and adjust themselves to the new expectations, complexities, differences, and values that they brought together. We can imagine the challenges and difficulties faced by the marginal group of couples in their marriages.

The third group is compromised of the **modernized couples**. These families usually are unfamiliar with the traditional forms of conflict resolution, or if they are familiar, are not be in favor of it. Thus, they adopt the western social or judicial forms of conflict management styles to resolve their conflicts. There are advantages and disadvantages to the traditional and western judicial systems. Applying the traditional problem solving approach through the gathering of family members and community leaders to listen to the problems and provide support to the individuals has its own uniqueness and strengths.

The traditional style of conflict or marriage resolution draws the couples closer to their relatives as they share their problems and receive ideas, encouragement, and suggestions. As in traditional cultural settings, parents are held accountable for their children's actions. The parents and family members would sacrifice their resources for the sake of their children or siblings. Happiness and well-being is strongly emphasized in the Mien cultural norm. Family will not be divided when problems occur; instead, they are drawn closer to each other through tough and challenging times.

There are several disadvantages to the traditional way of problem solving. An individual can easily win the case by bribing the mediator or inviting family members who can argue aggressively with power, reasoning skills or using a scapegoat technique. The mediator or community leader has the final judgment. The parties in conflict usually have to accept the resolutions made by the community mediator whether or not justice is served. The losing party would be forced to pay a restitution to compensate the mediator's, the victim, and individuals who were present at the meeting, to compensate for their time and effort in resolving the conflict. A dinner is expected to take place immediately following the meeting. This includes one or two live chickens (depending on the size of the group and the size of the chicken), some wine, rice, vegetables, and money of cash or silver coins. In most cases the individuals would end up having to borrow lives stock and money from a nearby relative or neighbor to pay for the restitutions. If paper money or silver coins were not available, the individual would have to negotiate for other agreeable options to pay the finds. In some cases, certain kinds of domestic animals would be accepted for the restitution. There were rare cases where a certain amount of crops could be substituted for the penalty.

The majority of westernized couples do not follow the traditional procedures in resolving their conflicts. They often rely on individually acquired problem solving skills or rely on the judicial system here to solve their marital issues. Most of the participants in this study are classified into the second group, the marginal. They still utilize family and community resources prior to seeking help from the judicial system. Parents, family members, pastors and community leaders or mediators are often involved with family matters in the community. Mien people in the U.S. still reside together as a community and maintain their daily social lives with strong clan and family connections.

The families in the U.S. who isolate themselves from the family, church and community resources have the highest marital confrontation and divorce rates. The more disconnected the couples are from their immediate family and community, the less resources and support programs available to strengthen their marriages and family conflicts. The study reveals that more and more Mien couples in the U.S. are seeking and adopting the freedom of independence and experiencing a higher volume of marital and family conflicts.

The modernized group has limited or no knowledge about the traditional problem solving methodology. They may have heard from their parents, grandparents or elders about how family or marital issues were resolved in Laos or Thailand, but they normally have no in-depth understanding about the procedures, complexities, advantages and disadvantages. As discussed earlier, the Mien traditional communication style is circular and indirect, which can easily cause multiple levels of communication barriers for couples and family members in the U.S, particularly for those who are from different generations. Due to the unfamiliarity with the conflict management techniques of their parents, grandparents or elders, it is almost impossible for those who are in the younger generation to follow the procedure or pattern in bringing harmony into a marriage or family. Therefore, since the modernized individuals and couples are more familiar with the communication styles and ways in dealing with differences in the U.S. over what was practiced in the past, they automatically apply the skills they know or have learned in their present culture.

The differences in handling conflicts can serve as one of the dividing factors among the people from different generations. The barrier between the modernized and the traditional groups is getting wider as both groups cannot find a common ground. The individuals and families in the traditional group see the modernized group as being "too Americanized" or being "too non-Mien." Whenever there is conflict or issues that exist between a family member or the married couple, it important for the modernized group to seek the advice and counsel from the parents, grandparents or elders. Doing so creates stronger connection and respect within the family circle. When the younger generation refuses to follow the traditional practices or fail to accept the advices given from the parents and elders, it creates a deeper bridge of trust, respect and communication among the two groups.

One central aspect to pay close attention to between these three groups is the religion or spiritual beliefs of the individuals and family members. Many couples and families not only have inherited linear or direct ways to share their thoughts, opinions, desires and needs with their spouses and family members, but they also have avoided practicing cultural norms that contradict the Bible. These individuals and couples perceive that the biblical values outweigh beliefs that doctrines that are created by humankind. They tend to be more opened in seeking support services and outside resources.

5. Love and Respect

The final component that contributes to the success or failure of a marriage is **love and respect**: everyone needs these and is entitled to them. People naturally want to be loved and respected by those they care about and those around them. Both attributes play an integral component in the development of a relationship. In a marriage relationship, one cannot exist and continue to function well without the other. Without love and respect a relationship would not succeed. They balance each other in a relationship as much as the body needs both left and right legs to stand, walk or run, and as well as needing the left and right arms to function properly as a unit of the body. Love and respect serve as the core elements in sustaining a relationship when other necessary married ingredients become diluted or fail. Love and respect cannot simply be excluded from a relationship. The deeper the growth within a family, the healthier the relationship becomes. The couple is able to understand and accept differences that arise in their marriage. They can enjoy their marriage and family life together in a well-nurtured environment.

Love and respect do not naturally exist in any relationship. There is no 'love pool' for anyone to simply fall into whenever he or she needs it. Many people have bought into the concept of "falling-in-love" and expect their partner to provide them with the love they want. Love and respect are the reciprocal constituents in any marriage relationship. A couple must mutually and cooperatively create, cultivate and nurture the love and respect needed to sustain and enhance their marriage. Love and respect need to be given and received in appropriate settings both socially and culturally. There are different kinds of love in our society. Instead of attempting to describe different patterns of love as presented by numerous researchers, I will briefly discuss six different kinds of loves, but only three are essential in a marriage relationship and family.

There are a number of different Greek words for love, as the Greek language distinguishes how the word is used. Ancient Greek has three distinct words for love: *eros, philia*, and *agape*. However, as with other languages, it has been historically difficult to separate the meanings of these words. Nonetheless, the senses in which these words were generally used are given below.

1. **Thelema** (θέλημα *thélēma*) originates from the Greek language (in modern Greek "*thelima*") means "will" and "intention." The Thelema form of love is automatically required from one person to another. Love is the law under one's strong will and desire. Thelema love is an esoteric and magical path to make one to understand one's life meaning and purpose. Intentional or self-willing love is full of unexplainable energy to do or accomplish something based on the one's life goal and mission. Thelema is about realizing your True Will, being all that you can be, and in doing so, helping to make the world a better place.

Within the world of Thelema, every man and every woman becomes a star in the universe. Each individual is unique and has his or her own path in a spacious universe. Therefore, each person can move freely within their existence without colliding into each other. Each person has his or her own path to travel, and all existing beings need to respect the right and privacy of others. Most Thelemites believe that everyone possesses a True Will which motivates their daily existence and directs their operations. This type of love also prohibits one from interfering with the will of any other person. Everyone within the Thelema world of love receives absolute freedom to follow his or her True Will and it needs to be honored and cherished by others. Since every True Will is different from person to person, no one can determine the True Will for another person. Each person must arrive at the discovery for himself and herself. Thus, true love can only exist when a person is united with his or her True Self in love.

As we can see clearly that Thelema love is a magical love, and it cannot and will not function in any marriage relationship as long as we are living in this imperfect and crooked world. This world does not have a clear path for any human being to roam without being crossed by others. A person may become a star but there is no separate world for each star—we all share the same common world. As human beings are weak, fragile, self-centered, incompetence outside the will of God, and are not freed from making mistakes or wrong doings that can bring injury to oneself or others, it is impossible for this type of love to exist, grow and flourish in any relationship that is formed by two different human beings.

2. ***Pragmatic*** love or ***pragma*** is the 2nd style of love. This kind of love is driven by the head, not the heart. Pragmatic lovers are practical. Pragmatic lovers think rationally and realistically about their expectations in a partner. Pragmatic lovers want to find value in their partners, and ultimately want to work with their partner to reach a common goal. This form of love comes with terms and conditions. A love relationship is built based on rational, practical criteria, certain conditions or standards. Some of the criteria include sharing common interests, the same culture or religion, having similar or related educational backgrounds, possessing certain

skills or talents that form the attraction in such ways that lead to mutual satisfaction. This style of love can be easily presented as a businesslike kind of love.

Within the pragmatic love style, individuals are searching for mates who possess compatible patterns that match their interests and expectations. There may be a list of criteria that an individual uses to determine his or her ideal mate. This checklist may include attributes such as appearance, height, weight, size, color of skin, educational background or financial stability of their ideal lover. It is a very critical form of love. Pragmatic love may not be a healthy form of love in most relationships. The common interests discovered by two people may or may not be the ultimate source of strength needed to maintain a long-term relationship. If the foundation of love is weak, the relationship will break or fall apart when other unrelated or uncommon attributes exist as the couple continues to live together. Common interests are crucial in a marriage; however, they should not be the only criteria. Couples should go beyond the pragmatic love level, which is the surface, and go deeper into other important areas that form the core of a love relationship.

3. The third type of love is friendship or brotherly love, known as ***phileo*** (φιλία *philía*). It includes loyalty to friends, family, and community. This kind of love requires virtue, equality and familiarity. In ancient texts, *philia* denoted a general type of love, used for love between family, between friends, a desire or enjoyment of an activity, as well as between lovers.

Friendship love has to do with equality of the mind and equal sharing of material goods. It involves with the familiarity of each other's strengths, weaknesses and needs. Spouses need to love and trust each other as close friends do if not better. In order for a casual friendship to grow and become a loyal friendship, it requires the individuals to spend time together to be build trust, respect and interdependence. Within a friendship type of love, a couple needs to spend quality time and energy to establish trust, love, and respect to strengthen the relationship. As close friends normally are free to have open discussions with each other on any topics and on any issues, couples also should have heart-to-heart talks on any matters that exist in their personal or marriage life. Therefore, friendship love is necessary in a marriage relationship. Philadelphia, one of the states in the U.S., has the meaning of brotherly love state. '*Phila*' means love and '*delphia*' means brotherly.

In some cultures, brotherly love plays a very crucial role in people's daily lives. Within the Mien and Hmong cultures, people from the same clan, truly value their kinship love for each other to a point where they may endanger their lives for the sake of their brothers or sisters. For some people, brotherly love plays a higher role and comes with a higher price than any other form of loves. Therefore, friendship love is also necessary within a marriage relationship. When couples can truly value and care for the well being of each other, they will have stronger love and firm bonding in their relationship.

4. Familial love or **storge** (στοργή *storgē*) means "affection" in modern Greek; it is a natural affection of between parents and children. It is mostly known for the mother's instinctual love for her baby. Storge love has to do with special bonding, caring and nurturing. There is genuine giving and receiving love between two people, as the mother freely and joyfully gives to her child and the child instinctively receives from his or her mother without any hesitation. Storge love is a very deep and warm inside feeling that happens naturally without any outside influences. Only the individuals in the circle can truly experience this form of love. People on the outside circle maybe able to observe but cannot fully sense the warmth and secured feelings experienced by these individuals.

Storge love takes place between family members. This is a certain sense of family affection that can only be developed, growth, and nurtured within the family. The core value beneath the storge love is the notion of "Blood is thicker than water." Storge love is a deep and abiding affection. It is an unconditional and conditional form of love. It is unconditional in the way that you love your child, parent or family, so you try not to find any faults in them or overlook of their weaknesses and mistakes. Because the love level between family members is so instinctually rich and great, individuals who hold the same family values can easily understand, accept, respect and forgive each other when a mistake happens. Storge love can come with conditions for many individuals in a family. As people's preferences, needs, desires, and expectations change throughout their course of life, disappointments, hurts, and pains may develop within the family. Thus, storge love can begin to lose its richness. Unresolved problems or issues within family members can dilute the rich meaning of the deep and abiding love.

An example of how family problems can destroy this form of familial love is divorce. When a child or children are caught in the midst of their parent's divorce or marital issues, it can create many different forms of personal and psychological problems to the children. Children may begin to hold grudges or resentments against one or both of their parents.

Storge love is viewed by as being kind, caring and supportive. As parents would naturally love, provide, protect and care for their children at all costs, spouses need to apply the same form of protective love for each others. As couples plan and strive to live and enjoy their lives together as long as they both shall live, they should apply storge love in their marriage appropriately. The four key action words in this form of love is **instinctive love**, **care**, **protect** and **provide**. Couples should give love and receive love as mother and child, without any hesitation or regret.

5. *Eros* (Ἔρως *érōs*) is passionate love, with sensual desire and longing. It is the love of beauty. The Modern Greek word "*erotas*" means "romantic or erotic love." This romantic type of love focuses on the beauty of a person. It could be facial beauty or body shape, size or height. The physical attraction of a mate or partner catches the eyes and grabs the heart of the other person. Romantic or erotic lovers delight in what they can capture with their naked eyes. Erotic lovers choose their mates by intuition or "chemistry." They are more likely to say they fell in love at first sight than those of other love styles.

Romantic love has its own values and weakness. A couple forming their marriage relationship based on romantic love alone will not go very far. Love has its boundaries, value and temperament according to the environment and other factors that the couples have created throughout the course of their marriage. Circumstances and life situations often present a different level of romantic love within a relationship. Romantic love alone cannot sustain or keep any married relationship from becoming cold or falling apart. When a romantic love fails to reach the expected degree, the couple's love relationship will become weak. Generally speaking romantic love usually begins with great intensity and gradually decreases as couples get older or become occupied by children and other life goals and responsibilities. As couples are living together, differences and issues are unavoidable aspects of life. Sooner or later, if relationship and personality differences are not minimized, they can gradually take over and eliminate the desires and expectation of romantic love. Often time marital conflicts can lessen the couple's love chemistry. The couple can maintain its richness or lose the original taste depending on the couples' willingness to learn and work through their differences cooperatively.

Romantic love is necessary in a marriage relationship when it is interpreted and applied correctly. Any marriage couple should have some level of desire and attraction to each other's body, especially for newlywed. As physical attraction is one of the love chemistries that draw a man and a woman into a love relationship, it is important for couples to learn how to accept, appreciate and value it as designed by the Creator. Romantic love should have its' boundary and limitation. It should not be shared with anyone or applied in anywhere outside of a marriage relationship. Any true love within a relationship should take root in a person's heart, mind, soul and spirit, not just in the physical form. Romantic love can be meaningful and lively in a marriage relationship when both spouses can truly understand, value, and nurture it beyond the physical level.

6. The final form of love is known as ***altruistic*** love or *agapē* (ἀγάπη *agápē*) in Greek. We can call it *amazing love*. This style of love has its uniqueness and strength in a love relationship. It is not common for people in general to accept and practice agape love. Out of all the variety forms of love, agape is the most difficult and challenging style of love. Other kinds of love come with different conditions and expectations, but agape love is known as "unconditional, divine or

self-giving love." Agape love is universal, eternal and undeserving love that comes from the heavenly above for the earthly living beings. It is an unselfish, caring and compassionate form of love that bursts out from God's own heart for all sinners in this world. It's a freely given type of love as God who loved the world and was willing to give His one and only Son, Jesus Christ, to die on the cross for the remission of man's sins and to establish a love relationship between God and man.

Agape love comes from the deepest part of a person's heart, mind, soul and spirit in revealing sincere thoughts, feelings and actions to others without expecting anything in return. It is a genuine desire given by God to love someone without expecting anything in return. Such love is patient, kind, does not envy, it does not boast, it is not proud, it is not rude, it is not self-seeking, it is not easily angered, it keeps no record of wrongs, it does not delight in evil but rejoices with the truth, it always protects, always trusts, always hopes, always perseveres, and never fails, as stated in the book of I Corinthians 13: 4-8, NIV (New International Version). According to this definition, agape love covers all areas of life. Couples who can understand, accept and apply this form of love in their relationship will see amazing results. It is believed that only those who have received agape love can apply the meaning in their lives. Individuals who have not experienced agape love will not be able to apply it in their lives or in their relationship.

The survey reveals that those who hold a strong belief in the Bible are able to create deeper love levels within their marriage and love relationship. Couples and families who attend church regularly and know the Bible well have better coping mechanisms toward the challenges that come across their lives. These people use less negative terms or phrases in their communication. Several participants indicated that they have learned from the different preaching and teachings in the church and through other seminars taught at couple's retreats, and they have learned to avoid using certain degrading terminologies or negative expressions in their homes. One couple stated that they prohibited anyone in the family to use the words hate, divorce, separation, cursing or swearing terms. Their children are never allowed to use God's or Jesus' name in vain. They are raised by moral and spiritual principles from the Bible to love, forgive, care and respect others just as Christ has done to sinners. This form of biblical teaching never existed in the traditional Mien circles. Now many are learning and adopting different sets of values and principles while they are making major transitions into their new cultures.

The forty-two couples who reported that they have healthy marriages revealed a combination of several forms of love as discussed above in their relationships. Through home visits, questionnaires, and other social contacts with many of these families, I have come to know many of them and their family members and have seen them hold strong to a certain levels of bonding in love and respect toward each other and the community. Despite the differences, challenges or conflicts that occur in their marriage, the deep-rooted love and respect the couple created bind them together. The stronger the love and respect that exists in the family, the more the family is able to withstand falling apart when circumstances confront them. Many of the participants in this study had overcome countless hurdles prior to coming to the U.S. Their past life experiences have brought both negative and positive impacts to their present lives. It becomes clear that love and respect prolong the family. A genuine love and respect binds the couples and family members together.

Within these family members there are different levels of social, economical, physiological, and intellectual backgrounds. Of all the participants interviewed for this research, those who have demonstrated their love, respect and acceptance of their partner's and family members' differences manifest a healthy marriage relationship. In some families, the husband, who is the head of the family and the main income provider, receives less income than his wife or children. In other situations the husband is unemployed or less educated than his wife or children. Thus, he may be perceived differently than his family members and the community. Some of the men in this study expressed their regret and unhappiness for not being able to obtain the educational and occupational skills needed to be the role models for their families and to function well in this modern society. Tears were shed both inwardly and outwardly when these men unveiled their feelings in being unable to provide for their families. Some of them had to depend on their spouses or children for language, culture and economical support. Although these men receive some levels of respect from their family members, they still feel insufficient and struggle with low self-esteem and self-image. Some do not receive the full respect from their family members and the community when they are incapable to fulfill their roles successfully.

There are several areas that make a Mien person feel like he or she is gaining or losing respect in the home and in the community. Some of these variables include a person's age, gender, marital status, the wellness of the family (especially the children), how much he or she is being loved and supported by the parents and family members, his or her socio-economic level, the educational background, and the leadership in the home and community. As the majority of the families being surveyed do not meet all these criteria, many individuals, (especially the husbands) are unsatisfied with the respect they receive from their spouses and children. Mien children born and raised in the U.S. have different concepts of respect for their parents and elders. In most cases the level of respect parents receive from their children has saddened their hearts and raised a major concern for the future generations.

Unlike in Laos or Thailand where parents and grandparents mainly supported and encouraged males to pursue higher education, females in the U.S. are being exposed to educational development as much as the males. The educational system in America provides equal opportunities to everyone regardless of their cultural, socio-economical, religious, gender, or educational backgrounds. Despite the availability and opportunity to high academic achievement, there are still a few families who try to convince their daughters or granddaughters to get married before they become "too old" to get married. Therefore, there are some women as young as fifteen, sixteen, and seventeen years old who are involved in serious relationships. Some of these high school students are engaged to be married to someone of their age or older. Some young adults are encouraged to get married as soon as they reach the legal age, while some already become parents before graduating from high school.

Young adults who are being pressured or encouraged by their parents to get married at a young age or before they have accomplished their educational goals often perceive their parents as being ignorant, illogical, misleading, and disrespectful. Fifty-eight percent of the respondents reported that they do not receive enough respect from their spouses who have a higher education than they do. They reported that their more educated spouses often disrespect them in their decision making, communication, resolving conflicts, financial management, and other family matters. Cultural norms, expectations, personal belief systems or behaviors acquired through life shape and motivate a person to act in certain patterns toward one-self and others. It becomes a clear-cut line that people in general want to be loved and respected for who they are despite their limitations, weaknesses, strengths, cultural and linguistic backgrounds, socio-economic status, gender, age or appearance. Love and respect are two of the most crucial elements in shaping the growth of a marriage and family.

Despite the different factors impacting the marriages and families of Mien people in the U.S., this study yields five important components that should be worth the attention of Mien married couples, parents, researchers, counselors, elders, community leaders, pastors/laymen, interested individuals, service providers, and researchers. The five variables that can enhance or hinder Mien's marriage and family relationships are summarized in a diagram on the following page. These factors are their educational achievement, religious belief, intercommunication, conflict management, and love and respect. It is highly suggested that further study in the realm of marriage and family development of Mien people in the U.S. is needed. As society changes and different level of life pressures are developing, Mien marriage and families will continue to be impacted by all angles of societal influence. It is only through the in-depth knowledge of the needs that exist within the individuals and family lives can family or service providers successfully provide the solutions to the brokenness of marriage and family. The five factors impacting Mien marriages and families are summarized below.

Figure 3: The Five Factors Impacting Mien Marriages and Families

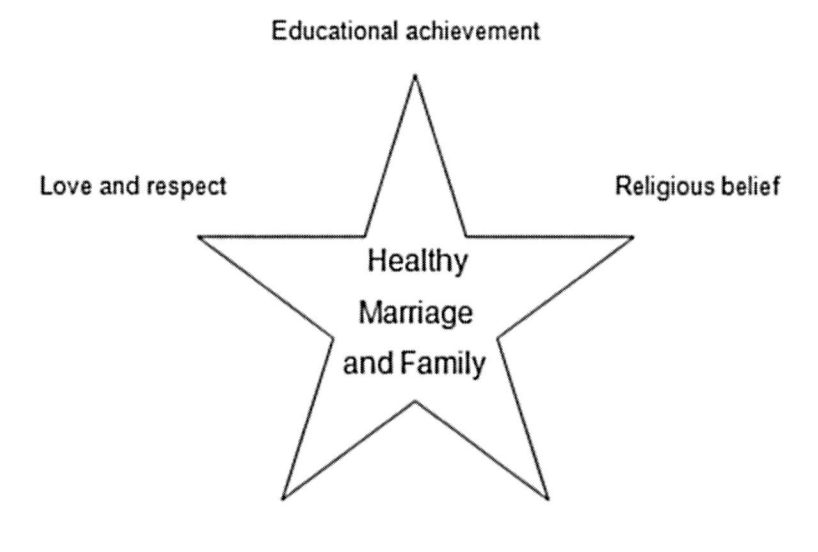

Educational achievement

Love and respect

Religious belief

Healthy Marriage and Family

Conflict management   Intercultural communication

Chapter 7

Intercultural Communication

Characteristics of Intercultural Communication

One of the greatest sources of stress and challenges in any relationship is the lack of communication. Communication takes place in many different forms: verbal, non-verbal, written, listening and technological. According to Ludden, an average person communicates through reading messages 13.3 percent of the time. Communicating through written messages, including letters, notes, memos, occurs on an average of 8.4 percent. The average person communicates through speech about 23 percent of the time. People in general listen more than they speak or write. The average person listens to communication about 53 percent of the time, through things such as television, radio, tapes, and live talk.

Often people experience difficulty in saying what they want to communicate in such a way that the other people can clearly understand them, making assumptions the message they are trying to communicate is understandable and acceptable, only to find out later that it was completely misunderstood. What can we do to be better communicators? How do we develop the skills necessary to say what we want to say in such a way that we are heard and then assured that we have been understood? These are some common questions that Mien couples and families are trying to discover for better techniques to communicate with their loved ones and those around them.

Inverse Communication Styles

The Mien have an upside down communication style which causes great confusion when spouses are trying to adapt to the western style of communicating. An inverse or upside down communication style is normally used in a negative connotation or as sarcasm. The communicated message always has an opposite meaning. This type of communication is usually take place between parents and children and spouses. It is inappropriate to use for parents, elders, quests, strangers or people in authority. Depending on the tone of voice and the context used, the message conveys the opposite meaning than what is intended.

For example, instead of saying, "Please, don't do that!" (*Maiv dungx zoux oc*), a Mien person would say "*Zoux longx deix oc*: meaning "Do a good job or do it well" or "G*unv zoux longx deix oc,*" meaning, "Be sure to do a good job." The word *zoux* means to do, *longx* means good, *deix oc* emphasizes expression. When something tastes something very delicious, people say, "*Kuv maiv kuv aah*", meaning "delicious not delicious." *Kuv* means delicious and *maiv* means not, and *aah* is an emphasizing expression.

Instead of saying something is good, they say, "*Longx maiv longx*", meaning "Good not good." *Longx* means good, *maiv* means not.

When someone wants to say, "Please don't go too long," a person would say, "*Gunv mingh lauh deix oc,*" meaning "You go ahead, go for a long time."

Therefore, information alone is not communication. Information is only potential communication. In order for communication to occur, we need to use information in the correct context. In general, people's egocentric attitudes create communication barriers within their marriage, families, in the workplace or other community settings. Mien men usually have higher egocentric behaviors than women. The Mien's patriarchal and male egocentrism can jeopardize their marriage and family in the U.S. Many wives and children who have become accustomed to western culture and communication styles are not compliant with the traditional male and adult dominant configured communication style. Fuglesang indicated that, "An egocentric, the inability to see reality from the viewpoint of others becomes the greatest communication breakdown. Massive egocentrism is, in fact, a pitiable state of mind because the beholder is, as it were, imprisoned by his own perceptions."

Communication goes through different processing stages. First, the speaker presents the information or message. Second, the receiver hears and receives the message. Third, the message is analyzed or taken apart for examination in the receiver's mind with the available interpretative tool he or she has at the time. Fourth, the message is synthesized or put back together. Finally, a response is given based on the final conclusion reached. How or how soon a person responds to the message is based upon the individual's understanding and interpretation of the message. An outward reaction comes from the inward interpretation of the information. The communication pattern is shown in the following diagram. Communication usually takes place in this five-step process:

1. Message sends
2. Message receives
3. Message analyzes
4. Message synthesizes
5. Message responses

Figure 4: Communication Pattern

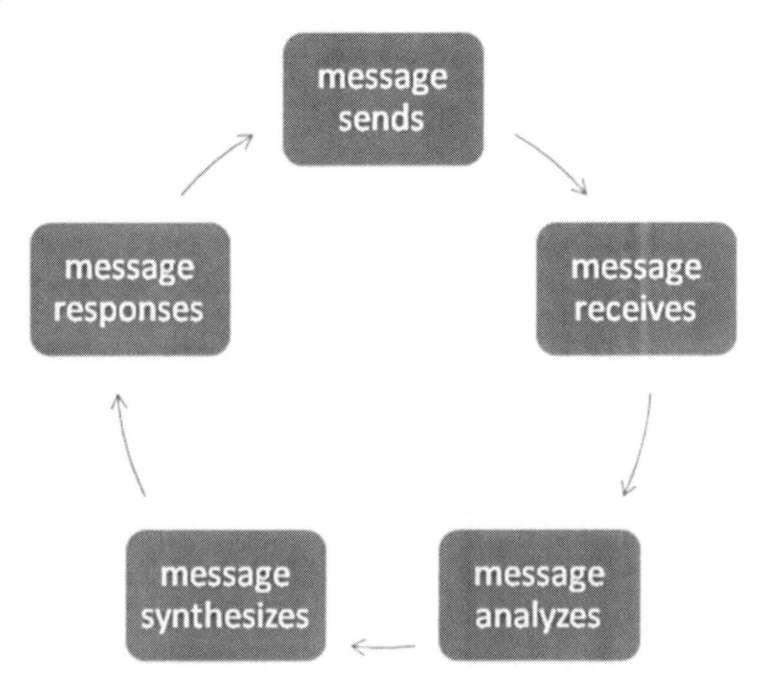

If the message is clearly conveyed, received, processed or analyzed, synthesized or formulated, then an accurate response will take place. If not, a communication barrier or problem will occur if the information has been lost or misinterpreted. The responses can be verbal or nonverbal. If information is not clearly presented, it does not contain any information and subsequent action or responses will miss the mark. Information is communicated from one terminal to another terminal. During the process of sending the information from one person to the other, the information is filtered and can lose the original authenticity. Information being received requires active attention in order to have accurate interpretation. A message sent and received should not occur in isolation from the content and context. Information can only contain its original richness if it is used in the right context. It should not be isolated from the events or objects themselves. Fuglesang best summarizes the importance of communicative language in the following:

"Language is a written or oral social habit formation facilitating our handling of reality with great economy. We recognize reality, or shall we say our raw experience, into consistent and reality communicable universe of ideas through the medium of a linguistic pattern. Without language, social formations are unthinkable."

Intercultural communication involves the sharing of concepts. Communication is a sharing of thoughts (Ludden and Marsha). Communication between spouses and family members occurs when people can clearly understand and agree on the topic, idea or issue being presented. To do so we need to understand how Mien people use language in the concepts of time, space, matter, and viewpoints in relation to the universe. Marriage means two opposite genders coming together as husband and wife in joining bodies, minds, souls and spirits. They are to love, support, encourage, understand, enjoy and strengthen each other in both happy and challenging times. The two people need to be responsible for themselves and their family. They need to create love, happiness, respect, trust and a lifelong healthy relationship. Marital conflicts can easily arise from misunderstanding in the daily marital and family communication out of personal and family needs, desires, goals and conflict management. Men and women are two separate beings. Physiologically, socially, mentally and emotionally speaking, they are created differently.

Communication Difficulty

At its core, communication requires a sender, a message and a receiver. It sounds like a simple process; however, many factors prevent communication from taking place. Some of the communication barriers are:

- Failure to understand the message
- Different perceptions concerning the meaning of the message
- Distractions
- Preoccupation
- Disinterest
- Competing messages
- Cultural differences between the sender and receiver
- Confused messages
- Making assumptions
- Confusing verbal and non-verbal languages
- Threats and ultimatums
- Actions that betray words

Communication is an interaction between two or more individuals and should be viewed in terms of specific instances of human action and reaction that are embedded in concrete life situations. There are three key components within the realm of intercultural communication—knowledge, motivation and skill. Knowledge is the necessary information that the two people interacting with each other need to have in order to effectively and properly carry on a conversation. Motivation is the positive affect toward the culture of the individual. This includes the empathy of the person's personal and cultural values. The third component is skills. This includes any necessary behavior required to act appropriately and effectively during a conversation.

Two other important terms should be clarified here as well. These are **intra-cultural communication** and **intercultural communication**. Intra-cultural communication refers to communication that takes place between couples or individuals sharing the same cultural background. When a conversation happens between two Mien people, it is considered intra-cultural communication. During intra-cultural communication, two people interacting implicitly share the same ground rules of communication and interaction, given the fact that there is little or no cultural gap. The second term is 'inter-cultural communication' in which the people come from different cultures, or from the same culture but have contradicting communication styles. Within any culture, when the generational gap widens, such as is the case with the Mien, communication barriers can easily occur without full awareness. Therefore, 'inter-cultural communication' is used interchangeably for individuals and married couples from different generations within the same cultural group, and those who are from different cultures. In inter-cultural communication, couples or individuals may be applying different forms of communication rules and expectations. Unless these communication rules are understood, respected or accepted it can create a huge gap for the two people when having conversations. Intergenerational gaps have broadened and widened, and for Mien people in the U.S. communication breakdowns begin to emerge in every home. Therefore, in order for us to keep things in the proper perspective, it is necessary to keep in mind how the term "inter-cultural communication" is used in this book.

One of the unique aspects of inter-cultural interactions is uncertainty and ambiguity concerning the ground rules by which the interaction will occur, and the meaning of signals. Because of the pervasive influence of culture on all aspects of the communication process, it is often difficult for couples or individuals from two different cultures or worldviews to operate similar signals interchangeably without any complexities. For example, in the foreword of the *Handbook of International and Intercultural Communication*, it is said, "Inter-cultural communication generally involves face-to-face communication between people from different national cultures." (Gudykunst and Mody) Richard E. Porter and Larry A. Samovar state that: "[the] inter-cultural communication process occurs whenever a message producer is a member of one culture and a message receiver is a member of another" (Porter and Samovar). Ting-Toomey describes inter-cultural communication as a process of "simultaneous encoding (*i.e.*, the sender choosing the right words or nonverbal gestures to express his or her intentions) and decoding (*i.e.*, the receiver translating the words or non-verbal cues into comprehensible meanings) of the exchanged messages." Porter and Samovar define the notion of communication as "a dynamic transactional behavior affecting process in which sources and receivers intentionally code their behavior to produce messages that they transmit through a channel in order to elicit particular attitudes or behaviors." According to this definition, they lay out eight specific ingredients of communication: source, encoding, message, channel, receiver, decoding, receiver response, and feedback.

Communication seems to take place in the following pattern. First, a person wishes to shares his or her feelings (happiness, sad, excitement or disappoint) with another human being conducts an internal activity called "encoding." Encoding is a communication process where verbal and nonverbal behaviors are selected and arranged according to the rules of grammar and syntax applicable to the verbal or non-verbal language being used to create a message.

It is important to point out that human communication is not a mechanistic way of thought processing, according to which communication is conducted on the basis of a determinate set of codes. Humans are not robots and communication can be shifted, changed, distorted or skewed by different environmental factors. When people can clearly understood the message being given with such a set of language or communication codes, one can conveniently comprehend the message of the other. Couples from different cultures or worldviews usually inherit uncertainty in both the verbal and nonverbal behaviors. Inter-cultural communicators generally engage with each other in a verbal language that is often not a native language for at least one, and sometimes both spouses, thus creating uncertainty in the meaning of the words they are communicating. Cultural differences in the use of all nonverbal channels can produce confusion in the messages for couples and family members.

A second characteristic of inter-cultural communication is the inevitability of conflict and misunderstandings. During inter-cultural communications, there are high chances that conflicts may arise when one spouse or both spouses misinterpret certain behaviors that do not conform to his or her expectations. When this occurs, one spouse often interprets those behaviors as transgressions against his or her value system. The repetition of this kind of unintended conflict can produce negative emotions, which are upsetting to an individual's self-concepts. These issues are inevitable in inter-cultural episodes with both spouses from different cultural systems because misunderstanding leads to uncertainty, and uncertainty contributes to communication barriers. Couples become impatient with each other or intolerant of the ambiguity, leading to further anger, frustration, or resentment. We know that even after uncertainty is reduced, conflict is inevitable because of the differences in the meaning of verbal and nonverbal behaviors across cultures, generations, and the associated emotions and values inherent in the cultural system.

Emotions play a very important role in our daily lives, especially in a marriage. Emotion shapes and molds people's lives and experiences. They give meaning and relevance to an individual and person's well being. Positive emotions include happiness, joy, satisfaction, pleasure, and interest. Some of the negative emotions are sadness, anger, disgust, fear, frustration, shame, hatred and guilt. Although these emotions are unattractive, they reveal something important about oneself and the relationship with other people, events, or situations. Within a married family relationship, how well couples deal with their negative emotions and resolve conflicts is a major determinant of success or failure of communication. One of the key to a healthy marriage relationship is the ability to resolve conflicts. Conflict resolution skills are one of the important ingredients to a happy marriage.

One may ask about the crucial role emotion plays in confliction resolution. When negative emotion is aroused during a conflict, it is easy for couples to be overcome by those feelings because they take over one's thinking and feeling. Even couples who are usually adept at thinking critically about things and who can act in positively moral and altruistic ways may not be able to think or act in such a manner when overcome by negative emotions. It is these critical moments in the communication episode—when negative emotions are aroused because of inevitable cultural or generational differences. Couples who can regulate their negative feelings are usually able to engage in a productive conversation. Once emotions are held in check and not immediately acted upon while being angry, disappointed or frustrated, couples can better engage in some aspects of critical thinking that can lead to a more satisfying outcome.

Cultural and generational barriers with overtones and implications are much more difficult to overcome than linguistic barriers, although it is always difficult to distinguish a sharp line between linguistic and cultural elements such as the Mien language and belief system. In most cases they are inseparable. There is an inevitable connection between the language structure of a culture and mode in which the families think, communicate, and act. Language is the most ordinary and distinctively human way in which people communicate their concepts and state their judgments. It is the culture of a person that motivates or permits the couples or individuals to think, behave and act within the given environment.

The Role of Culture in the Communication Process

"Absolute communication is impossible not only between languages but also within a language" (Park). To gain a broad understanding of intercultural communication between any two cultures, we need to examine the different linguistic and cultural components. These components include, but are not limited to, language structures, rhythm patterns, grammatical and lexical differences, idiomatic and metaphorical expressions, emotive meanings, and intercultural incongruence. However, it is not the sole purpose of this study to discuss all these variables. This study mainly discusses some of the communication differences that promote or hinder couples and families from understanding each other and building a strong marriage relationship.

Successful intercultural communication can never be accomplished without understanding the socio-cultural context of the target language. Even if we have a thorough grasp of their socio-cultural backgrounds, there still must be some degree of distortion and loss in the processes of transferring. It has been confirmed by Park that inter-cultural communication where distinctions depend much more on perceptual differences than on conceptual classifications, lead to greater divergences between languages and communication styles.

Mien people are characterized by their distinct language and clothing that uniquely denote who they are in society. Linguistic differences in expressing thoughts, wants, desires, happiness, hurts, pains and frustrations play a very crucial role in a marriage relationship. Culture and perception not only affect language lexicons, but also its function or pragmatics. Mien parents and spouses usually substitute a general noun "people" in the place of first person pronoun "I" when expressing one's unhappiness or frustration during a conversation with their children or spouses. Instead of saying directly that "I do not like what you do," or "whatever you are doing is not pleasing me," they would speak indirectly by using a vague noun in the place of a first person pronoun. For example, "*Mienh m'daaih maiv hiuv duqv mun lorqc*" in which sarcastically translates as "People don't have feelings." However, the actual implication of this phrase means "People have feelings, and what you do hurts me." Another example is, "*Yie maiv hiuv duqv mienh nyei hnyouv ndongc naaic nyei doqc*." In English it means that "I do not understand why people's hearts are so evil." This statement is directed toward the person whom the speaker is talking to. In most cases, it refers to the spouse or a child of the speaker. When a first person personal pronoun is being substituted by a third person pronoun or vice versa, it creates another confusing level of communication within any setting.

Mien language allows for pronouns to be dropped from sentences tended to be less individualistic and causes a huge form of communication barrier for spouses who are not accustomed to this kind of cultural norm. Culture, self-concepts, and individual values affect communication styles not only true for Mien culture but also for other Southeast Asian cultures as well.

Although Asian groups are substantively differed among themselves and should not be identified as one group, they, however, share social and cultural values that serve to determine goals, guide behavior, and maintain harmony within society. A major emphasis is most Asian cultures, particularly East and Southeast Asians, is the avoidance of all conflict—at the individual level, the family level, the community level, and the society level. By developing and abiding by strict rules of conduct, they unconsciously create a great deal of ambiguity and increase the likelihood of communication barriers among themselves. An important area to pay attention to is the source of the norms that may not be the same in every culture (*i.e.*, historical experience, religion, oral tradition), but the outcomes are similar. Some of the most common qualities include filial piety, direction of parent-child communications, self-control and restrain in emotional express, well-defined social roles and expectations, and shame as a behavior influence.

Each of these norms has been explored and discussed in international, cross-cultural, and American literature over the years. Acculturation to U.S. society has modified the extent to which each plays a role in the lives of Asian American families. Individuals are expected to behave in a more "Asian" manner when they are interacting with members of their own ethnic group and in a more "Asian" fashion with non-Asians. As a first generation Mien educator in the U.S. and someone who travels quite often to different states and countries conducting trainings, presentations and providing counseling services, I need to remind myself to be sensitive to the different generational groups of Mien that I work with.

Filial Piety

For Mien and other Asians, filial piety means the respect, honor, love, and obedience that children need to show to their parents automatically. It is duty and obligation that parents are being obeyed and respected regardless of age, social status, or physical and mental conditions. This form of unwritten cultural rule is expected to be fulfilled by all children both inside and outside of the home. In the traditional Mien family, filial piety involves unquestioning obedience, as the parent is expected to be the most knowledgeable and responsible for the well-being of the child. This form of interdependent relationship continues into adulthood and through the lifetime of the child, even when they become adults and parents themselves.

In an agrarian society, the older generation relies on their children and grandchildren for physical and financial needs. Retirement or pension of any kind was not only unavailable, but were unknown or unheard of concepts in the Mien culture. Children and grandchildren represented the social security for the parents and grandparents, becoming responsible for the care of their parents and grandparents when they aged or become disabled. In the event that their parents or grandparents passed away, the children and grandchildren would continue this form of rich and strong veneration by worshiping their deceased ancestors. This practice is especially true for the non-Christians, as discussed in the previous chapters.

Direction of Parent-Child Communications

There is a different level of communication between Mien parents and their children and grandchildren. Consistent with filial piety is the one-directional communication between parent and child. Information and direction are given to the child by the parent or grandparent. Children are viewed as "immature adults" and are not expected to have ideas or suggestions that are of import. They are taught not to argue or talk back with their parents or grandparents. Whenever an important decision needs to be made on the behalf of an individual or family, children are not to be involved in those decision makings for their minds are "still yet fully developed". For an example, when a child reaches a certain age and the parents have found the best suitable mate for their son or daughter, the child holds no ground of refusal but to gladly accept the plan, as parents know best about them and their needs. Once a soul-mate is selected by the parents, this person is believed to meet the qualifications and standards of the parents.

Another example is revealed in career choice, in which it becomes evident for parents and children in the U.S. Parents usually direct and persuade their children toward careers considered appropriate, in light of both the status associated with the careers and the potential earning power of an individual in that profession. Parents and grandparents who have not been able to gain a higher education or obtain the careers they desired, begin to develop their hopes and dreams in the hearts and hands of their children and grandchildren. Therefore, parents and grandparents usually steer their children or grandchildren toward certain career paths that they believe to be the most suitable for them. This means that inclusion in family business is an option for many Asians who are trained from an early age to work with other family members.

Self-control in Emotional Expression

As a general rule of thumb, one's outward expressions reveal one's inner being. Each person is viewed and praised or condemned by the way he or she conducts himself or herself in both private and public settings. Therefore, individuals are expected to control their emotions both inside and outside their homes. The open display of both positive (happiness, pride, love) and negative (grief, anger, hatred) emotions is unacceptable, especially in the Mien traditional cultural setting. There may be appropriate times and places to express such feelings, or they may be communicated through ritualized religious or creative activities.

An individual's inappropriate expression of emotions not only can bring criticism to oneself but also to the family. Thus, Mien children are taught by parents and grandparents at young age to restrain their emotions as much as possible and at all cost. In the events where parents are not available, the eldest child automatically presumes the authority and responsibility of a parent to monitor and direct the behaviors of their younger siblings. Therefore, when people are taught, expected and monitored to withhold their emotions from childhood to adulthood, they normally will continue to believe and behave so accordingly as they age. Individuals and married couples from this type of cultural environment usually encounter many different levels of relationship and communication barriers. The problem also continues to flow into other aspects of life, creating many barriers between the individuals and their western social service providers, educators, employers, psychologists, therapists and medical professionals.

Well-defined Social Roles and Expectations

Within the Mien and other Asian cultures, there are defined roles and responsibilities for individuals in the family. As men need to be equipped to deal with the outside world, women are to be prepared to handle the inside world for the family. Males are generally expected to assume the instrumental roles of provider, protector and peace-maker of the family. They are the purveyors of health and security for the family. While fathers are leaders for his children and wife, and grandfathers become mentors, teachers, and advisors for the adult males. They are to teach and train their sons and grandsons to become the most productive adults in society as much as possible, since the success or failure of their son or grandson reflect the character and reputation of the father and grandfather. Therefore, young men are taught to carefully observe, respect, learn and carry out the family expectations and cultural traditions.

Mien women fill the role of nurturing the family to maintain relationships and family functioning within the home.

A wife's role is to bear children and nurture them while managing the household chores. She is to gather vegetables from the fields and pounds rice to prepare meals for her family. Besides the family daily needs for foods, the domestic animals (pigs and chickens) also needed to be fed. She is to go into the forest or farms to gather enough foods to feed the domestic animals. With her very busy schedule, she also needs to embroider and sew clothes for her family. In addition to her own family, she also has many obligations to fulfill for her parents-in-law. She becomes the teacher and mentor for her daughters. She needs to prepare all her daughters to become "good wives" when the time come for them to be married. The success or failure of her daughters' marriages reflects on who she is in the community.

Roles and expectations within the family are clearly defined, with males and elders having more importance and impact than women and youth. While this is true within the family, it is also generally true within the community and the society, with business and governmental authority and decision-making power lying in the hands of males and elders. As women reach elder status, and if no men of their generation are still alive, they receive more power and responsibilities.

Shame as a Behavioral Influence

As discussed earlier, behaviors and attitudes of the Mien and Asians in general are never simply the reflection of an individual. An individual always plays a very important part of the whole picture. As there are many pieces to a puzzle and each piece is important to the whole picture, each individual within a family represents a unique part of the entire family. If an individual violates prescribed norms, it is considered a disgrace, and not only it is a disgrace for the individual, but it is a reflection on the entire family. Children learn at a very young age that if they misbehave or do not live up to the expectations of the family, the entire family is affected. This may merely mean that the whole family is embarrassed, it might involve the loss of family status in the community, or it could even mean ostracism of the family from participation in societal activities. Therefore, each person is responsible for the wellness or "good name" of the whole family. This form of expectations is highly regarded for children with parents in leadership positions. Thus, shame is a strong mechanism of control and influences individuals throughout their lives.

It is also important to keep in mind that culture differences impact not only on people's behaviors but also on the use of nonverbal communication. Although facial expressions of anger, contempt, disgust, fear, happiness, sadness, and surprise have a universal basis, cultures differ in the rules that govern how these expressions are used. Cultural display rules are rules of expression management that dictate the appropriateness of emotion display depending on social circumstances. As we know cultures also differ in other aspects of nonverbal behavior, including the use of gestures. Mien and Asian cultures differ from the western culture in many angles, but one particular difference is gesturing. Individuals are taught by their parents and grandparents that gestures or sign language are only applicable for individuals who are mute or deaf. Therefore, these individuals usually do not use gestures during a conversation with people who do not have hearing or speech impairments. The Mien and many Asians are verbal communicators who apply few gestures when having a conversation.

In addition to linguistic difficulties, people have to overcome the socio-cultural differences and pressures posed by western society. Communication for Mien families is a cultural as well as linguistic performance based on an underlying bilingual and bicultural competence. There are individuals who have developed Mien and/or English conversational linguistic skills, but have not fully developed the writing and cultural competency to mutually and effectively convey their message to their spouses and their children.

An individual, couple, or family generally organizes their lives in a network of communication depending on the language they are accustomed to and understand. Mien married couples and their families in the U.S. are confronted with cultural pitfalls at different points in both verbal and nonverbal communication within their family and community. It becomes clear that separating the Mien language from their cultural and social contexts can hardly be conceivable.

A crucial communication dimension to take note of is that Mien culture emphasizes self-denial or criticism. Praising oneself, spouse or children in public is considered to be prideful and impolite. Self-complimenting one's talents, skills, knowledge, success in tasks is viewed as a form of showing off. It can also be interpreted as a lack of moral character. Thus, Mien individuals who value and expect 'standing on ceremony' would not praise or compliment themselves, their spouses or their children in public. They would deny themselves being called "great" or "talented" in a particular job well done or for obtaining certain unique talents or skills. Public compliments or acknowledgement provided by others are viewed as positive but still can create embarrassment. Providing compliments on nicely dressed, beautiful outfits, hairstyles, skin tones, facial makeup, etc., almost always create red faces to those who are considered as traditional or old fashioned. For example, when receiving a praise for one's dress as being beautiful, one would respond by saying that, "Oh no, it's not beautiful. It's ugly." The greatest embarrassment is complimenting one's beauty. When a Mien woman is being acknowledged for her physical beauty, she would normally be embarrassed and responds with, "No, I am not beautiful, I am ugly," and walk away with a red face and a hidden joyful heart.

Circular Communication Style

Mien people for generations have been speaking both indirect and two-sided communication styles within and outside of the family. Traditional Mien elites communicate in circular or non-linear style in formal settings. People do not communicate directly to the point, instead they speak around the subject and expect the hearers or receivers to understand the message without having to repeat or request for clarification. It is considered an immature mind if the hearer requests explanation from the speaker or presenter. People tend to communicate around the subject or the main point in a circular format and expect the other person or people to comprehend the content of their message. It is also expected that an educated or wise person does not speak in a linear format. A linear or direct communication style indicates an ineloquent mind in a formal setting. Leaders and educated individuals in a formal meeting do not communicate the subject or the main point directly. Direct communication is normally used in storytelling, between close companions, expressed by immature minds such as children, and therefore adults are to speak in an 'intelligent' form of communication in all formal meetings and discussions.

In a non-formal meeting, traditional Mien speakers usually tell a story, recite an incident or an exciting event with great repetition. The speaker usually repeats certain phrases or actions several times that seem to be interested to them and or their listeners. The repetitive communication style occurs mostly when people are telling stories, jokes or sharing personal testimonies. This form of communication can be viewed as boring, not interesting, or unnecessary, but it is important to the speakers who are accustomed to this communication pattern. Unless the speaker is given the opportunity to do so, he or she would be disappointed and the conversation can be reduced or quickly ended.

A circular communication pattern applies to general Mien speakers, even between spouses, parents and children and with others. For example, instead of saying, "Please don't do that because I do not like it," Mien people would typically say, "*Gunv zoux longx deix oc!*" meaning, "Please do it well!" In a more confusing way, instead of saying, "Please don't do that, it displeases me, they would say, "*Yie maiv bieqc hnyouv maaih mienh ndongc naaic maiv haih hnamv hnangv,"* meaning "I don't understand how someone can be so inconsiderate of others." When a Mien person wants someone to know of his or her frustration, disapproval, irritation, resentment or any other dissatisfaction, communication is mostly expressed in idiom, proverb, implication or sarcasm. In the deepest part of their minds, the best way to get people's attention is to use words and expressions that penetrate directly into the hearts instead of speaking to the ears. They would use words to put guilt or shame on a person. It is believed that shaming and convicting words draw people's attention. Mien have an expression that "*Maiv nyeih mba'ndaauh gaatv, oix nyeih bouv piqv,*" meaning "You do not desire a light cut by an elephant leaf but a deep cut by an ax." (Elephant leaves are very sharp and tall in length. They form thick bushes and grow in many parts of Asian countries.) The implication of this sarcastic expression reflects that a stubborn person needs to be lectured by shameful words and harsh punishment. Kind words or light corrections are like dull tools that cannot perform a deep and precise cut, and therefore, don't get to the point.

Quite often Mien people expect their spouses or children to understand their messages by making indirect comparisons, complaints, compliments or comments to someone with direct implications to the person they are talking to. A person can be considered as retarded, "*ga'naaiv-hngongx,*" for not understanding the message after being given several indirect stories, statements, comparisons or proverbs to a situation or behavior. The speaker is not the one to be accused or blamed for having poor communication. It is almost always considered the hearer's ignorance or stupidity for not understanding the message.

Within the Mien communication pattern, there are some unexpressed levels of expectation on the communicator. Depending on a person's intellectual ability and social status in the community, people have certain unspoken expectations and social standards for him to know and behave. Issues may arise when a person fails to recognize his or her responsibilities as expected. There are layers of communication barriers between Mien people in the U.S., especially within the first and third generations.

Here is an example of how someone can unintentionally create a communication breakdown in a very strong-tide family by not being sensitive to the traditional Mien cultural expectations. A well-respected Mien community spokesman, born in Laos, grew up in a Thailand refugee camp, came to the U.S. as a teenager, became educated in the U.S., worked hard to become a Mien language and culture consultant, and unintentionally applied a western "direct" communication style with his wife's mother and her siblings. Five months prior to their eldest son's wedding, all his wife's siblings had decided to unite all the families to celebrate his mother-in-law's 70th birthday. It took a long time to plan since all his wife's five siblings were married and lived in three different states. Some of their children were grown, married, and lived far away. He, being the trusted and respected person not only in the Mien community, but also within the five families, assisted in planning and organizing the special event.

As it is a tradition for most Mien Christians to have a home service for such a special occasion, he was requested to give a sermon. He was delighted to accept the request since it was his mother-in-law's birthday, plus it would allow him the opportunity to bless her and compliment her in public for being a strong and courageous widowed mother, raising all five children in spite of a limited resources and poor environment. After the death of her husband in Laos while her children were still young, she decided to give everything she had to raise her children without being remarried. After witnessing many children being neglected and abused by their step-fathers and the widowed women not being loved as younger wives, she had decided not to get married and stay single for the rest of her life. She was determined to give her children all she knew and had, and she did. Through her strong faith and perseverance, she was able to bring all her children and grandchildren to the U.S. from Laos and Thailand. Today all her children are grown married and have their own families.

On the day of the birthday celebration, many of the church members accompanied her five children and their families. They came with gifts, smiling faces, appreciation and gratitude. After the opening prayer and songs, the sermon was given and tears filled the room. Each of her children gratefully expressed of happiness, joy, love, recognition, and appreciation. It was the best reunion for his mother-in-law and family ever. That was the first time he had personally witnessed the happiness of his mother-in-law in the twenty three years that he had known her. He remembered well that at first his mother-in-law hesitated for her youngest daughter to marry him for his family came from different regions of Laos and he was still young, uneducated and unemployed. He did not see the cheerful and happy face that he had hoped for on the day of their wedding. However, after seeing her being so touched by the sermon and the positive and uplifting testimonies given by his wife and her siblings, that moment made him feel so proud of his mother-in-law for enduring all the hardships and sacrifices to bring up her beautiful children. They enjoyed each other's company tremendously, eating and celebrating for two days. The food was great, children from different families intermingled well, and the fellowship was lively and fruitful. Everything went well and everyone seemed to appreciate the occasion. He believed things were well until an incident that occurred right at the end of the reunion, before their son's wedding.

On the second night of the family reunion, he and his wife cheerfully informed everyone of their eldest son's upcoming wedding and requested their presence. He and his wife had lived in the U.S. for over twenty-five years and were accustomed to the western styles of communication. They had forgotten to follow the three crucial steps in the traditional ways of communication with the families. First, instead of visiting each family in their homes separately in their homes to inform them about the wedding, seek their advice, get them involved, invite them individually, (which are the crucial steps in the Mien culture,) they did it the western way. They did not go through all the stages to open up the channels of communication, making everyone feel included. They gathered everyone together and announced the wedding. The second step they failed to take was the consultation. It was expected that being the youngest of the three daughters, she would consult with her two older sisters and her mother. The fact that she did not consult with them for advice was interpreted as disrespect. In this circumstance, the families felt that since they were not included in the wedding planning, they were excluded from the wedding.

The third violation came when he and his wife failed to request her youngest brother to be the "*Zouh Mienh*" meaning "the meal coordinator." Since there are two sons in the family, the sons automatically granted the honorable roles of "*Zouh Mienh*" for their sisters. "*Zouh Mienh*" has the responsibility to work closely with the groom's and the bride's families to coordinate all the meals for the wedding. "*Zouh Mienh*" is knowledgeable in wedding preparation, cultural values, and the food that is suitable for a wedding. On the day of the wedding, "*Zouh Mienh*" makes sure that all the well-prepared food is properly prepared, tasty and warm. He needs to be recognized by both sides of the family and rewarded with one of the pig's hind legs. According to the birth order, it was clear that his wife's youngest brother needed to be the "*Zouh Mienh*". Since they both lived in the U.S. for a long time, they unintentionally overlooked these three cultural expectations. They did not know that his mother-in-law and all of her siblings were deeply offended and decided not to attend both of the wedding receptions.

As soon as they realized the offenses, they both tried to repair the damage by calling and apologizing to everyone, but it was too late; their cultural and social values were violated. The trust was broken and the relationship that they had built for over twenty years was lost. There was nothing that they could do, except to pray and ask God to forgive them and restore their relationships in the future. The families' contacts have been interrupted by this one single event. This true personal story not only captures the significance of Mien cultural values, but also provides great insight into the complexities of the communication styles. We cannot afford to isolate a person's culture from his or her communication style. We can easily and mistakenly destroy a person or the whole family's relationship when we fail to recognize their cultural values and beliefs from the ways they conduct their lives regardless of the country or society they live in. Since the Mien has many unwritten and unspoken cultural values and expectations, it is very challenging for the younger generation to have understandable communication with their older relatives. The issue is even more crucial in married relationships when spouses are not from the same generation or cultural backgrounds. It becomes a greater challenge especially to those who are born and raised in the U.S.

Two-Sided Communication

In addition to the circular communication style, the Mien also converse in a two-sided communication pattern. They speak in ceremonial language at the same time they speak in a silent or in Mien known as 'heart language' or hidden language. A two-sided language takes place when the speaker speaks in a polite or "saving face" language, while the heart reserves an opposite meaning. Usually the words from the mouth are in contrast to the heart or mind. It is believed to be impolite, rude or unprofessional to publicly admit or reveal one's inner language. One is supposed to hide his or her inner language or feeling while expressing the outward language. Other people are to understand the real message without a clarification or repetition. This is especially true when speaking in a formal setting. This form of communication pattern can create confusions and assumptions to the receivers, especially in a formal meeting where people need to exchange the birthdays of potential spouses.

In the Mien culture, when two people are in love, before they can talk about uniting their futures together, it is very crucial for the young man's parents to match their son's birthday with the young woman's birthday for a healthy and prosperous marriage.

It is believed that incorrect matches of birthdays can create calamities or curses not only for the married couple or their children, but also for their immediate family members as well. To avoid this type of unwanted catastrophe happenings to anyone in the family, the boy's parents would take all the precautious steps to find the right match for their sons. The primary step is to send a close relative, someone who is knowledgeable to interpret the double-sided language, to request the girl's birth date. Depending on the girl's parents, if they do not have any strong objection to the young man and his family, they normally reveal the correct date of birth. However, in the case of any disappointment or disapproval from the girl's parents, they would withhold giving out the correct birth date. In any case, when a birthday is revealed, the girl's parents normally speak in analogy or in comparison to the nature, such as flowers, trees, crops or seasons.

Birth years refer to the Chinese zodiac. The annual cycle takes place in this pattern: *zeiv* (rat), *caauv* (cow), *yienh* (tiger), *maauz* (cat), *zaanh* (dragon), *zeiz* (snake), *hmz* (horse), *meic* (goat), *sien* (monkey), *youz* (rooster), *futv* (dog) and *hoiz* (pig). The birth months are being referenced to the different stages of flowers. An example for the month of January is used in the context of "*tauh huaa zuv zin yuoc kaai*", meaning the young blossoming flowers in January. So, it is up to the messenger to understand the analogy and provide the correct interpretation. It is also important to note that almost none of the communication happened in any written form, meaning the listeners would need to have a good, if not perfect memory, to retain the oral instruction. In many instances, when the messages were not clearly understood or remembered, it caused the family to make their best guesses and could lead into inaccurate result or unwanted result. The incorrect interpretations and incorrect birthdays have happened for some if not many couples.

Another example is when a man wants to be elected or appointed to a certain position; he would deny himself in possessing the qualifications or eligibility. When being requested to play a certain role or take on a certain position, he would downplay his abilities and try to come up with reasons or excuses to refuse the offer. In reality, he really wants what he is refusing, but he knows that it is the Mien way to deny one's knowledge, strength and skill. In his mind he believed that a true request has to be offered at least three times. Therefore, he would continue to refuse the offer or request at least a couple times. He would feel respected and gladly accept the offer or request when he is being convinced or persuaded by others.

On the contrary, he would be greatly offended if the request is offered less than three times or when the position is given to someone else. The two-sided communication pattern exists not only to men but also to women, and it occurs by "educated or matured" adults in both formal and semi-formal settings. Children being taught and observed by parents who applied double-side communication style would unconsciously adopt this form of communication. The two-sided communication style is still being preserved by some older generation Mien in the U.S. Individuals who hold a certain level of knowledge in the Mien's spiritual and oral languages commonly use this form of communication. Not everyone is capable of using the double-sided communication. Incorrect use of it would be criticized, laughed at, or shamed by the hearers.

Communication and Gender

It is true that different cultures value different styles of communication. Men and women communicate differently based on their neurological development. Research by linguistics on the topic of communication and gender in the U.S. has found that while women tend to speak up more in general in conversations, men tend to set the agenda by giving opinions, suggestions, information, while women tend to repeat (Watkins-Goffman).

Men and women have different body language. Women tend to gather themselves in, and men tend to stretch out. Men tend to spend a lot of time sizing each other up while women tend to seek closeness by self-revelation, with the goal of networking relationships. Men seek a hierarchy that concerns power and positions when they attempt to established relationships with women. Women on the contrary, tend to be interested in their positions, not so much with respect to hierarchy, but rather their positions in the network of relationships (Watkins-Goffman).

Communication is both verbal and non-verbal. When one sends a message, another person receives it and gives a response. An analogy in a situation that comes to mind is the game of 'throw and catch,' which is performed yearly in a Hmong new-year celebration. (Hmong are one of the ethnic groups who originated from China to Laos and now reside in the U.S. They have similar cultural backgrounds as Mien people and share the same language branch, Sino-Tibetan). During the Hmong New Year, people of different ages and backgrounds come to socialize and maintain this part of a rich cultural norm by tossing handmade balls out of cloth about the size of a softball to each other. Many have substituted the traditional handmade of cloth-ball to tennis balls.

On the day of the New Year, men and women, boys and girls dress up in their traditional costumes and select someone whom they like and want to communicate with or to establish a new relationship. After a short exchange of conversation, the two known or unknown individuals begin tossing the ball and communication begins at that point. As there are rules in any game, there are some basic ground rules for dropping the ball. A common condition for dropping a ball is to sing or chant in Hmong language. When one cannot sing or chant, he or she has to give away a personal belonging each time a ball is dropped. These can be a hat, belt, watch, necklace, ring, bracelet or outer layer of clothes. Single men and women usually establish this rule among themselves. The party that loses his or her personal items can claim them back by visiting his or her home after dark, usually after the family members are asleep. A love connection thus established at this point. Mien and Hmong people refer to it as 'love begins in the dark.'

The messages that a couple send in a relationship can be poorly expressed or misinterpreted. Not everyone possesses the same level of communication skills, like tossing and catching the ball. Sometimes the ball is tossed slower, faster, lower or higher, and the person who receives the ball needs to make appropriate judgment in order to catch the ball. With two experienced people who know how to toss at the right level and speed for easy catch, the game can last a long time and the couple can enjoy the conversation without interruptions or difficulties. Challenges come when one or both parties become too excited, insensitive, careless, prideful, or intentionally tosses the ball too hard, too high or too low—beyond the comfort level. One can easily catch the other off guard.

Communication in a marriage is very similar to this tossing and catching game. When a couple has developed a clear understanding of their own communication style and the style of their mates and are willing to make the necessary changes, they too can have a balanced and healthy relationship. Another point to keep in mind is that there are times when communication breaks down by unpredictable reasons, like a ball dropped on the ground that causes interruptions or consequences. When a couple misunderstands each other, problems start to develop. A small intentional or unintentional mistake can lead into ruin of the fun and joyful game. To ensure that effective communication takes place, translation must not only be capable of bridging the gap between languages but also between cultures.

Communication can be seen as behavior that is governed by norms and conventions. According to Hoffman, communication is culture-specific.

Social-Emotional Interactions

The traditional Mien family has shifted from a large size to an atomized husband-wife core. Women have gradually come to claim status and rights equal to men politically, economically, socially and culturally in the western world. Marriage places high emphasis on bringing happiness to individuals based on affection and equality between husband and wife. The mate selection process has become much more ambiguous. Young people receive more freedom to select their mates. Dating also has been shifted from private to more open in front of parents or family members and public scenes. Traditionally, young men and women did not date but met late in the evening in the woman's house while the rest of the family members were asleep. Traditional men and women's social-emotional values are much more reserved than today's men and women.

Although the expression of love in public is still not encouraged or widely accepted by Mien parents and elders in the U.S., young men and women openly reveal their affection in public places. Public display of affection was considered lacking moral values and character. Mien people used to say, "*saeng-kuv maiv hiuv duqv nyaiv*," meaning that only animals do not feel shameful or embarrassed with their behaviors. The expression of passion was not a free choice but restricted and prohibited by the culture and society. Love may be as real as in a traditional setting, but it is not as openly expressed as in the U.S. Publicly holding hands and dating is still foreign and strange to the majority of elders. Public displays of affection were considered as ridiculous and sometimes become a target of public scorn. One can easily verify this cultural norm by looking at any Mien photos taken either in Laos or Thailand. Almost all the pictures Mien families brought to the United State do not reflect their feelings of gratitude, happiness or joy. By observing photos Mien people took in their homeland or in the refugee camps, one would hardly find anyone with a smiling face.

When a Mien person is overjoyed with something or when he or she faces unhappy situations, it is a virtue to hide his or her feelings. A Mien man or woman never rushes to embrace, hug or kiss each other in public even after the couple or family members return from a long trip. The love is expressed inwardly while pressing oneself to behave well in masking the joy and happiness in public. Doing so can create a great moment of embarrassment. Expressions of love and hate are silently concealed instead of being outwardly expressed or stated.

Manners and Gestures

There are many unknown or strange gestures and manners between Mien's traditionally appropriate body language and the adopted Western cultural behaviors. Shrugging of one's shoulders in the U.S. is an indication for uncertainty or ignorance of a subject is a confusing concept for Mien who have not been accustomed to the modern culture. Mien belching, hacking, coughing, or hiccoughing appears to Westerners as impolite or offensive. In the Mien traditional cultural setting, belching after a meal indicates great enjoyment and satisfaction of the food. Hacking or making a hesitating sound after a nice drink is not considered as rude or impolite. It is a sign of enjoyment. However, the opposite is true in the U.S. Mien couples with different degrees of acculturation and assimilation have different interpretations and expectations of the new set of appropriate behaviors and body language. This is especially true with Mien children, youth and their elders.

The more assimilated couples and families would expect such "inappropriate behavior" to cease, change or give appropriate responses in excusing oneself each time they belch, sneeze or hiccough. Picking one's teeth right after a meal is common and acceptable in Mien culture. It is also common where some men might have a toothpick in their mouths while talking to another person. An Americanized spouse or family member would consider such behavior as impolite and should be avoided until one finds himself alone.

When the time comes for a family or group meal, children would patiently wait until the elders or everyone else is seated or gathered around the table before they start to pick up their eating utensils. The individual does not pick up his or her chopsticks, spoon or fork before the father, grandfather, or elder begins to eat first. Mien people usually talk while they eat, which contradicts Western cultural point of view, "A person should not talk when his or her mouth is full." To the Mien, it is indelicate to pick up food with your hands when eating, except eating sticky or sweet rice. Mien adopted the concept of using their fingers to eat sticky or sweet rice from the Lao or Laotian neighbors when they were in Southeast Asia.

Levels of Communication

There are different levels of communication in our cultures today. Researchers from the field of communication identified many unique ways people share information, ideas or requests. The following is one of the approaches presented by Helton in reference to Powell. In authentic communication, Helton refers to John Powell's five levels of communication as follows:

Level One: cliché or casual conversation. This conversation consists of casual conversation, greetings, and common courtesies both verbal and nonverbal. This conversation normally occur at work, school, or social gathering where people would just simple extend their greeting to someone they know or a stranger.

Level Two: Just the facts. A speaker simply restates what was seen, heard, or understood. This level of communication does not reveal anything personal about oneself or others. It is simply a slightly more complex mode of communicating with others. A person can be a message by relaying the message from one person to another, being a witness of an event or incident.

Level Three: Thoughts and ideas. The person states judgments on the facts that he/she received, and inserts his or her opinions and beliefs to those facts. At this level, two people in a communication mode are able to express themselves, but one or the other does not pursue the expression with evidence or backup. The conversation can be lengthy or short depending on the interest of the two parties. One or the other could decide to end the conversation by changing the subject or just simply walks away.

Level Four: Emotions and feelings. The person speaks or reveals from what is in his or her heart and mind. This usually occurs between two people who know each other well and do not worry about convention. It usually involves judgment plus evidence or justification. The two people, called a dyad, come to conclusions through mutual satisfaction.

Level Five: Intimate Communication or Confessional Communication. This level is reached through crisis, is being vulnerable, open, honest. The person speaks to share his or her hopes, fears, dreams, agendas, or urges. This level occurs between two people involved in a marriage or a significant relationship. People in this relationship seem to know intuitively what each other thinks or expects when having this level of communication. This level of communication involves sharing the heart, mind, soul and spirit. It includes seeking supreme power from God through prayers or petition.

One way for married individuals to understand each other is to know the importance of personality and difference. Myers and Brigg have identified different types of personalities, whose descriptions can be found at http://www.myersbriggs.org. "Our personalities cause us to believe and behave differently in the same circumstance. Our personalities can lead to approach life in entirely different ways," (Helton, 1999:80). Understanding a person's personality type helps us better know the person and his or her preferences and tendencies. These personality traits include: extroversion, introversion, intuition, sensing, feeling, thinking, judging, and receiving.

The first set of traits, introversion and extraversion deal with how people prefer to interact with the world. The introverts prefer to deal with inward issues like concepts, ideas, thoughts, and images. The extraverts focus on the outer world of people, objects and actions.

The second set of traits are intuition and sensing, focusing on how people gather information. Intuitive types rely on hunches, impressions, and gut instinct. People of this trait prefer the abstract, big picture, and broad strokes. They love imagination and make predictions. The sensing type is the opposite. They focus on specifics, details, and the concrete. They pay attention to what actually happened instead of the future or what could happen.

The third set of traits, known as the feeling and thinking, refer to how people prefer to make decisions after they have collected the information. The feelers base their decisions upon personal values and how others may be impacted by the decision. They value harmony over clarity. In contrast, 'thinkers' will generally base their decisions on logic, critical thinking, objectivity, and facts. They regard searching for truth and fairness as more important than making people happy in a time of decision making.

The final set of personalities and traits pertain to know how people orient themselves. The judges are more structured, organized, detailed, and systematic. What is most important to them are orders, rules, plans, systems, and control. Percivers on the other hand value spontaneity, flexibility, curiosity, and open-endedness (Helen).

Negative Interactional Patterns

Helton indicated four harmful interactional patterns during a marriage or family conflict. These patterns are polarizing, reacting, using global terms, and distorting messages.

First, *polarizing* occurs when the person expresses his thoughts and opinions even more strongly or rigidly than he actually believes. It is an attempt to power the other person over to one's side of opinion by exaggeration.

Second is *reacting*, in which a person allows someone's behavior or influence to control his or her own.

Third is *'global terms'*, in which one is generalizing in describing behavior. Examples of global statements are, "You are always messy!" "You never listen to me." "He or she will never change."

The final pattern during conflict is *distorting messages*. It is a negative response pertaining to one's listening skills, self-perception, and self-esteem.

There is no doubt that many couples find themselves trapped in their daily conversation with their spouses in one or more of the different communication patterns. Individuals acquire certain communication styles and patterns of life from their parents, siblings, peers, schools or the socio-culture they experience as children and adults. Once a person has developed a comfort zone or habitual technique, he or she may or may not realize the positive or negative impact of their communication patterns in relation to their spouses, family members or others. It is difficult for people to understand each other if their communication patterns or expectations are out of alignment. People cannot make self-correction or improvement if they are not being aware of the effect of their communication or behavioral patterns. In the next chapter, I will discuss about some of these changes and differences for Mien parents in the United Sates. Some of these differences include their beliefs and family structure.

To summarize this chapter, it is crucial for spouses to realize just how profoundly men and women differ from each other. Male and female brains are dramatically different anatomically, chemically, hormonally, and physiologically. Those differences cause fundamentally different ways of thinking, feeling, and behaving. Instead of polarizing these God-given gifts and talents as barriers in any relationship, it is best to appreciate and honor those differences. In a marriage and family relationship, we should not be frustrated by the gender differences, we should decide to respect them and learn how to work with them instead of against them.

In a marriage, it is necessary for both spouses to understand the differences in how men and women process information. The female brain is highly empathetic, with a low ability to compartmentalize, a high ability to multitask, a low ability to control emotions, a relational orientation, a low project orientation, a low ability to "zone out," a tendency to think and feel before acting in response to stress, a cautious response to risk, and a tendency to cooperate with other females. The male brain is highly systemized, with a high ability to compartmentalize, a low ability to multitask, a high ability to control emotions, a low relational orientation, a high project orientation, a high ability to "zone out," a tendency to act first and think later when faced with stress, an aggressive response to risk, and a tendency to compete with other males.

In terms of communication, women reveal their needs, wants, happiness, frustrations and other physical and emotional feelings more in verbal form than men. While men's conversations tend to focus on facts, women's conversations tend to emphasize the feelings behind the facts. Men solve problems best by thinking about one issue at a time, usually on their own. But women generally need to talk through problems with someone else to process their thoughts. Men approach situations with a strong desire to make decisions and take action, whereas women sometimes just want to talk about how they feel about those same situations. Men tend to speak directly and use words literally, while women tend to speak indirectly. Therefore, a wife needs to give her husband the time and space he needs to think through issues on his own. She needs to be willing to work with him to find solutions that they both can both act on. After that she can speak to him in direct ways so that he can clearly understand the issue or the concept. On the same line, a husband needs to listen to his wife when he shares his thoughts and feelings about any issues or topics.

In a nut shell, communication is always a matter of interpersonal action and reaction between communicators. We should not be quick to draw conclusion or boundary line between intercultural and intra-cultural communication in terms of difference of language being spoken between spouses or family members. We can see that inter-cultural and intra-cultural communication happen at a certain location and time where there is an encounter of humans in a particular environment. Both involve clusters of language codes and aspects of culture with varying degrees of similarity and difference between the sender and receiver of the message. Both depend on mutual understanding, respect and negotiations between the individuals.

Table 3: Comparison of Mien and American Communication Styles

Mien/Asian Traditional Communication Style	U.S. Communication Style
1. Talkative is un-Mien	1. Talkative is Americanized
2. The more you talk the less respect you receive	2. The more expressive you are the more you are known
3. Speak the words and hide your feelings	3. Speak your minds and be and be direct to the point
4. Speaking your mind is out of your mind	4. Speaking your mind reveals your mind and is strongly encouraged
5. Feelings are kept to oneself	5. Feelings are expressed to others
6. Think more, speak less	6. Think and speak of one's thoughts
7. Guessing for the unknown	7. Hiding out the truth
8. Expecting others to know the unstated subject	8. Telling or explaining the subject
9. Passive and respectful in getting one's needs and desires	9. Assertive, aggressive to meet one's needs and desires
10. Affection in public is shameful	10. Physical affection is acceptable and common
11. Observe for information	11. Ask questions for information
12. Love is unexpressive	12. Love is verbalized and expressive
13. Unhappiness is revealed in the face known as "butv qiex" or being silent and holding grudges	13. Unhappiness is revealed through words and actions
14. Appreciation is expressed through foods, gifts, or through offering favors without being asked	14. Appreciation is revealed in verbal or in written form
15. Struggles, challenges and problems draw couples and family members closer	15. Struggles, challenges and life issues often push or pull couples and family apart

Chapter 8

Mien Cultural and Marital Issues

Changing Roles of Mien American Families

The changing of family roles within the Mien American culture is similar to that of other Asian-Americans in the U.S. The impact of acculturation on families and its subsequent impact on the family roles and family structure of Mien and Asian-American families in general has become a concern to both educators and researchers. Of the many Southeast Asian families in the U.S., the Mien are from the most rural background, and therefore have the least familiarity with Western culture, the lowest levels of education, and the most difficulty in guiding their children through the Western cultural system.

Many Mien and other Southeast Asian families have experienced severe trauma through the war and years of suffering in the concentric refugee camps. They developed high incidences of post-traumatic stress disorders (PTSD), affecting the education and well-being of both parents and children. As children learn English and adapt to the Western culture much faster than their elders, the generational gap between parents and children is complicated by cultural and linguistic differences in understanding. Children often assimilate rapidly into the modern culture while their parents try to acculturate and adapt as much as they can, but find it much more difficult to change their ways of thinking that have long been ingrained in their minds. While trying to assimilate, many parents also have the fear that their offspring are losing their mother-tongue and forgetting or disregarding their traditional cultural values.

In addition, the roles of parent and child are often forced to reverse, as children often become the main language brokers for their parents. Many parents become frustrated at not being able to help their children with homework (even young elementary school children) and fear looking "ignorant" in front of their children, teachers, and other parents. The educational background of these parents, as well as their cultural values, also has a strong impact on parent involvement in their children's education.

"Any examination of contemporary changes in Asian American families must first and foremost look at the diverse immigrant population among Asian Americans and the changing roles of Asian American women since 1965. Only after the passage of the 1965 Immigration Reform Act has the gender balance between Asian American men and women reached parity. The earliest immigration laws in the late eighteenth and early nineteenth centuries worked to perpetuate a distinct gender imbalance among Asian Americans. Along with their dramatic increase in numbers, a high percentage of Asian American women also work outside of the home," (Fong).

With the decline of the U.S. economy and the increase in financial need for families across the nation, parents have been pressured to seek employment that will provide sufficient income to support their loved ones. As a single income has become almost impossible for a family with even one child to live on, mothers are forced to leave the home to work and bring home more money to supplement the fathers' income.

Labor force participation and full-time employment have both positive and negative consequences for Mien and other Asian working women in the U.S. Women are being challenged by the demands of their families and society to compete in the workforce as much as men do. Earning livable income is equally important for men and women. Stable employment also enhances social skills, helps in cultural assimilation, and contributes to positive self-image inside and outside of the family. It also elevates one's sense of personal value as a contributor in the family. The fact that a woman is earning her share of income can, in some cases, create a more egalitarian marital relationship where there was originally the traditional or authoritarian family structure. This tends to be the case for the more educated, second-and third-generation Mien and other Asian American professionals.

The first Mien family arrived in the U.S. on 1975: Mr. Kao Chiem (*Gauv Jiem*) and Chua Meng (*Juov Mengh*) Chao, who currently reside in Portland, Oregon. I learned this information learned at the 30th Annual New Year celebration at Cal Expo in Sacramento, California, organized by the United Iu-Mien Community, Inc, where I was the keynote speaker. The majority of the Mien families began to arrive in the U.S. in the early 1980s through to the late 1990s.

Due to financial need, many people started working as soon as they were able to obtain employment instead of attending school. When both the wife and husband worked, there was limited time for couples to spend together, or with their children, or on household tasks. This was particularly true for working-class families in which one or both parents were working more than one job, or working irregular hours. Balanced family time is hard to establish when families are holding two or more jobs or while in school or receiving training.

An important strength of Mien and Southeast Asian families is their commitment to the extended family. As such, Mien families have larger average household sizes compared to the total U.S. average. Families usually consist of five or more members. Larger household sizes for Mien and other Asian families are due for the most part to living arrangements that include relatives outside of the nuclear family unit.

The large extended Mien households are a reflection of three factors. First, these households tend to have more adult children living at home while they are completing their higher education or vocational training. Second, more elderly relatives live with the families as they age, as opposed to in assisted living residences as is common for American families. Some of their challenges in America include the lack of English proficiency to communicate their needs and problems with their providers and how to access community resources. Many adult and seniors lack formal education and are not equipped with employment skills as required in Western societies. In addition to language and cultural barriers, many elderly individuals become co-dependent on their children and grandchildren for transportation needs. Compounding these problems, many elderly refugees suffer from depression, post-traumatic stress disorder (PTSD), sleep disorders and anxiety. To the Mien and other Asians, mental illness is a stigma, which precludes seniors from seeking help from outsiders. Many elderly refugees from Southeast Asian countries believe that mental health ailments are a disgrace to the particular person, and to their whole family and community. Due to the strong family interconnections within the family groupings, placing an elderly person in a retired facility or nursing home can create more emotional and psychological problems. These challenges often present significant obstacles for them to live alone in a separate independent housing facility.

Third, established families often host friends or relatives that are in need of short-term housing due to the loss of employment or relocation. Not surprisingly, an even higher percentage of Mien families live in large and extended households. The limited space creates a privacy issue for many couples and their children. In some cases, in order to avoid the confined environment for space and privacy, some wives have left their husbands instead of complaining and trying to make changes over which they had little or no control due to cultural reasons. Mien people believe that the "goodness" of a group outweighs the "goodness" of one's self. An individual within the family or group is expected to avoid causing any pain, hardship or issue for selfish reason as much as possible.

Mien women still bear most of the responsibilities of cooking, domestic chores, and child rearing even in dual-income families. Thus, having extra people living in the household can create high levels of stress and marital conflict among spouses and their children. Domestic violence often escalates and erupts for many of these families who struggle over power and control. In addition, many other issues, such as addiction to gambling, alcohol, drugs and spousal abuse, exist but are not as common as in Laos or Thailand, since many individuals are becoming aware of their rights and can access law enforcement and the judicial system for protection and prevention.

Traditional Mien extended family structure has long been based on the hierarchical principles of the dominance of males over females and elders over the young. This kind of organizational structure works to instill a strong sense of individual dependence on the larger family unit.

Clinging to the safety and security of traditional values is one way Mien families try to endure the dramatic relocation away from their homeland. The younger and more modern adults who are born and raised in a new culture are constantly challenging the family roles, patterns, and authorities in the U.S. Older women often exercise considerable power in their households, especially when they work outside the home. In some cases, Mien American women begin to assume the primary role as family "breadwinner," because female-dominated service sector jobs are more easily available for the women than low-skill jobs sought by the men. This gender-reversal situation may be temporary as the husband takes time to obtain educational or technical training that will eventually enable him to gain more skillful employment, or the shifting of roles may be a permanent change. Nonetheless, tensions arise as the traditional role of the male as the primary breadwinner for the family is often undermined in the U.S. by economic necessity. Along with gender relations, Mien families confront major shifts in authority roles between young and old. Children and young adults who have grown up in the U.S. have better English language skills, educational opportunities, and job training skills than their parents. In many cases, the children become interpreters and cultural brokers for their parents.

Parenthood

Parenthood has become more of an option for some married Mien couples in the U.S. Through available educational programs and support services in family planning and decision-making, spouses have more information enabling them to choose to delay parenthood or not to have any children at all. Having the opportunity for education and occupational development, some spouses have decided to postpone parenthood and pursue personal endeavors. Obtaining a high school diploma and college degree opens a new dimension of family life and personal enrichment goals for many wives, in particular. It is not surprising for today's Mien women to obtain an education level higher than their husbands. Their strong commitment, persistence, perseverance, and motivation have driven them to higher educational and occupational achievements despite their multiple roles in the homes.

The availability of education in the U.S. has encouraged and motivated men as well as women to seek education that they have not dreamt of in their native countries. This is particularly true for many Mien women in Laos and Thailand where parents only encouraged and supported their sons to receive basic education. Very few Mien women were granted the educational opportunity by their parents or grandparents within the Mien agrarian society. A woman's primary responsibility in the family was to be a "good daughter" who was obedient, loyal to her parents and elders, a diligent worker in the field, tending to the domestic animals, sewing and babysitting. Thus, the only child rearing and communication skills they received for their later married lives were mainly from observing their parents and grandparents. When things went well, people kept things quiet within the home. When mistakes or problems occurred, many lectures and much attention was given. This was a normal communication pattern in the Mien traditional culture. When being lectured or criticized for any reason, the communication usually was one-way. An "obedient or a good son, daughter or daughter-in-law" was not expected to talk back, but to show humility by looking down and paying close attention when being lectured. Eye contact was never allowed when confronted by a parent or a person in authority. It was considered rude, disrespectful and disobedient to gaze at a person during a conversation.

Although some Mien families have lived in the U.S. now for a lengthy period of time, it is possible that some still have not fully acculturated to the western cultural norms, especially in marriage and family communication and parenting. Within the few Mien educators or college graduates, there are only a few individuals who may be able to distinguish the differences between the traditional and non-traditional communication styles and expectations within a married setting.

Throughout the many years of my teaching and training Mien parents and children in the states of Washington, Oregon, California, Alaska and Canada, I have discovered that parents and grandparents seek options, new ideas, techniques and parenting styles to bridge the intergenerational gap between spouses, parents, children and grandparents. Many of them have never heard of the different communication techniques and parenting skills that are available to couples and families.

Marriage

According to research on marriage and family and societal culture, men generally seem to be more reluctant to marry than women. They marry at an older age than women. Married people are happier than single, divorced, separated, or widowed individuals.

According Waite and Gallagher, married people live longer, are healthier, have fewer heart attacks and other diseases, have fewer problems with alcohol, behave in less risky ways, more satisfied with their sexuality needs and have frequent physical intimacy with their spouse, and become much wealthier than single people. There is much research data that compares and contrasts the advantages and disadvantages for married and single people. The following briefly highlights four of the benefits married couples enjoy—better financial management, longer life, better mental health, and a brighter spiritual worldview.

Financially speaking, household and family needs often cause the couple to evaluate their income and expenses in a more balanced fashion. Mien people have a saying that, "*Maiv gaengh dorng jaa maiv hiuv duqv hmei-nzauv jaaix*, which translates to be, "You don't know how expensive salt and oil can be until you are married,." Meaning, a person does not know the value of money until he or she is married. Unmarried people usually make money and spend money based on their personal desires. In the back of the minds, they say to themselves that, "This is my money, and I get to choose how I want to use it." Their spending pattern creates a direct impact on their own lives more than on anyone else. Therefore, the lesser obligations they have on how to spend their money, the harder it is for them to control their spending habits. Single people who live alone are responsible for all their monthly expenses.

On the contrary, married couples usually have dual incomes and are able to share their living costs, such as food, insurance, furniture, medical bill, car payment, child care, utility bills, etc. When one person becomes ill or encounters an emergency, gets into an accident, loses his or her job, or needs emotional support due to stressors, the spouse is there to help. Married men are more successful in work as well, getting promoted more often and receiving higher performance. They also have higher attendance and are more punctual at work for they know the value to maintain a job in order to provide for the family. Married individuals usually have better time management and set priorities according to their needs of their families. They normally learn how to live on a balanced family budget instead of individualized spending habits. The financial needs of one's family may form the encouragement and motivation for one to gain the knowledge and skills to become successful provider.

Longevity becomes another benefit for married people. The longer a couple stays together in their marriage, the more years they will enjoy their lives together. Single men have mortality rates that are 250% higher than married men. Single women have mortality rates that are 50% higher than married women (Ross et all). Married couples have approximately ten years less risk of dying from cancer. Single people when become ill spend longer time in the hospital, and have greater risk of dying from surgery (Goodwin et al). Married women are 30% more likely to rate their health as excellent or very good compared to single women, and 40% less likely to rate their health as only fair or poor compared to single women. Based on life expectancies, nine of ten married men and women alive at age 48 are alive at 65, while only six of ten single men and eight of ten single women make it to 65. Married men may have better immune systems as well, either from support or from nagging to monitor blood pressure, cholesterol, weight, etc . . . and may be at less risk to catch colds" (Cohen et al).

Married men are half as likely to commit suicide as single men, and one third as likely as divorced men. Widowed men under 45 are nine times more likely to commit suicide as married men (Smith, Mercy, and Conn). Married people report lower levels of depression and distress, and 40% say they are very happy with their lives, compared to about 25% in single people. Married people were half as likely to say they were unhappy with their lives. Single men drink twice as much as married men, and one out of four say their drinking causes problems. Only one of seven married men says the same. One out of six single men abstains from alcohol, but one in four married men do (Miller-Tutzauer et al).

Men and women who never marry are happier than those who separate or divorce. Apparently, it is much better never to have tried marriage than to have tried and failed (Collins). Separation and divorce become very common options for people to escape or avoid their relationship differences. Men and women generally do not have balanced power, not only in the Mien or Asian cultures, but in most cultures. Within a Mien married family, men tend to have greater power than the women. The power can be based on superior resources in occupational prestige, income, education, and participation in outside organizations. When women have more of these resources than their husbands, their relative power in the family generally increases. A woman's domestic power usually changes when she begins to have children. Her child or children divert her attention, focus and resources on becoming a nurturer and provider. As the size of a family increases, family differences also become unavoidable. When conflicts happen in a family, couples typically say more negative things to each other than they do to strangers and outsiders. Therefore, to understand the Mien people and their marital problems means to have some background knowledge about their cultural norms and the hierarchy within the family that consist the concepts, values, and assumptions about life that guide their behavior which are widely shared among the family members, community and outsiders, such as the issues discussed in previous chapters.

Understanding the difference between cultural guidance and individuals is an important step in understanding Mien family values and the marriage system. Mien culture consists of ideas that are transmitted from generation to generation, rarely with explicit instruction, by parents, teachers, religious figures, and other respected elders. There are various factors that have affected Mien and other Asian marriages and family communication. Some of these variables include the changing of spousal roles, the increased prominence of common-law marriage in the U.S., the frequency of divorce and remarriage, and the shift from agricultural to industrial and technological world. All these and other factors have complicated the Mien traditional system and pattern of family and marriage. The role designations of mother, father, and child are no longer clear or being preserved for individuals and families living in the western society. The complexities of western culture create more confusion and barriers for Mien families to manage and maintain their spousal and parental roles. The society expects and demands fathers to participate in their children's lives by providing day-to-day physical and emotional care that is difference to how parents and children were raised in their homeland. It is true that most textbooks and literature available today for classroom teaching and pleasure reading are written by non-Asian scholars and deal with the subject from an alien context. In a field like communication, where social and cultural factors play such an important role, it is reasonable to expect that the teaching must be based with the appropriate social and cultural context.

Mien Marriage Problems

The problems facing Mien marriages and families in the U.S. can be seen and explained from different points of view. The result of this study yields five major factors that impact the success or failure of Mien marriages and families in the U.S., as shown in chapter 6, figure 3. These variables are the educational achievement, intercultural communication, love and respect, religious belief, and conflict management. In addition, there are eleven other prevalent elements that cause marital and relationship issues, and they are summarized in the following sections.

1. **Lack of competent and certified marriage counselors.** Currently, there is a Mien state-certified marriage counselor in California and a marriage counselor in Washington State. The majority of today's Mien college graduates are from the fields of business or technology. Other graduates have major in education, social services, health care, and real estate. Certified counselors who are both linguistically and culturally competent in Mien are lacking, particularly in the areas of marriage and family, mental health, substance abuse and rehabilitation counseling. By having available counselors and therapists who are knowledgeable about the academic, social, psychological and spiritual needs of these families, will surely help individuals and families to understand their issues and obtain possible solutions. Once their barriers and challenges are minimized, people can gain hope, strength and the appropriate resources to improve their lives.

2. **Financial barriers.** The majority of families do not have solid employment that offers benefits for counseling services. Without sufficient benefits from their employers or solid income to cover the counseling fees, individuals and couples are not able to access counseling services. The low socio-economic status forces both parents to work and leave their children to be cared for by child-care providers, family members of friends. The conflict in work scheduling has caused many couples to have problems with their children, and some end up paying very high prices. Many children become rebellious against their parents because they are not meeting their social and emotional needs. Parents are not able to be home when the children need them. Some parents have double employment and have very limited time for their spouses and children. Family activities or quality time become hopes and dreams for some families. Their marriages become weak and children are forced to become self-sufficient or independent when no adults are available to care for them. Independency gradually develops unconsciously. In many cases, it is too late for parents to make up for family time that has been lost. Some teenagers rebel against their parents when love, support, and attention were absent from in childhood.

Lewis and Feiring indicate that culture contributes to shaping the events that families engage in as a collective unit, and family eating together regularly is one of a few family events that transcend cultures and its families. Mien families in the U.S. who are demanded to work on swing shifts or have conflicting schedules with other family members, are not able to have regular meals with their families as much as they would like. In Laos and Thailand, families worked on their own schedules and at their own times. Very few people wore watches or had a clock in the house to tell time. Now that they are living in America, their lives are being programmed and governed by time. Living in a fast pace society has created many unexpected challenges and barriers for couples, parents and children. Individuals who are not able to transform their minds and bodies to follow the time system cannot and will not become successful or productive in a time-governed society. People who don't know how to manage their time effectively will eventually allow the time to manage them. So, either a person will manage the time or the time will manage the person. Since we are living in a time-driven society where family members have different work schedules, having a quality family time for most families becomes a dividing factor in relationship building.

3. **Cultural barriers.** Counseling has been an alien concept to most Mien and other Asian families and couples. Those who are not accustomed to or familiar with the nature of counseling may have developed a misperception that counseling is only designed for people with mental illness. These individuals would think that "normal or regular" people do not need counseling. They do not understand the benefits of counseling services. Many are concerned about confidentiality since they live in close proximity of their family members, friends and relatives in the community. Disclosing family problems, especially sexual topics, are usually prohibited by the culture. When one discloses his or her marriage or sexual problems, it is considered to be selling one's family reputation which can potentially cause the individual and family members to lose face. Thus, the notion of 'face saving' can hinder certain individuals and families within the Mien and other Asian communities from seeking professional counseling services.

4. **Trust level.** It is not easy for Mien and Asian couples to build trust with an unknown service provider. Throughout their lives, the Mien and other Southeast Asian adults and elders have had their trust broken by many different levels of people in Laos and Thailand that created many myths and uncertainties in their minds. Their negative life experiences with the government, soldiers in the refugee camps, and their fellow countrymen often time become barriers for them to reach out for helps from someone outside of their immediate family members. The uncertainty of keeping secrets or confidentiality that can lead to legal issues hinder individuals from sharing personal and marriage issues with someone who has not gained their trust. Therefore, many couples are reluctant to seek counseling or professional helps from outsiders.

5. **Different communication styles.** The circular communication pattern Mien couples acquired from their traditional homeland is being practiced in a linear communication society and often pre-

sents one of the greatest hindrances in a marriage growth and development. As intercultural marriages are becoming more common within the Mien community circles, communication limits between spouses becomes inevitable. The communications barriers and differences are discussed in details in chapter six and seven.

6. **Unparalleled teaching and disciplining techniques.** The unparalleled teaching and disciplining techniques between eastern and western cultures impose a strong communication breakdown for parents and grandparents. Grandparents play a crucial role in their children's lives and in the lives of their grandchildren as well. They have the duty to teach and discipline their grandchildren in the presence or absence of their parents. Since corporal punishment creates legal issues in the U.S., many Mien parents are confused or feel helpless to apply appropriate and effective disciplining strategies.

7. **Unexpressed appreciation, affection, compliments or praise.** Physical and emotional affection becomes an issue for second—and third-generation married couples. Giving praise or compliments to spouses in public arenas and within the family setting imposes another set of expectations for marriages and families in western culture. Individuals, couples and families who are still functioning in the traditional cultural zone still withhold themselves back from expressing appreciation, affection, and compliments to their spouses or children. This has created many different levels of misunderstanding and frustrations for individual spouses or children who have become accustomed to the Western culture of giving outward praise.

8. **Poor problem solving skills/conflict management.** Due to limited educational backgrounds, many couples lack the necessary conflict management skills in resolving their marital issues, and parents are not able to improve their child rearing or disciplinary skills. Most parents learned that the corporal punishment of whipping, leaving marks and bruises on a child's body, is prohibited by U.S. law. If they continue to discipline in the same way, they will eventually have to face Child Protective or Adult Protective

Services. In some unfortunate cases, children turned their parents into some complicated legal issues. The traditional problem solving techniques have worked against many Mien parents in the U.S.

9. **Large family size.** The size of Mien and other Southeast Asian families ranges from two to eight plus children. Sometimes married and or extended family members live together in one house. The lack of sufficient space for all family members, especially for the married couples who need privacy, often creates family and marital conflicts. Older children need quiet places for schoolwork and personal conversations on the phone are not always possible. Limited bathrooms and space for family or social activities become other challenges for the large extended family.

10. **Different marriage and family expectations.** The traditional roles and expectations for daughters and daughter-in-laws pose another family conflict. Daughters and daughter-in-laws in the U.S. not only cannot but do not follow the traditional expectations and requirements as they learn and become assimilated with Western culture. The traditional roles for daughters and daughter-in-laws to squat before a father-in-law, prepare three hot meals a day, feed the domestic animals, tend the fields, pound rice, gather fire wood, do laundry, and keep the house clean are not realistic in this country. A more in-depth discussion of these roles and issues can be found in chapter two.

11. **Unfamiliarity with available resources.** Language and culture barriers have prevented many individuals and families from participating and taking advantage of the available resources in the community for couples and families. Transportation and getting directions are some of the additional problems for elderly or limited English proficiency individuals. The vast majority of elderly Mien and Asian people are unfamiliar with the judicial system in America, especially in the arenas of domestic issues. Although traditionally divorce was legal, it was not common and Mien in general strongly oppose it. The unfamiliar system, financial burden, language and transportation barriers become a stumbling block for couples to obtain resources.

Chapter 9

What Marriage is and What Marriage is Not

People from all over the world may have different interpretations or expectations for marriage. Even people from the same culture may see things differently than the larger group. Regardless of these differences, many people would agree that the common definition of marriage is a social, spiritual and legal union between a man and a woman. The union of two people into one marriage is sometimes identified as matrimony. Marriage is an institution in which interpersonal relationships are acknowledged by the people of that culture, the state, or by religious authorities. Civil marriage is the legal concept of marriage as a governmental institution, in accordance with marriage laws of the jurisdiction. If a marriage is recognized by the state, by the couple's religion, and/or by the society in which they live, then marriage changes the social status of the individuals who enter into it.

There are many reasons people get married. Some of the more common reasons for marriage today are:

- to legitimize a sexual relationship,
- to fulfill religious obligations,
- to make a public declaration of love,
- to escape an unhappy home,
- to satisfy parent's wishes,
- to start a family,
- to meet the obligation of an arranged marriage,
- because of a pregnancy (to save face),
- for financial needs (to pool resources/to get tax breaks),
- for vengeance on one's spouse or parents, to gain citizenship,
- coercion,
- fear of independence,
- fear of loneliness,

- fear of societal judgment,
- being sold in slavery (human trafficking)

If a marriage is formed through any of the reasons listed above, however, its foundation will be too weak to withstand the pressures that will challenge the relationship. In reality, it is evident that even for those couples with a strong marriage foundation, who had the free will to choose their mate, prepared with years of courtship, and even completed the appropriate premarital counseling, there are still many challenges they must overcome to keep their marriage healthy. When a marriage is formed in a manner other than through free will and free choice, and a genuine bonding of love through mutual agreement and satisfaction, a true happiness and healthy relationship cannot occur.

Our social and work lives are built around image. People have different views and expectations prior to getting married and will carry out these ideas throughout their marriages. The principles couples develop in their marriage relationships can help them or work against them. Mien people usually think of marriage as a system for producing children for their ensured care and lifelong support, to carry on family traditions, and to increase the Mien population locally and globally.

Married couples have vision of direction in their daily life together. In most cases, having a healthy marriage is an ultimate goal for married couples in all parts of the world.

Forming a family is much easier than *maintaining* a *healthy* marriage and family. Many Mien couples and families struggle with numerous social, environmental, cultural, linguistic and economical difficulties. "American family and marital relationships are often stretched to the breaking point by the demands of dual careers, financial concerns, and competing outside commitments and activities. Support from extended family has also deteriorated over time and are bringing challenges that our grandparents never imagined" (Wemhoff).

The problem of communication in a marriage is not esoteric. The unbalanced pattern of intercultural communication has become a concern in research studies. Communication is one of the most fundamental characteristics of human society. To be human is to communicate with one's fellow beings. The purpose of communication is to be able to know each other, to share experiences and aspirations and, therefore, to help each other achieves greater progress.

"Cultural change is the most difficult issue to deal with, as it touches upon the very personality and values of people as individuals and members of society" (Goonasekera). Gloria D. Feliciano first published a study on marriage communication in an Asian country in 1973. According to her, communication research in Asian countries started in the late 1950s and early 1960s from Asian journalists and doctorate graduates in the west, particularly the U.S. The developmental communication studies included agriculture, health, family planning and education. In Thailand, communication research was done with the focus of communication effects on the individual, Goonasekera.

"Understanding the theories and concepts in intercultural communication does not automatically lead to culturally sensitive behaviors. In fact, it is not uncommon to find individuals who are extremely knowledgeable about theories regarding cross-cultural and intercultural effectiveness, who possess the best of intentions yet who are ineffective, who possess the best of intentions, yet who are unable to demonstrate their knowledge in their actions" (Brislin and Yoshida). They add that, "certain skills, such as the ability to tolerate ambiguity, manage stress, establish realistic expectations, and demonstrate flexibility and empathy are helpful tools in all types of cross-cultural adjustment."

Maintaining a healthy and balanced family requires a lot of hard work to cultivate, prune, and care for a healthy marriage. It is like planting a young fruit tree that requires two dissimilar individuals to work together throughout the different seasons to provide the best nurturing and caring. Despite the challenges brought forth by the environment, the couple must cooperatively work together to keep the tree healthy so that it will become fruitful. As a young fruit tree needs healthy soil, water, fertilizer, and sufficient heat energy, the couple is required to examine one's strengths and weaknesses while learning about the strengths and weaknesses of their mate. Effort, commitment, energy and time are necessary to sustain a healthy tree that would bear fruit; likewise, the couple also must be willing to strive to build effective and healthy communication methods. They need to get ready to handle challenges while they learn to love, understand and accept each other. Once the couple has identified each other's strengths and weaknesses, they are to fully commit themselves to utilize their strengths to improve their weaknesses. There are many healthy common grounds in a relationship, and it is the responsibility of the couple to discover the best possible knowledge, skills, and resources to enjoy each other and support the relationship.

What "Marriage" is NOT:

1. Marriage is NOT a game.

A game is entertainment designed for people to enjoy, either by themselves or with others, or to occupy their time. Games have different topics, contents, actions, speeds, levels, and age appropriateness. The contents and actions of games are not reality. Skillful players can produce different results than less skilled players. Each game comes with certain rules and procedures, and all players need to follow the rules. Players cannot enjoy the game if they are not familiar with the rules. Understanding the rules and procedures can be a challenge for those who are not able to read or understand the language used in the game. In order for these individuals to play the game, they have to be taught by someone who is knowledgeable.

On the same line, games are not created for everyone. Those who have no passion or desire for a certain game would not want to play. Those who play can quickly lose interest in the game if it is too complicated, too easy, or does not match their interests. When players cannot defeat their opponents or produce the results they desire, they often stop playing it. While some quit playing the game, others may hand it over to someone else, sell or trade the game for something else, or throw it out. Games are entertainment, and people quit when they get bored or lose interest. Therefore, marriage is not a game and people should not treat their marriages as games. In a marriage, a couple should not follow the contents, rules, strategies and techniques created by others. They need to establish their own marriage roles, responsibilities, goals, and commitments to nurture their married relationship.

2. Marriage is NOT a sport.

Sports are activities that are governed by a set of rules or customs and often engaged in competition. The term 'sports' commonly refers to activities where the physical capabilities of the competitor are the primary means of determination of the outcome—of winning or losing. Sports are not only fascinating but also enormously entertaining. Although some may argue that sports and politics aren't a comfortable mix, in the end it's hard to keep the two separate. In sports, the rules and regulations are bound to change. Many rules in different forms of sports have changed over the years. Some rules and regulations are written, not by the players, but by some knowledgeable individual, group or entity, and differ between countries. Many sports are seasonal. When the season or tournament is over, the games and practices cease. Therefore, marriage is not a sport.

3. Marriage is NOT a business.

The main purpose of a business is to make profitable gain, and to attract and keep customers. Its basic function is to solve a customer's problem or need in a reliable fashion. One customer's problem becomes business to be solved for the business owner. The business engages a person's or couple's time, attention, or labor, as his or her principal concern or interest, whether for a long or short period of time. The central focal point of a business in making money for personal gain can cause an individual, couples or groups to become dishonest manipulators and enemies to others. In a business world, the good for oneself outweighs the good of others. In a business meeting, participants are to follow a certain agenda, usually not of one's own. The main focus is to persuade and get people to buy into one's ideas, plans and objectives. Therefore, marriage is unlike a business and should never be treated as such.

4. Marriage is NOT a contract.

Legally speaking, marriage is a contract with certain rights and responsibilities. But we must distinguish between legal marriage and covenant marriage. In a legal marriage, if one party does not live up to the contract, then legal actions can force them to do so or to end the marriage with an equitable settlement. In a **contract marriage**, if one of the partners doesn't live up to their end of the contract, then re-negotiations are in order. If an amicable agreement isn't reached, then the marriage is allowed to end with an "equitable settlement." So a contract marriage is essentially, "You do your part and I'll do mine," or *else!*

Contracts are important—the problem arises when we come to view our marriage only as a contract or a series of contracts. When this happens, we have become totally secular in our thinking and have abandoned the biblical view of marriage. The Bible views marriage ultimately as a covenant although contracts may be an important part of carrying out our covenant. There are general characteristics of contracts. We know that most contracts are often made for a limited period of time, deal with specific actions, are motivated by the desire to get something we want, and are unspoken and implicit. While marriage is a legal contract to be honored, and informal contracts within marriage often help us effectively use our differing skills to our mutual benefit, Christian marriage is much more than a contract. This "much more" is to be discovered in the word *covenant.*

Marriage is uniquely beneficial to society because it is the foundation of the family and the basic building block of society. It brings significant stability and meaning to human relationships. It remains the ideal for the raising of children. It plays an important role in transferring culture and civilization into future generations. Marriage is not merely a private contract, but a social institution of great public concern.

A contract is a legally binding exchange of promises or agreement between two or more people. A contract is a promise that must be kept between the agreed parties. Breach of a contract is recognized by the law and remedies can be provided. Contracts come with terms, conditions, and deadlines. People make different contracts throughout their lifetimes. Sometimes written contracts are required, (*e.g.*, when buying a house or a vehicle); however, the vast majority of contracts can be and are made orally, like borrowing something from someone and promising to return it at a certain date and time. A contract is a legally enforceable agreement between individuals or entities. Contract activity has a very broad and expansive meaning. It can be an agreement between two or more parties, especially one that is written and enforceable by law, or a formal agreement between parties. If a marriage is formed as the basis of a contract, it is designed to be broken.

What "Marriage" Is

1. Marriage IS like a tandem bicycle.

A marriage is like a tandem bicycle with two wheels held together by a strong metal frame. The wheels represent the roles and responsibilities of the husband and wife, and the frame serves as the core values, strengths, and commitment that hold the marriage together. As wheels without the frame cannot function properly, husband and wife cannot have a meaningful marriage without sharing the same beliefs and moral principles. In order to have a safe and enjoyable ride, both wheels need to be the same size, with the same amount air, and balanced. When one wheel spins and the other refuses to cooperate, problems will arise. In term of position, the husband is the leader of the family, and he should be taking the lead. The leader needs to know the way, have good vision, provide proper steering, know when to speed up, slow down or make a stop, and avoid any dangers on the road. When the front wheel leads, the rear wheel needs to follow; otherwise calamities will occur when both wheels work against each other. Whenever the front wheel stops moving and only the rear wheel spins, the task becomes not only difficult but problematic. One wrongful act can lead to many unwanted problems.

In this analogy, we can see the importance of the leader. Whether the husband or the wife leads the family, that person must lead with a clear direction and confidence. Although husbands are called by the Word of God and society to lead their family, in some situations the wives may need to fulfill that role when necessary. In actuality, we know that some husbands fail to lead their families. In this kind of situation, the wife is obligated to provide the guidance needed for the family. By the same token, we can use a unicycle to represent a single person or a single parent. Riding a unicycle is like a person going through life challenges without a balanced wheel or an assistant. Whether we want to accept it or not, everyone goes through life as if being in a race. It does not matter how skillful an unicyclist is, there are many challenges and disadvantages compared to those with regular bicycles that have equal and balanced wheels. Communication, cooperation, respect, balance, and equal support not only serve as necessary keys in bicycle riding, but are equally important in a marriage relationship.

2. Marriage IS like a pair of scissors.

Scissors come in different shapes, sizes, colors, densities, textures, sharpness, and functions. Some are made for children; others are designed for adults or professional usage, such as tailors, barbers or hair stylists. While medical professionals use them in clinics and hospitals for surgeries, others use them as cutting tools in factories and industrial companies. In schools and offices, scissors are used for different educational and occupational purposes. Scissors have changed in recent years to reflect trends in styles and shapes. Regardless of who developed them or how they are made, they are all designed for one purpose—to cut.

As two different sizes of material come together to form a pair of scissors, two different people come together to form a marriage. Couples are like a pair of scissors, two people with two different bodies, minds, souls and spirits to form a union known as husband and wife in a marriage. As scissors can only fulfill their designed function when both arms are working together cooperatively, a marriage can only flourish when both the husband and wife are in harmony with each other. In order to be called a pair of scissors, both arms must stay intact as a whole. Likewise, in order for a marriage to exist, there needs to be a husband and wife living and cleaving to each other. However, when both arms are working against each other, they are not only unable to cut anything, but create great difficulties for the person using them. In a marriage, when the husband and wife each decide to go in opposite directions, problems develop. When an arm of a scissor is disconnected with the other piece, it is no longer considered to be a pair of scissors. It automatically loses its value and purpose. The same is true for a marriage. When both spouses do not agree with each other and choose to go separate directions, the relationship is broken and there is no marriage. In order for a marriage to be happy and thriving, both spouses must be willing to work together cooperatively as scissors.

3. Marriage IS like a pair of chopsticks.

Mien people are famous for using chopsticks. When two people become husband and wife, they are like a pair of chopsticks. As a single chopstick is weak and is unable to pick up food, the husband and wife need each other to work together as lifetime partners. As a pair of chopsticks are stronger and are able to pick up foods for oneself and others, the husband and wife can accomplish the family's tasks more successfully if they cooperatively support each other as a team and do not work against each other. As chopsticks can be made from different kinds of materials, such as bamboo, plastic, wood or even metal, as long as they are equal in length, size and work together, they can accomplish the tasks in a meaningful way.

The greatest analogy for the appropriate usage of chopsticks is to view the top piece of the chopstick as the husband, the bottom piece as the wife, and they both are held together by a strong hand, the hand of God, their Creator. The husband, being the head of the family usually positions himself on the top, and the wife, the supporter and helpmate, positions herself below her husband. Once they recognize, accept and respect each other's roles and positions as they are designed to be, they can easily eliminate many of the common daily marital conflicts and issues. They both can then enjoy each other.

4. Marriage IS a covenant.

A covenant, like a contract, is an agreement made between two or more persons, but the nature of the agreement is quite different. **Marriage is a sacred covenant designed and blessed by God.** In marriage, God joins two persons into one (Genesis 2:24; Matthew 19:5; Mark 10:8). Originally, marriage (and family) was created by God to reflect His image in humanity. Because of humanity's fall into sin, marriage (and family) exists to magnify the worth, excellence, and glory of God in restoring His image in humanity through the gospel of Jesus Christ. Human marriage exists to preach the gospel of God (1 Timothy 1:11). God intends every human marriage to represent the divine marriage of God to the new, redeemed humanity (the Church, Christ's bride —see Ephesians 5:22-32; Revelation 19:7-10 and 21:9-27) through the death, burial and resurrection of Jesus Christ.

Marriage is a covenant of lifelong commitment between a man and a woman, not a contract which can be subject to early termination. Marriage certainly involves contractual aspects such as compromise, bargaining, and many meetings of the minds over time, consideration, terms and conditions. True marriage involves much more than what can be said in words. A covenant marriage is one of teamwork. It commits to "find the best solution to any problem at hand." Each person is committed to the vow they made to their spouse, even if their spouse doesn't live up to their vow, but also are committed to the vow they made to God.

A covenant marriage does not have a fixed period of time like most contracts. It is agreed upon and to be fulfilled for life. A true covenant marriage is not based solely on mutuality, but instead involves the agreement to sacrifice, persevere in love, remain steadfast in sickness and health, for richer or poorer, sharing the good and the bad, the joys and the pains. The characteristics of a covenant relationship are different from contractual marriage. Covenants are initiated for the benefit of the other person. In covenant relationships, people make unconditional promises. Covenant relationships are based on steadfast love. Covenant relationships view commitments as permanent and require confrontation and forgiveness whenever necessary. It is being committed to the vow two people made to God; to love and honor the spouse God has given us. The married couple needs to know that when they break their vow to their spouse, they are breaking their vow to God!

Chapter 10

Marriage and Relationships

Marriage is a heavenly ordained gift of love. Marriage is predestined by God and given to a man and a woman to morally and lawfully commit them into a lifetime relationship. The two individuals become one body, one soul, and one spirit living in a balanced and harmonious life before God and before man. Marriage is an interesting and challenging lifelong journey. The success of a marriage requires both spouses to gain self-awareness, develop effective communication skills, and have a strong commitment to strengthening each other as lifetime partners.

A married couple witnesses in many ways. They need to realize that how they treat each other in their marriage is a witness to everyone they come in contact with as to what the love of God is all about. Whether couples know it or not, they are witness to their children as they live their married life in front of them. How couples treat each other when they are in public and in private is a way of communicating their beliefs and core values without words. One's marriage is a witness of one's love for God. A marriage is a witness of how God can empower and transform those who belong to Him. A true marriage is a revelation of God's amazing love and forgiveness given from heaven above to earthly human beings. A real marriage brings glory and honor to the creator and sustainer of love, marriage and family.

When a man and a woman begin their marriage or life-time relationship without God, it is like buttoning one's shirts in the wrong order. The basic steps to buttoning a shirt can be likened to a marriage. When we begin by putting the first button into the right place, the rest of the buttons will fit perfectly into their proper locations. The shirt will be evenly placed on the body; the person who is wearing it feels comfortable and any potential embarrassment will be avoided. However, if the shirt is buttoned incorrectly, the person who is wearing it is uncomfortable, and feels embarrassment when others see it. Similarly, as a shirt has buttons that need to be placed into the right location, a marriage relationship needs to begin with the proper steps as designed by God. When marriages happen outside of God's design and plan, they are not under God's provision, care or protection when issues and conflicts arise. As humans are imperfect and full of weaknesses, we cannot resolve our own issues and challenges without God's support and guidance. Often when we try taking things into our own hands, we end up creating more problems and a bigger mess. Instead of fixing the problems, we create another layer of problems for ourselves and others. However, the Bible has very clear life and relationship principles for individuals and married couples. If, and only if, people are willing to **accept**, **admit** and **apply** the Biblical truths into their lives, can they have a healthy and balanced relationship with their spouse, children, relatives, friends, and others.

The Two Crucial Dimensional Relationships

The two most important dimensional connections for every individual are horizontal and vertical relationships. These two relationship dimensions are equally necessary for any active and functional individual living in this world. They need to be equally offered, received, valued, supported, cultivated and balanced in order for love and harmony to co-exist in one's life. Out of all of the relationship and communication patterns presented herein, the two most crucial relationships for any individual are vertical and horizontal relationships. The health and well-being of an individual or married couple is determined by the connection and communication between these two relationships.

1. **Horizontal Relationship.** This is a relationship a person has with other human beings. The relationship includes one's spouse, children, parents, grandparents, siblings, relatives, friends, neighbors, employers, co-workers, classmates, care providers, authorities, superiors, club members, nature, and general contacts or fellowship with other humans and living beings. The relationship one has with other human beings and the environment has significant value to one's social, physical, emotional and psychological health and wellness. A person simply cannot fully enjoy himself or herself without having a

good and balanced relationship with the people in his or her life. We can come to love and value ourselves, accept the strengths and weaknesses, and appreciate the unique differences when we can truly love and appreciate others.

The first crucial human relationship we have and need to establish and maintain is the connection with our immediate family members. This includes our spouses, children, parents, brothers and sisters, and grandparents. Some very important questions that we need to ask ourselves are, "What kind of relationship do we have with our spouse, children, parents, siblings and grandparents? Do we love one more than the others? Do we favor or value one over the others? How do we share our resources with these family members? How are we spending time with each individual family member? How do we accept and respect the unique differences in characteristics and personalities of these individuals?" There may be different levels of connections and love relationships between these family members. Although the love relationship one has with his or her spouse is not the same as with the children, parents, siblings and grandparents, the relationship between these family members still plays an important role in determining a person's self-actualization and the values of other human beings. When someone has a broken relationship with one of his or her immediate family members, he or she has a relational issue that may prevent him or her from having a healthy relationship with others, especially in a marriage relationship. Spouses who have a poor relationship with their parents or siblings may also have difficulty cultivating a healthy relationship with their spouse.

In addition to the importance of having strong connections with one's immediate family members, everyone also needs to have a balanced relationship with their extended family members, friends, neighbors, co-workers, subordinates, superiorities, classmates, service providers, people in places of authority and other human beings. A well-balanced and successful person, particularly in business, needs to have good communication, not only with his or her nuclear family and acquaintances, but also with the people he or she interacts with in social and professional settings. Almost every day of our lives, we find ways to get along with and enjoy life with many different kinds of people. Some of the common places we meet people are stores, schools, work, churches, temples, synagogues, parks, theatres, libraries, hospitals, clinics, gymnasiums, clubs, associations and organizations. In each one of these locations, we need to treat each other with respect regardless of our backgrounds.

Last, but not least, we all need to live in respect and harmony with the laws of the land and nature. This includes respecting our environmental resources, such as lands, waters, plants, trees, domestic animals and wildlife. To live harmoniously with nature is to understand and accept natural forces. The better we can understand, accept, and appreciate what the Creator has provided for human beings, the better we can live in harmony with nature. The knowledge and education we receive from our parents, teachers, the Bible and schools about physics, chemistry, meteorology, biology, physiology, metallurgy, and much more about our eulogies and origins, we come to live so much more harmoniously with nature. Nature looks at our complicated relationships with one another, the healing qualities of human friendship, and the endurance, faith, healing, and unconditional love that is given freely by our animal companions. If we desire to live in harmony with Mother Earth, we must act as her guardians, always placing her needs before the profits we can make from exploding her natural resources. When we look at the earth as a living organism we realize that, like other living organisms, she needs to be nurtured and cared for in a living manner.

When people strive to live in harmony with nature, they are interested in discussing and making changes that are necessary to our daily lives that will positively affect the world around us. People will learn why organic gardening and farming is the hope of our future and why some of the old ways of doing things are more efficient and safer for us and the environment. If we live in harmony with Mother Earth, we will learn that flowers should not be valued only for their beauty and fragrance alone, but that there are also healing qualities in their blossoms, leaves and roots. The flowers brighten our days here on earth, lifting up our spirits; and they may also hold the key to better health. Preserving flowers and other natural resources not only can provide the appropriate habitats for wild animals, but helps to preserve them as well.

When couples live in harmony with nature, they become more conscious about the environment and enjoy spending time with each other by going for long walks, jogging, hiking, swim in the ocean, camping and sleep in the open space or any other activities that can enhance their relationship. Native Americans believe that the Creator put everything on this earth to live together harmoniously, be used respectfully, and to be replenished whenever possible. The general rule is we are to take nothing that we don't need, and use everything we take. By living in harmony with nature, we not only make the environment more hospitable, but they help renew the resources available and honor the Creator and His gifts and each other. We are related to all creation as a world-wide family. Everything and everyone has a part to play in the big picture, and we could not exist without all the players. All of creation deserves our respect.

Couples also need to find ways to understand, accept, respect and value each other for which they are created. As people need to learn about their environment, adjust themselves to live appropriately without harming themselves or the Mother Earth, individuals and couples should do the same in a relationship. We need to change things that can be changed for the betterment of everyone and accept those that cannot be changed.

2. **Vertical Relationship.** A vertical relationship plays a very crucial role in human life. This is a relationship with the Creator God, who has the power to give life, bless life, and take away life. Everyone born into this world is seeking a savior,

whether we know it or not. Our souls search for security, belonging, and a relationship with the Creator. The moment we become conscious about ourselves and our environment, we begin to look for life meaning and purpose. While some people go through life quietly, others ask important questions and work hard to find the answers. One of these questions is, "What is the meaning or value of life? What are we looking for in this world? Why are we here?" Some people may respond by saying that their family, parent, job, house, car, jewelry, boats, or airplane is their top priority in the meaning of life and why they exist. Still others realize that God is most important in their life.

Many things in people's lives can be considered important and valuable. Depending on the person's view of God and humanity, he or she would establish price tags on things that are available to him or her. Our priorities are also set based on what we determine to be important and necessary in our lives. We nourish relationships with those we love, and we develop close attachment to certain materialistic things that we like or need. People seek opportunities to advance themselves in society by attending prestigious schools, receiving quality training and practical life skills that will lead to high salaried employment or honored positions. Some parents are working very hard to send their children to school either locally or abroad so that the children will attain knowledge from certain elite schools and in certain careers. While some parents can afford to send their children to famous and expensive schools, others could not and feel helpless and hopeless for the educational success of their children.

In Asian cultures, some children become idols for their parents and grandparents. This is particularly true for parents and grandparents who lack formal education and are not able to receive higher education while living in the U.S. These individuals place their future hopes and dreams on the educational success of their children or grandchildren. Thus, parents and grandparents place great pressures on their children or grandchildren to major in certain subjects that would bring perceived respect and high income into the family, such as a medical doctor, lawyer, engineer, or civic role. Once their son or daughter receives the college degree, the family places high hopes and expectations on that individual. Often the different levels of expectations can become overwhelming, if not impossible, to meet. Worse yet, when the individual fails at his job, such as being fired due to some inappropriate behaviors or illegal matter, it affects the entire family. Depending on the nature of the failure, disappointment, shame or humiliation can fall on the family. Many are able secure employment so that they can put food on the table for their loved ones, to have shelter and to take care of other responsibilities. Every day we spend many hours and endless effort to care and provide for our physical needs. Often, we become so focused on our physical needs and neglect our spiritual needs. We spend a lot of money and time feeding our bodies, making sure that we have enough to eat, at least two to three meals a day. Mien have a saying that, "*Mienh kouv laaix sung nzuih, nziouv kouv laaix norm biuih*", which means that "A man works hard because of his mouth (needs foods), and ants have to work hard for their hole." Every month each person spends literally hundreds of dollars on foods to give us health, strength and life, but how much attention do we put into building the health and wellness of our spiritual lives? We need to equally provide, protect, and care for the needs of our physical and spiritual health.

A person's spiritual health serves as a core foundation to his or her overall well-being. When a person has established the right relationship with the Creator spiritually, he or she then will have the inner passion and outer desire to do well and love those around him or her. Without it, a person cannot successfully develop and maintain a human relationship. Although, both vertical and horizontal relationships are important, we should be reminded that horizontal connections do not last forever. All horizontal relationships or connections only last temporarily. Since human life will someday come to an end, any horizontal connections we develop will eventually come to an end. Vertical relationships, however, are eternal. If we only have horizontal connections and no vertical relationships, we will come to great disappointment and despair when the relationships are no longer available.

Today, there are many people who do not have a relationship with God. They rarely give God any thought and just mind their own business. Some feel that God put them here on earth, and they should just do the best they can to live and enjoy life. They believe that people should eat, drink, get married and be happy while there is opportunity. On the other hand, there are those who work very hard at trying to live their life for God. They dedicate their lives to serve God through serving others locally, nationally or internationally. They are involved in lots of activities in their homes, church or neighbors. They are very busy doing that they believe is God's will for their life. They form small groups, large groups and become preoccupied with their daily spiritual activities. There is a major different between doing things, getting work done, and staying busy for God versus having a close and personal relationship with God. Often time people become too busy with ministry work and fail to have a personal relationship with God. It has become clear that there is nothing in life that could be, or should be, or of any greater importance than our personal relationship with God. Our vertical relationship affects every aspect of our lives. This includes our life goals, career choices, where to live, who to socialize, the meaning of marriage and family, how we raise children, how we love, respect, and treat others, the ways we manage our finances, and how we conduct ourselves in this vast world.

After having discussed the importance of having a vertical relationship, how does one go about developing and nourishing a relationship with the Almighty Creator? After all, He is the creator of the heavens and the earth, and I am just His creation. How can I develop a relationship with Him? Why would He want to have a relationship with me? Since He owns the whole entire universe, what good can I offer Him? How can an imperfect person like me be engaged in a relationship with the perfect, holy and righteous God? While there are many other similar questions and a number of simple, yet dynamic aspects of this topic, I can assure you that creating a relationship with the Creator God is not as complicated or difficult as what most people think. Everyone has at least a friend. Some people have many and variety of friends. Therefore, we already know how to form a friendship with someone and how to keep that friendship alive. The first step in a relationship building is not to be fearful or skeptic about the person, but to simply approach that person and begin a friendly conversation. Once you have developed enough trust level with that person, you would have broken some of the relationship building barriers, and your friendship will eventually begin to grow.

Likewise, when you want to establish a vertical relationship with God, it just takes a simple conversation. You would need to talk to Him, speak to Him, and present whatever topics, issues or needs to Him. The process is very simple, yet, for so many, sadly they feel unworthy or fearful to speak to Him. For many it is due to sin consciousness or condemnation that prevents them from seeking God. Some people's past life experiences or their present life circumstances cause them to feel unworthy or fearful to approach God. Instead of facing God for solutions, answers or cures to their needs, they choose to distant themselves away from Him. Regardless of our past history or present life conditions, we should not run away or avoid having a relationship with God. We all need Him, and He desires to have a close relationship with everyone and anyone who are willing to come to Him. The God of the universe is a loving, forgiving, kind, and gracious Lord and Savior. It is true that sin has separated human beings from God. The Bible tells us in Isaiah 59:1-2 that, "Surely the arm of the LORD is not too short to save, nor his ear too dull to hear. [2] But your iniquities have separated you from your God; your sins have hidden his face from you, so that he will not hear." Because sin became the barrier between us and God, He took away that barrier through His Son, Jesus Christ. When Jesus died on the cross, He did not only take away the barrier between God and man but established a new human-God relationship. Although Christ died to pay for the sins of the entire world over thousand years ago, the power of the Cross is still remains today. The Cross is strong enough to carry the weight of the world, calls sins, and long enough to reach the heaven from the earth for anyone who is willing to walk on it. Roman 5:8 tells us that, "[8]But God demonstrates his own love for us in this: While we were still sinners, Christ died for us." The Word of God promises in Roman 10:9-12 that if you confess with your lips that Jesus is Lord and believe in your heart that God raised him from the dead, you will be saved.

Spirituality is not synonymous with religion. Spirituality refers to a felt need to be in harmony with some higher unseen order of things. Human being simply cannot fully live at peace with themselves, not mentioning the peace with others and the nature, without first establishing a firm relationship with the Creator God. Spiritual connection with the source of life provider gives the primary source of strength, wisdom and guidance to any human relationship building. A man cannot and will not be able to live at peace with himself unless he is at peace with God. Religion, at its best, is simply one way of expressing one's spirituality. Spirituality assumes a higher order to which humans must conform—if we are to find peace. Harmony cannot be achieved by changing the "order of things" to suit our preferences. Harmony comes only from changing our actions to conform to the "higher order." A life lived in harmony with God, people, and nature is its own reward not only in this world but also in the eternal world.

The following chart shows the importance of having both vertical and horizontal relationships. There are great benefits to having both relationships and disadvantages for having just the horizontal relationship.

Table 4: Summary of Horizontal and Vertical Relationships

HORIZONTAL RELATIONSHIP	VERTICAL RELATIONSHIP
1. Love relationship is necessary, but Conditional	1. Love relationship is necessary and is Unconditional
2. Help and support are necessary, but not always available	2. Help and support are necessary and always available
3. Resource is limited and may not be available when needed	3. Resource is unlimited and accessible when the need is necessary
4. Relationship comes with term, condition, and price	4. Relationship is free and all costs were paid for in full
5. Communication is temporary, changing, and can be vague or confusing	5. Communication is everlasting, unchanging, and understanding
6. Relationship comes with unrealistic expectations and disappointments	6. Relationship comes with clear expectations and joy
7. Relationship comes with many unavoidable issues, hurts and pains	7. Relationship comes with room for growth, healing, and restoration

I would like to summarize this chapter by saying that a man's own BEST in society only serves as his Basic External Skill Test, and not necessary his BEST accomplishments in the eternal world. Therefore, the BEST of a man should not be measured by what he is able to do with his available resources, but by what he is able to accomplish without any resources. As a man came with nothing into this world empty handed, he shall take nothing with him when he leaves this world. Therefore, a man cannot produce anything good by himself without the resources that God has already created and provided in this world. A man can only use his intellectual and physical skills based on what God has allowed him to do. Without the proper creation and functions of a man's body and mind, how is he able to apply his cognitive and physical capabilities in creative ways? Before a man can do anything useful with his hands, feet or body, there needs to be proper body mechanical communication and function of the brain, nerves, organs, muscles, and bones. Therefore, a man is simply helpless on his own without the primary source, energy, strength and provisions from his Creator.

According to the Word of God, I would like to highlight the following spiritual truths:

1. Your **ATTITUDE** toward others determines your **ALTITUDE** with God. (Mathew 22:39; 1 John 3:16). The way we love, accept, respect, and treat others reveal many attributes about our relationship with God. If we say we love God and are obedient

to his commandments, we need to show it through the way we interact and live in harmony with others. We cannot claim to be children of God and live opposite lifestyles to the teaching of the Bible. The closer we walk with God, the stronger and healthier relationship we have toward our spouses, children and neighbors. The farther we are from God, the more distant we are with our loved ones, and the relationship with others becomes weaken and less healthy.

2. Your **BELIEF** about the values of life is revealed in your **BEHAVIORS**. (Mathew. 6:19-21). The lenses we use to view, understand and determine the meaning of life usually reveal through our behaviors toward the relationship we build and connect with our spouses, family members, neighbors, co-workers, classmates, authorities, etc. Unless we gain the full understanding to the values and meaning of life, we cannot behave appropriately toward others and the Creator God. When a person or couple has the right perspective about God and human natures, it will change the way we behave and treat each others. Every human life is precious and valuable to God regardless of our past, present or future activities. If we know and accept the values of life as designed by God, we will learn how to appreciate life and live a life according to God's purpose. This will change the way we conduct ourselves and complete our daily activities in both private and public places.

3. Your **LOYALTY** toward God reveals how you **LOVE** and honor your spouse and others. (Luke 10:27, Mathew 22:7, Deuteronomy 6:5, Mark 12:30; Proverbs 3:6). The commands in these Bible passages direct us to "Love the Lord your God with all your heart and with all your soul and with all your strength and with all your mind'; and, 'love your neighbor as yourself." The two greatest commandments given by the Creator for all human beings are to first, love our God with everything we have, and second, to love our neighbor as ourselves. The message is very clear, strong and thought provoking. To love God with all of our heart, mind, soul and strength means to change from self-centeredness to God-centeredness. It means

to fully surrender ourselves and everything that we have or owned to God for He is the creator of all things, the giver of all things, and He can take away anything at anytime. We came empty handed into this world, and we acknowledge Him for providing all that we have in this world. It means to completely yield ourselves to His Lordship. To love God means to give up our rights to our self-government, to do whatever we want, whenever we want and however we want, to follow His righteous commands and principles.

The second highest command is to place others above ourselves. Mathews 7:12 says "So in everything, do to others what you would have them do to you, for this sums up the Law and the Prophets." This biblical passage tells us to treat our neighbors with love and respect regardless if we want to or not. Doing good deeds to others is a basically a great thing to do in life. Every street corner and neighbor needs people to be nice and treat each other with kindness and respect. It also means to apply the golden rule in our daily steps. Meaning we need to "treat others in the same way we want to be treated", instead of "do to others before they do unto you."

4. Your **VIEW** of Jesus Christ and your life circumstances determine your **VICTORIOUS** or **VICTIMIZED** life style. The way we perceive the truth about the creation of the universe and humans play a significant role in how we view and manage our daily activities. Some crucial questions that are related to this statement include, who is the creator of man and the universe? Who is God and who is Jesus? Is Jesus God's son or just a prophet? If Jesus was God's son, did he die, buried and rose again on the third day? Was Jesus God himself or just a mere man? Is human existence in this world designed by God or through some unknown forms of super natural power? Our answers to these questions will determine the way we view ourselves, our world, how we conduct our daily life activities, and how we handle our life conditions. If we believe that Jesus was fully man and fully God and that he came into this world not to condemn the world nor to glorify himself, but he came

to bring grace, hope, healing and salvation to all fallen human beings so that they can become sons and daughters of God through the atonement of sins done at the cross of Calvary, then we can have a victorious spiritual life while living on earth. If not, we will always become victimized by the bondage of sins. Sin will take power over our lives, and we will become subject to God's wrath on the Day of Judgment. If we accept the truth about God's redemption and atonement of human's sins, the truth will set us free from the penalty of sins. (John 8:32-36). The Bible tells us that Christ has overcome the world and that all power on heavens and earth has been given to him. (John 16:33). Christ not only holds the truth, but he also holds the key of life and death. He is the creator and life sustainer. The only way to receive the victory from the bondage of sins or the power to conquer life and death is to receive God's son, Christ Jesus as our Lord and Savior. There are no other means or alternatives.

5. Your **WILL** before God reveals the **WAY** you **WALK** your life here on earth. (James 4:10). In life we yield ourselves to so many things and in many different ways. As a child we yield ourselves to the provision, nourishment, protection and guidance of our parents. In schools we yield ourselves to the rules and regulations of the schools and teachers. At work we yield ourselves to the policies and expectations of the company and our supervisors. As citizens we yield ourselves to traffic regulations, authorities, and the laws of the land. In a marriage relationship, we have certain roles, responsibilities, needs, expectations, and boundaries for ourselves and our spouses. Everywhere we go we learn that people from different cultures have different cultural norms, values, and codes of conduct. In order to live in harmony with people and society we need to follow and obey certain standards and principles. We simply cannot avoid them or change them to fit our needs or desires. When we ignore the cultural, society and individual rules, standards, requirements and expectations, we know that it is difficult, if not impossible, to maintain the peace, joy, and harmonious relationship. In fact, there are consequences

and penalties associated when one or more of the written or unspoken rules or life guiding principles are broken.

What does it mean to submit our will before God? One way to show our submission to God is by accepting and obeying the rules of the land, authorities and people we encounter in our daily life, especially those God has entrusted under our care. We cannot be submissive to God's holy commands when we become law and relationship breakers. Laws and rules are necessary for all human beings. The true nature of any rule is established to help people live in peace and harmony between man and God and between all human beings on earth. Laws and rules should be developed to protect and prevent people from creating harms to one, others, and God's creation. Laws and rules have come a long way since God gave the first man and woman, Adam and Eve, in the Garden of Eden, and everyone ought to follow them. Laws and rules were in God's plan from the beginning to guide and direct human beings to live a righteous lifestyle before God and man. As there are signs on our streets and highways to prevent us from causing harms to ourselves or others, so there are signs of life's road to remind us of our how actions toward each other and the nature play an important part in our society. Without laws and rules, life would be in chaos everywhere. All laws ever made by man are derived from the original ten laws or commandments given to man by God in Exodus 20:1-17. There are additional biblical references to help us understand the origin of rules and laws, and they can be found Micah 4:1-5; 1 Kings 21:1-15; Galatians 3:24; Romans 13:8; Ephesians 20:1-17; and Genesis 2:15-17. If all rules are legitimate, people should not abuse them but uphold them and apply them appropriately.

Chapter 11

Recommendations and Suggestions

This final chapter contains recommendations and suggestions for married couples, counselors and therapists, community leaders, pastors and clergymen, and researchers to better understand and meet the needs of the Mien and other Southeast Asian minorities in their marriages and families. Through my research, I have found that there are studies on Asian families and marriages in general, but not specifically on Mien families and marriages. Asian American divorce rates are relatively low compared to the national average. However, most community leaders and pastors have witnessed a rise in marital conflicts and the divorce rate. Fong reported that the divorce rate for Asian Americans was just 5 percent. This figure increased from the 3.7 percent divorce rate among Asian Americans in 1990. Japanese Americans, who are considered the most assimilated of the Asian American groups, had the highest overall divorce rate at 5.4 percent in 1990. At the end of the spectrum, South Asian Indians had the lowest divorce rate at 2.1 percent as indicated below.

Table 5: Asian American Households and Family Characteristics

Group	Percent under 18 Living with Two Parents	Percent over 15 Divorced
All	73.0	8.3
Asian Pacific Americans	83.6	3.8
Asian Americans	84.6	3.7
Chinese	81.6	2.8
Filipino	80.9	4.4
Japanese	86.1	5.4
Asian Indian	91.8	2.1
Korean	89.0	3.8
Vietnamese	76.6	2.9
Cambodian	71.0	2.5
Laotian	82.6	2.4
Hmong	86.2	1.7

Source: U.S. Bureau of the Census, 1990 *Census of the Population, Asians and Pacific Islanders in the United States* (Washington, DC: U.S. Government Printing Office, 1993).

The results of the research conducted for this study yield some interesting insights on how intercultural communication and other variables combine to enhance or hinder a marriage or family relationship. The final research analysis and insights have some meaningful implications for parents, religious and community leaders, service providers, and researchers. We all should take note that one's cultural background and educational achievement level, religion or belief system, intercultural communication, conflict management, and love and respect are some of the major components impacting today's Mien marriages and families in the U.S. The broad range of data gathered has contributed greatly to the outcome of this study. The cooperation from the participants was invaluable and proved very thoughtful and informative.

A key point to remember in regards to this subject is that making general statements or assumptions about any ethnic group without thorough background knowledge can easily lead to incorrect results. Mixing the Mien with the general Asian or Laotian population is a prime example. There are some similar cultural values between the Mien and the Hmong, Lao or Thai; however, each culture is governed by a separate set of cultural values, making them distinct from one another. We should take extra caution not to lump the Mien with other ethnic minorities in the general cultural framework. The Mien form their own unique ethnic group just as the Hmong, Lao, Thai, Cambodian or Vietnamese.

RECOMMENDATIONS FOR COUPLES

The following relationship-building tips are recommended for married couples to consider and try to adopt in their marriage relationships if they do not already do so.

Love and Respect

When two people have chosen each other to be lifetime mates through marriage, they each have the responsibility and accountability to love, cherish, support, and strengthen their marriage with all of their will and power. Here are some more specific suggestions for fostering love and respect in a marriage:

> ***Love your spouse with genuine love and respect.*** Love is neither inferior nor superior. Love is one-size-fits-all. People in every part of the world, every culture, gender, and age need love and want to be loved. In a marriage, both you and your spouse need to create equal love, respect, trust, and relationship security regardless of theirs or your cultural and economic background. True love is like super glue that can attach two people together for life. Spouses are different in many ways and yet can be equal in love. Genuine love does not care about shapes, sizes or colors. Everyone and anyone can receive love and give love.
>
> ***A genuine love within a marriage is not self-centered, but for the betterment of your spouse.*** A true love is sacrificial, giving, active and perseverant. The main focus of a genuine love within a marriage is not to see through each other, but to see each through the challenging moments. It is like a couple sitting in front of a fire place—when some sparks of fire suddenly landed on both people's heads, to show that each one is willing to first put out the fire on the other's head prior to putting out their own. Genuine love seeks the opportunity to do good for your spouse instead of taking advantage of his or her weakness. The focus is on your spouse instead of on yourself.
>
> A genuine love is unlike this Mien couple, Mr. and Mrs. Dangc, who used to live in Laos and Thailand, and have shared with me their life testimony. Before they become Christians, they did not know about a genuine love and practiced self-centered love. One day, as they were passing through a nearby village, a large, angry dog was trying to protect his owner's property by

barking and attempted to attack them. When the husband saw the huge and aggressive dog, he immediately stepped back and pushed his wife to be on the frontline. Thank God, the wife was able to rescue herself and her husband in that dangerous situation. Instead of running away, which could have been deadly, she immediately got down low in a squatting position and spoke calmly to the dog. After a few seconds, the angry dog slowly made his way back into his owner's home. From this story, the husband's immediate reaction was an example of self-centered love, as opposed to genuine love. And, on a lighter note, the moral of this story is, 'every strong man needs a stronger woman'.

Try to be quick to examine yourself and slow to judge your spouse. It is much easier for us to see the mistakes and weaknesses in others, and we often fail to recognize our own faults. Depending on a person's cultural and educational background, self-analysis or evaluation is not something that was taught or discussed for some people. To elaborate this concept in a literal sense, for example, in a cultural environment where a mirror is not available, it is hard for someone to know exactly how his or her face looks. Thus, if there were something on his face, he would not know it unless someone else pointed it out to him. We do need to hold a mirror to ourselves, however, and should try to examine ourselves and make all the necessary changes before trying to change our spouse. In other words, the appropriate changing of oneself can lead to the appropriate changing of our spouses. We need to remove the barriers that block us before we can begin to help anyone else.

True love and respect empower you in achieving a stronger marriage. True love in a marriage becomes a very powerful force, like the steam engine of a train. The degree and intensity of the steam can move the engine and the engine moves the entire train. In a marriage, once there is true and genuine love, couples can overcome any life challenges and still be able to reach their destiny sooner or later.

On the other hand, without the power of the steam, the train cannot go anywhere or fulfill its duties regardless of the quality of the engine or how light the load. This is also true for any married couple. When a real and true love is missing from a marriage, no money, power, looks or expensive jewelry can ignite the love fire of the two people. If a love can be purchased or restored by any other means, other than true and genuine love, it only becomes a show and destined to end sooner or later.

Take initiative to fulfill your given roles and responsibilities within the family to the best of your ability. We should not ignore the needs and well-being of our spouse or children. Given the context of an evolving society, there is no set standard of family roles and responsibilities for husbands and wives. Regardless of one's social and cultural norm or setting, strong family involvement brings the best result for the marriage and family stability, especially for the fathers to fulfill their roles in the home. This crucial marital aspect has been studied and reported by Wilcox that, "Paternal involvement is positively associated with the economic achievement, educational attainment, and emotional health of children." He continues to say that, "Conservative Protestant married men with children are consistently more active and expressive with their children than unaffiliated men and are often more engaged with their children than mainline Protestant fathers."

In a marriage relationship, the husbands and wives share some interchangeable roles. These are easy to remember as such: the husband has at least four primary duties to fulfill—he is the **Provider, Protector, Peace Maker,** and **Promise Keeper** for his family. The wife has at least 3 crucial roles to play—she is the **Nurturer, Nutcracker,** and **Nobler.**

- As a **provider**, the husband is the bread and rice winner for his family. He works within his ability to provide foods, clothes, shelter, and income for his family the best he possibly can.

- As a **protector,** he is to seek and provide physical, social, emotional, and spiritual security and well-being for his family. He is to be certain that his wife and children are free from any potential harm. He should be alert and ready to walk in front of them, behind them, and beside them whenever necessary. He should be willing to put his life on the line for his family at any time and at any cost.

- As a **peace maker**, he provides a loving, caring and healthy home environment for his children. He needs to guide, direct, correct and discipline his children with appropriate and effective parenting technique. Regardless of his background, he needs to avoid applying the traditional Mien parenting style where the father is the commander or dictator in the family at all cost. In the traditional Mien parenting method, parents used corporal punishment where a child can receive different forms of physical beating, such as flicking or pinching the ear, knuckling the head, beating with a stick, and kicking or punching. Besides the physical beating, condemning and shaming words were used to bring humiliation to the child so that his or her inappropriate behavior would change. While receiving the correction or discipline, the child is to be silent and not to talk back to the parent.

In addition, as a peace maker means he needs to model and create healthy social, emotional and spiritual relationships among his family members. Whenever an issue arises in the family, the matter should be resolved with a positive and constructive outcome. The father should be the one to create peace, maintain peace and apply his peacemaking model in the home—and not leave it up to his wife. The wife or mother also has her roles to fulfill in the home. She can give advice and support, which are very necessary, but she should not take the lead to peacemaking in a family.

- As a **promise keeper**, he is to lead his family with honesty and integrity. The Golden Rule applies in every situation, especially in a family. Children learn the values of family and life principles by observing and being taught by their parents. As we are living in a very selfish and self-centered society, many people do try to take advantage of others for their own benefit. Honesty and integrity are absent from their life principles. Therefore, a father has the role and responsibility to be a promise keeper in two major areas: one to keep the marriage vows made to his wife, and two, to fulfill his fatherly responsibilities to his children. He should be a man of integrity. What is a man of integrity and how is integrity maintained? The word "integrity" comes from the mathematics word "integer" which means to "be whole and unified", "to be complete and open". It means to be "consistent". What is on the inside is shown on the outside, and there is no hidden agenda. A person of integrity is not double-minded and straight forward. He keeps his word to his family and everyone around him even if it hurts him. He is to be careful about making commitments because he keeps them all.

Integrity pleases God and He honors those with an upright heart. 1 Chronicle 29:17 says that, "I know, my God, that you test the heart and are pleased with Integrity." Integrity provides security and preserves the upright man from stress and many life issues. Proverbs 10:9 tells us that, "The man of integrity walks securely, but he who takes crooked paths will be found out." Integrity guides the upright man through grey pitfalls of life. Proverbs 11:3 explains that, "The integrity of the upright guides them, but the unfaithful are destroyed by their duplicity. Integrity gives a man credibility and influence. Therefore, a married man is a promise keeper with high integrity because it pleases God, keeps him out of trouble and is beneficial to his family in all settings.

The wife's three major roles are **nurturer**, **nutcracker**, and **nobler**.

- As a **nurturer**, she provides the fundamental and most important needs for her children. In addition to providing food, clothes, blankets and safety to her children, she maintains her family and makes sure everything is in the right order. A mother is not only the greatest nurturer for a child, but she is also the giver and sustainer of life, from pregnancy and throughout their childhood. Physically, she is responsible for the nursing and rearing of her children, and making sure that they receive proper nutrients for good health and growth. Emotionally, she is to love, care for, and guide her children to become effective communicators and contributors in the family and society.

- As a **nutcracker**, she is the one to turn on and off the family's lights. She is an alarm clock and a security alarm to her family. She does not sleep when someone becomes ill or when one of her children has not returned home. She keeps watch over her children and family needs more than her own. She can go to bed with an empty stomach as long as her children are not starving. She cuts, cooks, and cleans for her family, not out of obligation, but with great joy and happiness. She has cuts, bruises, and blisters on her hands from her hard work. As a nutcracker, she sheds tears and sweats for her family; often unnoticeably. She balances the family's income and expenses. She becomes the time and money keeper for the family.

- As a **nobler,** she is very conscious of the basic needs of her children and family. Often times she becomes the only available nurse to her family. She knows who has good health and who needs medical attention. She is quick to diagnose their symptoms and applies the best possible remedy to their illness without being asked or delayed. In addition, she is the first and most important teacher to her children. She is responsible for her children's physical, emotional and spiritual habits-including cleanliness, order, conversation, eating, sleeping, manners, time management and general propriety of behavior before God and others. She knows when to turn on, turn off and adjust the temperature of the house. The kitchen is her world and she needs everyone to respect and honor her rules in it. She knows when the refrigerator is full or empty and what kind of food to get. She knows when the oven is warm or hot. She knows when the water pressure is high or low. She is the thermostat of her house. She knows which room is clean and which room is messy. She knows who is wearing clean or dirty clothes. At night she knows which doors and windows are opened and closed. She knows who is present and absent from the home. She knows where to shop, what to buy, how much to buy and how to prepare it.

Avoid, at all cost, physical, verbal, or emotional harm to others. This means that neglect or abuse of any kind should be eliminated and avoided at all cost. In a marriage, there is no room for any spouse or anyone in the family to abuse another.

The best gift a father can give to his children is to love their mother with respect and sincere love. A father cannot give his children any more valuable gifts than to love their mother, his own wife. If he truly loves her, he is to remain faithful, honest, and caring for her and the children. The Mien have a saying for a married man that, "*Ndiangx nzueic maiv taux meih gomv biauv, sieqv nzueic maiv taux meih zoux aqv.*" This means that once your house is built, you may see other nice trees, but you should not cut them down to build your own house.

The best gift a mother can give to her children is to respect their father, her husband. Respecting her husband means to be faithful and love him as who he is. The Mien have a saying for a married woman that, "*Nie nzueic maiv taux meih zong nzox, dorn nzueic maiv taux meih zoux nqox.*" It means that once your clay-fire-pit is built, you may see more nice dirt or mud, but you cannot gather it to build another clay-fire-pit. (Traditionally, the clay-fire-pit serves as the main cooking stove for the entire family.)

Do not neglect your family by spending your time and money on addictive or abusive activities or substances, such as gambling, alcohol, drugs, or tobacco, but instead be honest and faithful to each other in all aspects of your private and public lives.

Intercultural Communication: Impacts on Marriage and Family Relationships

Give your spouse the most precious gift that you can give, and that no one can take away—that is your time, attention and sincere heart.

Communication

The following twelve recommendations are for married couples to avoid communication barriers. Both you and your spouse should try to apply the following directive and assertive styles of communication. Here are some suggestions for couples to consider:

- During a conversation, when you are not certain what your spouse is trying to communicate, you should try to repeat what you have heard to verify your understanding is correct or not. Asking for clarification is the first step to good communication. When you clearly understand the message your spouse is giving you, you can properly answer the question without creating a barrier.

- You should try not to make assumptions or try to think for your spouse. When you try to guess what's on your spouse's mind, it will put you out of your mind. Guessing or making assumptions on what your spouse is trying to say can cause more harm than good. It is not helpful to you or your spouse for it will only lead you to deeper communication problems. Whenever you try to think for someone, most likely the result is wrong. You should not test the depth of a river with both feet.

- You should try to be an attentive listener. Attentive listening skill does not come naturally for anyone. It is a skill that one needs to develop and continue to improve. There is a difference between listening with your ears and hearing with your heart. In a marriage relationship, it is highly suggested that couples learn to be quick to listen and slow to talk. There is a reason why God gives people two ears and a mouth so that we can do more listening than talking. During a conversation you should try to listen more than talk. Being an attentive listener means facing each other while having a conversation—that is why God positioned our ears facing the front and not facing the back. Although face-to-face communication is different from the traditional Mien way of talking to each other, attentive listening is necessary in a marriage relationship.

- You should try not to interrupt your spouse when he or she is speaking. Each person needs to take turns and respect what the other person has to say. Interruption only creates communication break downs and more potential unintended problems. Interrupting someone during a conversation can cause your spouse to feel disvalued and disrespected.

- You should avoid being critical or judgmental of each other while expressing your feelings or needs. You should try not to prejudge your spouse before knowing the whole message. Instead, you should try to study and understand your spouse as a person who is different than you. God creates man and woman with different gifts, talents, and communication capabilities.

- When you are expressing your feelings of hurt or frustration, you should speak with "I feel" statements rather than "you" statements in a low tone and calm voice. In this way you are not accusing your spouse, but mainly expressing your feelings without any accusations or blame. Your spouse would rather hear you say, "I'm feeling hurt or upset," than to hear you say, "You cause me pain or make me angry." "You" statements cause people to feel blamed or accused and are counterproductive to healthy communication.

- Honesty is a good policy in any setting. You should learn to communicate honestly with your spouse and children. You should try not to ignore your spouse's feelings. The more you can acknowledge his or her feelings, the more your spouse will open up to share his or her feelings. At the same time you should not make fun of what your spouse feels. Husbands, try to refrain yourself from giving an answer or solution unless your wife asks for one. Often times, the wife is not looking for an answer, but she just needs you to listen to her as she is trying to form some emotional connection with you. When women feel free to speak, they feel respected and encouraged to express themselves.

- You should try to avoid using the trapping words of 'never' and 'always' in your discussion. These words are used when one is frustrated or irritated and they can cause a spouse to feel unfairly accused. The more you use these wall-building words, the more barriers you are creating between yourself and your spouse. When you use these words, you are usually exaggerating and not communicating precisely your thoughts and feelings.

- You should avoid blaming, shaming, or calling names when one feels frustrated, hurt, or angry whenever possible. Blaming and shaming statements cause both you and your spouse to feel disrespected and disvalued. Instead of building a bridge of understanding, you are burning or tearing it down. Blaming, shaming, and name calling is like pouring unwanted salt or hot chili on your spouse's soup. For example, the name calling of "*ga'naaiv-waaic, ga'naaiv-doqc, ga'naaiv-ciouv or mienh waaic mienh, mienh doqc mienh, mienh ciouv mienh*", meaning "a bad person, an evil person, a mean person" should be avoided.

- When you and your spouse are having a heated or angry discussion, you should try to use a pausing, cooling down, and rethinking strategy. You should try to pause yourself, take a deep breath, reprogram your thinking, and calm yourself down before continuing the conversation when you or your spouse becomes angry at each other. Anger usually controls the actions and words of the person. Words that come out from an angry person are usually not positive or encouraging. Using destructive or hurtful words during a conversation is like pouring gasoline into an open fire. To protect you and your spouse from getting burned, you both should take a step or two back and let the fire simmer down before continuing your discussion.

- You should avoid holding grudges, or in Mien "*maiv dungx butv qiex*" for an unresolved issue. Holding grudges on issues and not being able to resolve them through healthy communication can result in harm to both spouses. Holding grudges for long periods of time usually isolates you and your spouse and thus creates further poor communication.

- You should avoid using any form of threats, as it is common in the Mien culture. This is especially important for men who are accustomed to the traditional way of getting things done their way. Using threats in the U.S. can be detrimental to your relationship. Threats not only can destroy trust in a love relationship, but can also lead to legal action. Threats do not resolve conflicts but only create more conflicts.

Conflict Management

Conflicts exist in every relationship, particularly in a marriage. Conflicts exist for various reasons and are not necessarily negative. It is impossible for human beings to avoid having any form of misunderstanding or conflict in our lives, especially in a love relationship. As there is no human being who is flawless; therefore, mistakes and issues are unavoidable within any marriage. Conflicts exist to demand couples to adopt and acquire the necessary tools to maintain and repair their marriage and family when problems arise. For example, a mechanic has to go through years of training in order to be equipped with the appropriate knowledge and tools to perform well at a job. He has to be knowledgeable to repair vehicles of different years, makes and models. The more tools he has, the easier for him to counter the mechanical problems. Conflicts in a family or relationship are inevitable. It makes a major difference for couples or people who live together to understand who they are as individuals, as a group or family, what they value themselves and in each other, and how they perceive the world in which they are living. The conflict that grows out of individual characteristics can be a positive force in their relationship. It provides an opportunity for them to explore new ideas and solutions to problem solving. Wemhoff said it well that "In marriage, conflict helps individuals recognize possibilities and points of views that they never knew existed."

Conflict avoidance can be harmful in a marriage. The main issue in any conflict can be boiled down to the understanding of the conflict, accurate interpretation of the conflict and proper management of the conflict. How couples handle their conflicts can enhance or hinder their long-term relationship. In any life circumstances people can become constructive or destructive in the process of resolving the issues. Due to the gender communication differences, expectations, and cultural values, couples normally do not possess the effective conflict management skills in today's complex society. Below are some suggestions for married couples:

- When resolving conflict, select an appropriate place and time for discussion. Avoid discussing sensitive issues in the presence of children. Parents may need to wait until their spouse is ready to discuss the problem and when children are not present.

- Acknowledge the conflict and agree on the topic(s) that need to be addressed. You may have several or multiple of issues that need to be resolved. However, you may need to prioritize which topic you want to address first and which ones can be addressed at a later time. Acknowledging the issue is the beginning step in resolving the issue.

- State the issue clearly. Focus on the present issue and try not to bring back issues from the past that may or may not relevant to the present conflict. Bringing back issues that cannot be changed can be a waste of time, energy, and is of no benefit. Husbands generally are not interested in discussing issues in the past and wish that their wives would not try to "revive a dead horse." Reciting an unpleasant experience or memory from the past often creates additional pain, regret, frustration or isolation in a relationship. Sometimes, it creates more harm than good.

- Focus on the problems one at a time. One should start to resolve smaller problems first before hitting the more complex ones. The progress or positive results one achieves from the

- Avoid traditional circular or guessing communication style. The new wine in the old wine's skin concept helps us to understand that people change as the society and environment changes. Applying the traditional circular communication style in a directive and open communication culture may not be very productive. Spouses are to be attentive to each other's communication styles as well as their children and family members.

- Avoid making assumptions and interruptions during a conversation. Be respectful and good listener as much as possible regardless of the person's age, gender or title.

- Husbands do not try to win over the discussion or issue as most men do in conversations or dissolutions, but seek logical resolutions to your problems. Winning over an issue and losing one's character can be an expensive price to pay. Husbands from Asian countries should realize that winning at a discussion does not always promote a high quality of a man. Instead, one's aggressiveness can destroy one's good character. Therefore, reaching a meaningful conclusion should be the ultimate goal in a discussion.

Married couples have the power to transform their marriages if provided with the proper tools and techniques. In order for a marriage to flourish and last, there needs to be a strong commitment to make the necessary changes even though it may involve pain.

Religious Belief System

Consciously or subconsciously, everyone has developed some level of principles and moral values that guide his or her life. These moral codes or standards serve as the foundation to how a person conducts his or her daily activities. There are many different forms of religion and belief systems in our modern world. It is suggested that each one of us should carefully select some healthy and productive life principles to guide and direct us in our daily lives. The following are some suggestions for couples to consider:

- Take time to carefully study meaningful life principles and resources to guide one's life and the lives of those around us. The couple should make sure that they have sufficient knowledge before making a hard decision that can potentially impact one's marriage relationship, family, and career. The choices you make today should be the choices that you can live with tomorrow.

- Most religions teach followers to live a balanced life with humanity and the universe in peace and harmony. However, not every religion provides accurate truths about humanity and God. Our society pays heavy attention to the physical needs but often overlooks or neglects our spiritual well-being. Both are equally important. We should not ignore either one of them. One crucial self question is, "How are we meeting our spiritual needs while we are accomplishing our daily tasks and aiming for our future goals?" Physiologically, our human bodies depend on three necessary life-sustaining elements: food, water and oxygen. What about our spirits and souls? How are we caring for our spiritual wellness? One should seriously consider adopting meaningful life principles for the sake of the body, mind and spirit. Not all truth is absolute truth, and everyone is encouraged to find the real truth. The Bible is a reliable source to begin.

- As parents, both spouses have the responsibilities to pass on their belief systems to their children and grandchildren. Be sure that the moral life principles parents provide to their children are beneficial to both physical and spiritual wellness.

RECOMMENDATIONS FOR COUNSELORS AND THERAPISTS

The role of a counselor and therapist is to help an individual, couple or group to live a healthy and balanced lifestyle between the Creator and the creation. People in all walks of life need to understand who they are before they can understand others or their environment. Helping people to gain the right perspective of these differences is just the first stage. The approach should not just end here. A counselor or therapist can help point out these differences, as they surface, sort out the differences into an understandable format, and guide a couple to resolving them in the most appropriate ways that lead to a better relationship. Couples need to understand that differences are not intentional and that misunderstandings are merely the result of expectations that are not realistic. Once the couple gains the correct perspective and assessment about their difference, it can strengthen their relationship. More importantly, counselors and therapists of Mien or Asian clients should strongly and carefully take into consideration the cultural components as discussed in this book prior to providing the counseling service.

Married couples from most Asian countries were not being exposed to any formal personal or marital counseling. In the culturally diverse communities, differences may be expected to exist in the communication styles of spouses, family and community members. Establishing relations with the community is one of the best approaches for counselors to take. The term marriage counseling did not exist in the Mien vocabulary until they resettled in the U.S. Even in the U.S. today very few have correct view or knowledge of what marital counseling is and the context of a counseling process. They need to be carefully and patiently educated. The greater populations of Asian clients consider "counseling" as mainly designed for "mentally ill" individuals. Therefore, couples who do not consider themselves as having any forms of mental or psychological retardations have no need for counseling. These are some areas for counselors to keep in mind. They should:

- Be patient in taking time to explain the counseling process in clear and easy to understand language to limited English-speaking clients. This includes any and all financial involvement, confidentiality, one's role and responsibility as a counselor and their roles as clients.

- Try to help clients feel trusted, comfortable and accepted before probing into their personal or relationship issues. Counselors need to establish trust and respect before discussing personal matters. Without proper trust and respect, one's counseling service can be in vain or early termination.

- Be very careful to approach culturally sensitive issues and taboos when working with diverse ethnic clients, especially refugees and immigrants.

- Educate clients about legal and financial issues. Clients need to know what is expected of them financially and any potential legal actions. That means the service providers need to discuss family and personal financial expectations and concerns openly. It also means to clearly discuss any concrete plans for the future and unexpected circumstances. Surprises can destroy trust. Again, it is important to take note that most Asian clients do not reveal their frustrations, disagreements, negative emotions or even request for clarifications from a provider of whom they consider a knowledgeable and respected individual.

- To provide a quality service to Mien or other ethnic clients may require that the counselor do some extra reading about their culture, personal and family backgrounds and specific needs.

- One of the best ways for counselors to understand their clients' needs is to improve their relations with the diverse groups of clients, parents, pastors, shaman, and community leaders or representatives they will encounter.

Many untouched topics in their homelands include mortgages, checking and saving accounts, retirements, pensions, life or health insurances, wills, estate planning, career choices, schooling, sports and activities, or plans for honeymoons for newlywed couples. These topics were never discussed in an agrarian society. Now they become strange and yet necessary topics for couples to understand and make decisions about. Let's take the honeymoon concept as an example. One would have to be taught the meaning of a honeymoon and the importance of it. Newlywed couples were not only bewildered by the concept of a honeymoon, but they would also be limited by their financial standing in choice of romantic activity. Almost everywhere people went they would see trees, mountains, rivers, rice fields, cornfields, wild animals and domestic animals. One can freely be entertained with natural live music from the birds and insects in the woods and forest. There were no hotels, television, transportations, fancy clothes, social clubs or restaurants for newlywed couples to enjoy.

Today many studies show that money and financial planning are a prime source of conflict in marriage. Money serves as an emotional link, power and struggle within a marriage. One's family origin and cultural background, early life circumstances and the images he or she received from his or her peers or media combined have a dynamic influence on a relationship. As counselors, you should:

- Offer preparation or premarital counseling to engage couples in accessible facilities, such as churches or community centers. Pastoral guidance and language assistance is provided to couples and families in most churches.

- Provide education on marriage, family and parenting in bilingual and multicultural settings, such as schools, churches, and other community organizations or associations where they are more accessible to couples and families.

- Provide social, psychological, and career counseling for youths and the elderly. The majorities of parents who lack a firm foundation of Western education are unable to coach or provide meaningful information or support for their children's social, emotional and career needs. Often parents depend on educators and counselors to assist their children in pursuing their future goals.

- Recruit ethnic minority counselors. Where possible, efforts should be made to attract suitable candidates from minority ethnic groups into counseling services. The recruitment should be designed to increase the knowledge of minority cultures amongst established counselors as well as encouraging those in difficulty to seek help.

- Training—counselors need to be aware of different cultural values, beliefs, and expectations in marriage and family. Multi-disciplinary training or seminars are necessary.

Counseling is not a common practice for Mien and other ethnic cultures from Asian countries as briefly discussed earlier. It is a new approach to resolving marital issues. Most couples are not familiar with the counseling concept and have misconceptions of counseling services. Many people think that counseling and psychotherapy are only for people who are "crazy" or who have mental disorders. Thus, the shame and stigma that is associated with counseling may be barriers for the use of mental health services.

Due to the strong connection with their immediate or nuclear families, couples often seek help from within (close relatives or family friends) before approaching outsiders. This is to protect the collective "face" of the family. Marriage and family professionals are often among the last group to be contacted for marital or family issues. The lack of trusted, bilingual and bi-cultural mental health professionals poses another barrier for couples seeking psychological assistance. Transportation and child-care can be other limitations for clients seeking professional help.

The role of the family in the daily lives of Mien Americans cannot be overstated. Whereas Americans tend to be more individualistic, Mien and other Asian Americans view family above all else. Personal matters are generally kept within the family. It is uncommon for a couple to go outside of the family for the resolution of personal or family matters as it is considered as rejection or rebellion against the family. When a family member seeks assistance outside of the family, it is viewed by the family members that they are not caring, sufficient or competent enough to meet his or her needs. Mien people view the etiology of mental illness as a personal weakness that can be controlled by disciplined thinking and the avoidance of morbid thoughts rather than sharing their weaknesses with a stranger.

Highly acculturated couples are more aware of psychological resources and are more willing to explore outside professional help. On the other hand, for the less acculturated or elderly people, it is still considered taboo and causes them to lose face. Family members are not supposed to get outside assistance for their marriage and family issues unless the inner resources are diminished. Any issues being addressed and resolved outside of the family boundary is considered as shameful and un-Mien.

Another factor that prevents Mien Americans and other Asian Americans from seeking counseling is that they tend to experience stress physiologically; and therefore help may occur from medical professionals rather than mental health professionals.

Seeking psychological help by Asian Americans is contingent on their level of acculturation and assimilation. The highly assimilated individuals are more aware of the resources for psychological help and are better able to utilize these resources. They are able to recognize the need for psychological evaluation and are more tolerant of the stigma that is attached to mental health problems. They are more receptive to accepting referrals or recommendations from their physicians or judiciaries for psychological or chemical evaluation or treatment. As a court interpreter for many years working with the Mien, Hmong, Lao and Thai communities from juvenile to municipal and superior courthouses, I have witnessed the struggles and challenges of the judiciaries to explain the laws to individuals who lack total understanding of the system. Often the courts could not make appropriate referrals to clients due to language and cultural reasons.

Counseling Mien Americans: The Invisible Minority

Counseling Mien American couples, individuals or families, like all intercultural counseling, requires extensive awareness and sensitivity. However, familiarity with the culture is not enough; it is also critically important to address the issues of the person or family before making generalizations based on one's knowledge of the Mien or other Asian cultures. Therapists should not treat Mien clients as a homogenous group with other Asian Americans. Service providers need to have a full assessment of a client's social, cultural, occupational, and educational background such as their generational status, socioeconomic status, migration experience, the length of residency in the U.S. and their present and past belief systems. Counselors must also assess the extent to which their clients identify with their own racial and ethnic group and the majority group, their sense of perceived prejudice, the ethnic composition in the community of their upbringing and of their current community (i.e., whether they are the only Mien American family in the community or they reside and work in a predominately Mien community), and how all of these affect their general social-emotional-psychological adjustment and functioning.

Hardworking, disciplined, polite, and passive are some of the many attributes of Asian Americans or Mien Americans. The Mien perceive themselves as the "invisible minority" within the minority in the U.S. The psychological and social needs among the Mien in America have gone unnoticed by the larger society. Besides the Mien there are many cultural groups within the Asian American population who share certain cultural values, regardless of ethnic background, and these values must be appreciated if culturally relevant counseling is to occur. It is unsafe to make sweeping generalizations about Asian Americans in general because each group has its own distinctive cultural background, unique historical experiences and reasons for immigration.

In addition, there are myths that need to be acknowledged and dispelled within the minority groups. Clearly there are Asian Americans who are very successful, many even in the stereotypical fields of science and technology; they also have a higher average income than other minorities and a low divorce rate compared to the Mien. For example, the Hmong in the U.S. who share the same linguistic and cultural background as the Mien, have more educators, such as attorneys, medical doctors, computer engineers, and a senator. Currently, there is only one certified Mien medical doctor. However, the myth extends to all Asian Americans, who came to the U.S. as refugees and have inadequate educational and occupational skills. Using the myth of Asians as a model minority, based on the successful images of a few elite individuals, has a very negative effect on the general population of Asian Americans, such as the Mien. Several mental health concerns and psychological afflictions, such as threats to cultural identity, powerlessness, feelings of marginality, loneliness, hostility and perceived alienation and discrimination remain hidden under the model minority myth. The society's belief that Asian Americans experience fewer difficulties has made it easy to overlook the negative issues with the Mien American community.

Many community leaders, educators and community members acknowledge that the Mien Americans do not seek mental health services in general. It is crucial for counselors to be aware that Mien Americans' infrequent use of mental health services is not an indication of a lack of psychological problems. Guilt and shame are two core values by which the Mien Americans are raised and these two values dictate their social behaviors. Many may prefer a 'silent misery' of psychological suffering instead of openly seeking the help, which is considered as shameful or a failure in life. It has a very high negative effect on their self-esteem and self-worth. The combination of language and cultural dilemmas force many individuals to be silent in society. They prefer to self-suffering instead of causing the family suffering. Biting one's tongue, swallowing one's pain, and hiding one's guilt, shame and suffering is a common psychological issue to Mien individuals who have been brought up in a passive society.

The low or no self-value concept serves as a brick wall for many Mien adults and elders to overcome. It blocks many from furthering the knowledge and skills they brought from their homeland. In some cases it totally hinders them from becoming who they are and their potential for future success. It stunts their social, spiritual, intellectual and personal growth. The silent misery limits many individuals from helping themselves and weakens their family relationship. There are five common reasons as to why Mien Americans often underutilize mental health services.

1. Given that the majority of Mien Americans are foreign-born, and that counseling is not commonly practiced in Laos or Thailand, Mien Americans are not familiar with and have a misconception of counseling.

2. Many Mien Americans think that counseling and psychotherapy are only for people who are mentally ill or "crazy". Thus, the shame and stigma that is associated with counseling-seeking behaviors may be barriers to using of mental health services.

3. Providing the fact that there is a strong family orientation within the Mien culture, members often seek help from within (close relatives or family friends) before approaching outsiders. This is to protect the collective "face" of the family. For Mien family members who have severe mental problems, mental health professionals are the last to be contacted.

4. The traditional role of mental health professionals in consulting with clients in a closed-door office is not attractive for Mien Americans who are reluctant to step into the mental health agency. Meeting alone with a counselor in a closed-door environment creates an uncomfortable or alienated feeling to clients who are used to an open-door family meeting. It contradicts the traditional way of solving problems by bringing in parents and family members from both sides of the party.

5. Many Mien Americans underutilize counseling services because of a lack of mental professionals who can speak their language and who can empathize with the relationship between their cultural adjustment experiences and their present concerns.

RECOMMENDATIONS FOR RESEARCHERS

I personally would like to acknowledge any interested researchers on the topics of Mien or Asian cultures in the U.S. or overseas, especially in the field of marriage and families. As mentioned earlier that resources is limited on the needs, challenges and strengths of marriages for the Mien and Asian families. When conducting a research with any refugee or ethnic minorities, researchers are recommended the following seven basic suggestions.

1. Researchers should take a precaution not to include Mien with other Asian groups, such as Asians or Laotians in their studies.

There are many ethnic minorities from Asian countries and the term Laotian covers all the different sub-cultural groups from the country of Laos.

2. Due to the limited literature, resource and study on the lives of Mien people in the U.S., especially in the field of marriage and family, immediate attention is needed. Similar or different surveys are needed to further the data. It is highly suggested to collect larger data in order to get a better result for each area being studied. Securing sufficient funds to cover the expenses, for example paying the interpreters, translators and participants for their time, effort and information to assist the researcher is needed.

3. To receive a primary source of data is to personally observe some of the regular community events or ceremonies. You may need to provide your own language and culture broker for your studies. One of your most reliable resources for a knowledge interpreter or translator is to contact the community leader for a competent interpreter and a calendar of annual cultural events.

4. When working with a Mien interpreter or translator, be aware of the age and gender issue in the Mien community and make sure that the person is linguistically and culturally competent. If this person doesn't hold a good reputation in the community, the researcher will not be able to get full participation and cooperation.

5. In order to produce accurate results from any culturally related studies, it is necessary to have some background knowledge of the culture. Researchers can do so by contacting the key community leaders, clan representatives or pastors for primary or secondary sources of information.

6. It is necessary to keep in mind when working with the Mien community to first inform by the husband or the head of the

family and or community leader for appropriate approaches, permission and supports.

7. It is crucial to have both spouses be present during an interview. It is not appropriate to meet just the wife without the present of her husband, since the husband is the decision maker in his family.

RECOMMENDATIONS FOR PASTORS AND LAYMEN

As pastors and laymen at a church setting, one of the goals is to provide quality support services to assist people in your congregation to reach for spiritual, emotional and social wellness. People who are seeking help from the church may see the pastor or laymen as their last resort to the life challenges they are facing. Thus, pastors and laymen have the opportunity and privilege to help the individuals or couples find hope, encouragement and solutions to their individual and family issues. Here are some suggestions to consider:

1. Provide a structured counseling program to assist your congregation for emotional and spiritual help, hope and healing.

2. Train and equip the lay clergy men at your church for marriage and family counseling support service. These people can assist the pastor when needed. The more staff a church has the broader services a church is able to provide to both the members and others in the community.

3. If a church has a counseling service available, the staff and church leaders need to promote, encourage and educate couples and families to utilize a church's available counseling program since culturally and linguistically appropriate counseling service is limited in the Mien community.

4. Encourage one's congregation to utilize other available professional services in the community whenever possible. Since most of the limited and available counseling resources

are unfamiliar to Mien people, they need to be educated and encouraged to obtain any available resources for self and marriage or family improvement. Provide a list of resourceful and helpful service providers for the congregation.

RECOMMEDATIONS FOR COMMUNITY LEADERS

Community leaders often play a crucial role in the health and wellness of marriages and family relationships in the community. As Mien elders and less acculturated individuals often cite and drill on an old concept that "Mien people are unchanging owls", they obviously unveil their emotional, psychological and social frustration, anxiety and concerns as they continue to reside in the U.S. They need the community leaders to lead, guide, encourage and assist them to gain self-sufficiency and other necessary skills to be functional community members. Their inability to provide for themselves and their families can place them in many awkward positions that can lower their self-esteem and self-worth. As the Mien communities become bombarded by the complexities of society and seeing families become weakened, fragile, and broken, many lose heart and hope about the future of the Mien language, culture and family. Community leaders are armed with the following suggestions:

1. Encourage community members to seek professional help when needed. This includes medical, psychological, judicial and mediating assistance whenever appropriate.

2. Encourage, educate, and motivate community members to seek counseling services for their marriage, social, emotional, and mental issues. This includes any counseling services available in a church setting that are made available for individuals and couples.

3. Recommend engaged couples for pre-marital counseling. They can contact their local churches for referral or recommendations to free counseling programs. For example, Mien Evangelical Church located in Tukwila, Washington, provides free pre—and post-marital counseling services to its members. Interested

individuals may contact the church. There are bilingual and bi-cultural counseling services available upon request.

4. Avoid applying traditional mediations or problem solving skills that are in conflict with the judicial system in the United States.

5. Be knowledgeable about the cultural, social and political changes in the United States and inform the community members as much as possible.

6. Assist the elderly and those who lack English literacy to access the different resources and services in the community, such as literacy development classes, citizenship classes, housing, financial and loan programs, healthcare, childcare, safety, tenant's and landlord's rights and responsibilities, legal services, and other social services. The city and county have attorneys and knowledgeable speakers to provide free trainings on these and other available services in the community.

7. Invite guest speakers to present important topics to community members (with a qualified interpreter) during the annual new-year celebrations and other community events.

8. Community leaders are the role models and they should strive to live their private and public lives above approach for others to follow.

9. Organize community events to promote and preserve Mien language and culture in healthy and productive setting.

10. Provide primary literacy classes for interested individuals to learn how to read and write their mother language since public schools do not support them. Churches and community centers are some supportive organizations to begin.

It is my sincere prayers, hopes and desires that the information and data provided in this book becomes a useful resource to all of my readers.

The Mien people in the U.S. and other parts of the world have come a long way and also have overcome many obstacles and challenges to be who they are today. May the words spoken and the ideas shared in this book be a ringing bell or a flash of light, to open the minds, hearts and spirits of my fellow Mien brothers and sisters, motivate each and everyone to reflect on our past history, examine our present life situations, make all the necessary life changes to strengthen ourselves and those around us, and move forward with high hopes and a positive attitude toward the future.

REFERENCES

A Report of the Intergovernmental Affairs Committee, 1989. The New Domestic Agenda: A Strengthened American Family, A Strengthened Economy. The Council of State of Governments, Iron Works Pike, O.P. Box 11910. Lexington, Kentucky.

Allison Ryan, M.A., & Paul Pintrich, Ph.D., Gender Differences Found In The Way Boys And Girls Solve Math Problems. [On-line] Journal of Educational Psychology, Vol. 89 No. 2 pp 401-402. http://www.apa.org/releases/math2.html

Arcus, Margaret E., Schvaneveldt, Jay D., Moss, J. Joel. Handbook of Family Life Education: Foundations of Family Life Education, Vol. 1&2. Sage Publications, Newbury Park, London, New Delhi.

Banks, J.A. 1979. *Teaching strategies for ethnic studies*, 2nd edition. Boston, Allyn and Bacon.

Brehem, Sharon S. 1985. Intimate Relationships. Random House, New York.

Brislin, Richard & Yoshida, Tomoko 1994. Intercultural Communication Training: An Introduction. Sage Publications.

Bumroongsook, Sualee 1995. Love and Marriage: Mate Selection In Twentieth-Century Central Thailand. Chulalongkorn University Press.

Campbell, A. 1981. The Sense of Well Being in America: Patterns and Trends. New York McGraw-Hill.

Carstensen, L. L., Gottman, J. M., & Levenson, R. W. 1995. Emotional behavior in long-term marriage. *Psychology and Aging 10*(1), 140-149.

Chao, YS, 1998. Southeast Asian Cultures In Transition: A Study on How Cultural and Environmental Factors Influence Students' Academic Achievement. Pacific Asia Press, A Greenshower Corp.

Collins, Randall, 1986. Sociology of Marriage and Family: Gender, Love, and Property. Nelson-Hall, Chicago.

Cox, Martha J. and Brooks-Gunn 1999. Conflict and Cohesion in Families. Lawrence Erlbaum Associates Publishers.

Dill, Bonnie T, 1986. Our Mother's Grief: Racial Ethnic Women and the Maintenance of Families. Research Paper 4, Department of Sociology and Social Work, Memphis State University.

Dunjvin, Maj. Debra, Walter Reed Army Medical Center, Washington D.C., December 2001, Monitor on Psychology, Volume 32, No. 11

Eichler, Margrit 1997. Family Shifts: Families, Policies, Gender Equality. Oxford University Press.

Ferree, M.M. 1990. Beyond Separate Spheres: Feminism and Family Research. Journal of Marriage and the Family, vol. 52, pp. 866-884.

Filsinger, E.E. 1988. Biological Re-examined, the Quest for Answers. In E.E. Filsinger (Ed.), *Biosocial Perspective on the Family* (pp. 9-38). Newbury Park, CA: Sage.

Fong, Timothy P. 2002. The Contemporary Asian American Experience: Beyond the Model Minority. Pearson Education, Inc.

Fuglesang, Andreas 1982. About Understanding: Ideas and Observations on Cross-Cultural Communication. Dag Hammerskjold Foundation.

Gladure, B.A. 1988. Biological Influence Upon the Development of Sexual Orientation. In E.E. Filsinger (Ed.) *Biological Perspectives on the Family* (pp. 61-92). Newbury Park, CA: Sage.

Goonasekera, Anura; Beng, Yeap S. and Mahizhnan, Arun 1996. Opening Windows: Issues in Communication. Stamford Press, Pte Ltd.

Gottman, J.M., & Levenson, R. W. 1992. Marital processes predictive of later dissolution: Behavior, physiology, and health. *Journal of Personality and Social Psychology, 63*(2), 221-223.

Gottman, J.M., & Levenson, R. W. 1999. Rebound from marital conflict and divorce prediction. *Family Process, 38*(3), 287-292.

Gottman, J.M., & Levenson, R. W., 2000. The timing of divorce: Predicting when a couple will divorce over a 14-year period. *Journal of Marriage and the Family, 62*(3), 737-745.

Gudykunst, W., and Mody, B., 2001. *Handbook of International and Intercultural Communication.* Newbury Park, CA: Sage.

Gudykunst, W. B., Gao, G., Schmidt, K. L., Nishida, T., M., Leung, K., Wang, G., & Barraclough, R. A., 1992. The influence of individualism-collectivism, self-monitoring, and predicted-outcome value on communication in ingroup and outgroup relationships. *Journal of Cross-Cultural Psychology, 23*, 196-213.

Hall, Edward T. 1959. The Silent Language. New York: Doubleday.

Her Majesty's Stationary Office, 1979. Marriage Matters: A Consultative Document by the Working Party on Marriage Guidance. Home Office in Consultation with Department of Health and Social Security, ISBN 011401574

Helton, Jeff and Lora, 1999. Authentic Marriages: How to Connect with Other Couples Through a Marriage Accountability Group. Moody Press, Chicago.

Hoffmann, Charlotte 1996. Language, Culture and Communication in Contemporary Europe. Multilingual Matters Ltd.

Jim, E. & Suen, P. 1990. *Chinese Parents and Teenagers in Canada: Transitions and Conflicts*. Vancouver, B.C.: Canadian Mental Health Association.

Kacha-Ananda, Chob. 1997. Thailand Yao: Past, Present, and Future.

Institute for the Study of Languages and Cultures of Asia and Africa, Tokyo.

Kiel, Anne Cohen, 1998. Unpublished Thesis, Effects of Acculturation on Immigrant Families: Parent-child Relationships in Asian-American Families. University of Washington.

Kim, M.S., Hunter, J. E., Miyahara, A., Horvath, A. M., Breshahan, M., ^ Yoon, H. J., 1996. Individual vs. Culture-level dimensions of individualism and collectivism: Effects on preferred conversation styles. *Communication Monographs*, 63, 29-49.

Larimore, Walt and Barbara, 2008. His Brain, Her Brain: Howe Divinely Designed Differences Can Strengthen Your Marriage, Grand Rapids, Michigan.

Lee, J. 1974. The styles of loving. *Psychology Today*, 8, 43-51.

Lee, J. 1998. Love-styles. In R. Sternberg & Barnes (Eds.), *The Psychology of Love*. New Heven, CT: Yale University Press.

Lerner, Daniel 1976. Asian Communication: Research, Training, Planning. East-West Communication Institute, Honolulu, Hawaii.

Lewis, Michael and Feiring, Candice 1998. Families, Risks, and Competence. Lawrence Erlbaum Associates Publishers.

Lewis, Paul and Elaine. 1984. Peoples of Golden Triangle. Great Britian by Thames and Hudson Ltd. 500 Fifth Ave. New York, NY 10110

Ludden, Marsha 1992. Effective Communication Skills: Essential Tools for Success in Work, Social and Personal Situations. Jist Works, Inc.

Lucas, Richard E. *Cross-Cultural Evidence for the Fundamental Features of Extraversion.* September 2000, Vol. 79, No. 3, 452-468. Journal of Personality and Social Psychology,

Mattessich, P., and R. Hill, 1987. "Life Cycle and Family Development." In: M.B. Sussman and S.K. Steinmetc, eds. *Handbook of Marriage and Family.* New York: Plenum Press, pp. 437-469.

McManus, Michael J. 1995. Marriage Savers: Helping Your Friends and Family Avoid Divorce. Zondervan Publishing House.

Metowbian, Albert 1971. Silent Messages. Wadsworth Publishing Co. Belmont, CA.

Moschetta, Evelyn and Paul 1998. Marriage Spirit: Finding The Passion and Joy of Soul-Centered Love. Simon and Schuster.

Olsen, C.S. Russell, and D.H. Sprengkle 1984. "Circumplex Model of Marital and Family Systems VI. Theoretical Update. In: D.H. Olsen and P.M. Miller, eds. *Family Studies Review Yearbook. Volume 2.* New Delhi: Sage Publications.

Park, Myong-Seok 1979. Communication Styles in Two Different Cultures: Korean and American. Han Shin Publishing Co.

Porter, Richard E. & Samovar, Larry A, eds. (1988). *Intercultural Communication: A reader.* Fifth edition. Belmong: Wadsworth Publishing Company. 1988.

Porter, Richard E & Samovar, Larry A. (1988). "Approaching Intercultural Communication". In Porter, Richard E. & Samovar, Larry A, eds.

Quinn, M.J., & Tomita, S.K. (1997). *Elder abuse and neglect: Causes, diagnosis, and intervention strategies.* (2nd ed.). New York: Springer Publishing Co.

Rogers, Everett M. & Hart, Williams B. (2002). "The Histories of Intercultural, International, and Development Communication". In Gudykunst, William B and Mody, Bella, eds., 1-8.

Rossi, A. 1984. Gender and Parenthood. *American Sociological Reviews*, vol. 49, 1-19.

Sabbatini, Renato Ph.D., Are There Differences between the Brains of Males and Females? [On-line],http://www.epub.org.br/cm/n11/mente/eisntein/cerebro-homen.html

Saracho, O.N. & Spodek, B. 1993. Understanding the Multicultural Experience of Early Childhood Education. Washington, DC: NAEYC.

Savin D, Sack WH, Clarke GN, Meas N, Richart I (1996), The Khmer adolescent project: III. A study of trauma from Thailand's site

Silove D, Manicavasagar V, Beltran R, Le G, Nguyen H, Phan T, Blaszczynski A (1997), Satisfaction of Vietnamese patients and their families with refugee and mainstream mental health services. *Psychiatric Services* 48: 1064-1069

Smith, Larry E. 1981. English for Cross-Cultural Communication. The MacMillan Press Ltd.

Summerfield D (2000), Childhood, war, refugeedom and 'Trauma': Three core questions for mental health professionals. *Transcultural Psychiatry* 37: 417-433

Ting-Toomey, Stella. (1999). *Communicating Across Cultures*. New York/London: The Guiltford Press.

Troost, K.M. 1988. Sociobiology and the Family: Promise versus Product. In E.E. Filsinger (Ed). *Biosocial Perspectives on the Family* (pp. 188-205). Newbury Park, CA: Sage.

Uba, Laura, 1994. Asian Americans: *Personality Patterns, Identity, and Mental Health*, New York: Guilford Press, New York.

UNICEF (2002), Adult wars, child soldiers: Voices of children involved in armed conflict in the east Asia and pacific region. http://www.unicef.org/media/publications/adultwarschildsoldiers.pdf

U.S. Department of Health and Human Services (1999), *Mental health: A report of the Surgeon General* Rockland, MD: U.S. Department of Health and Human Services, Substance Abuse and Mental Health Services Administration, Center for Mental Health Services, National Institute of Health, National Institute of Mental Health

Waite, Linda & Gallagher, Maggie, 2001. The Case for Marriage: Why Married People Are Happier, Healthier and Better Off Financially. ISBN: 978-0-7679-0632-6 (0-7679-0632-2)

Walker, D.K., and R.W. Crocker. 1988. "Measuring Family Systems Outcomes." In: H.B. Weiss and F.H. Jacobs, eds. *Evaluating Family Programs*. New York: Aldine de Gruyter, pp. 153-176.

Watkins-Goffman, Linda 2001. Lives in Two Languages: An Exploration of Identity and Culture. The University of Michigan Press.

Wemhoff, Rich, 1999. Marriage: The Best Resources To Help Yours Thrive. Resource Pathways, Inc.

Wilcox, W. Bradford, 2004. *Soft Patriarchs, New Men: Howe Christianity Shapes Father and Husbands*. The University of Chicago Press.

Winch, Peter. (1997). "Can We Understand Ourselves?" *Philosophical Investigations*, 20:3, 193-204.

Zeitlin, Marian F. et al. 1995. Strengthen the Family: Implications for International Development. United Nations University Press

CPSIA information can be obtained at www.ICGtesting.com
Printed in the USA
BVOW070659291012

303974BV00010B/1/P

9 781449 764524